Everything on the Table

Plain Talk About Food and Wine

COLMAN ANDREWS

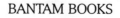

BANTAM BOOKS

New York   Toronto   London   Sydney   Auckland

EVERYTHING ON THE TABLE

A Bantam Book / December 1992

BOOK DESIGN BY CAROL MALCOLM-RUSSO

ILLUSTRATION BY ROXANNA BIKADOROFF

CALLIGRAPHY BY LUC-RAPHAËL BESSIÈRE

Library of Congress Cataloging-in-Publication Data

Andrews, Colman.
Everything on the table : plain talk about food and wine / Colman
Andrews.
p.   cm.
Includes bibliographical references and index.
ISBN 0-553-09021-6
1. Cookery, American.   I. Title.
TX715.A56667   1992
641.5973—dc20   92-10891
CIP

Published simultaneously in the United States and Canada

Bantam Books are published by Bantam Books, a division of Bantam
Doubleday Dell Publishing Group, Inc. Its trademark, consisting of the
words "Bantam Books" and the portrayal of a rooster, is Registered in
U.S. Patent and Trademark Office and in other countries. Marca Regis-
trada. Bantam Books, 666 Fifth Avenue, New York, New York 10103.

PRINTED IN THE UNITED STATES OF AMERICA
BVG   0 9 8 7 6 5 4 3 2 1

FOR PAULA AND MADELEINE

*"If I could compose music
about eating and drinking
I would do so."*

—WILLIAM CAINE, *THE GLUTTON'S MIRROR*

Contents

ACKNOWLEDGMENTS ix

INTRODUCTION: EATING AMERICA 1

  WHAT IS A TACO, ANYWAY? 1

  FOOD WITHOUT FEAR 7

Part I • Gourmets and How We Got That Way 23

ONE GOURMET WITH GARNISH 25

TWO ROOTS 33

THREE THE UNBEATABLE SWEETNESS OF FRYING 41

FOUR COOKING BY EAR 53

FIVE THAT WAS NO CUISINART, THAT WAS
  MY KNIFE 69

SIX I CAN'T BELIEVE YOU ORDERED THUMPER 79

SEVEN WE EAT WHAT WE WANT 89

Part II • Waiter, There's a Flaw in My Soup 101

EIGHT RESTAURANT CRITICS NEVER HAVE A
  NICE DAY 103

Contents

NINE SILAS AND ME   117
TEN WHY SEAN CAN'T COOK   125
ELEVEN DOWN WITH THREE-STAR RESTAURANTS   133

Part III • Satisfied Appetites   141

TWELVE SEVEN RESTAURANTS   143
THIRTEEN WAKING UP IN ROME   163
FOURTEEN CLAUDE'S CHALLENGE   171
FIFTEEN HAMBURGERS AT CHEZ PANISSE   183
SIXTEEN IF YOU ARE DETAINED AT CALAIS ...   189
SEVENTEEN SOMETIMES A CIGAR   199

Part IV • Wine as Money, Wine as Life   205

EIGHTEEN THE EMPEROR'S NEW WINE   207
NINETEEN LIQUID GOLD AND EMPTY BOTTLES   217
TWENTY SNIFF THIS   223
TWENTY-ONE I THINK WE'RE ALL BOZOS IN THIS
  WINE SHOP   229

Part V • Side Orders   235

TWENTY-TWO CHICKEN À LA KING AND
  BIDIMENSIONAL PIRANHA   237
TWENTY-THREE THE NOTEBOOKS OF CAPTAIN
  CAMILLE   249
TWENTY-FOUR MEANWHILE, BACK AT THE RANCH   265
TWENTY-FIVE THE BLUE BAR BLUES   273
TWENTY-SIX RUMINATIONS   281

BIBLIOGRAPHY   299
RECIPE INDEX   303
GENERAL INDEX   305

Acknowledgments

ECAUSE THIS BOOK IS LARGELY AN EX-pression of my opinions about food and drink, it seems appropriate for me first of all to thank some of the people who have helped shape those opinions. Chief among these are: Claude Caspar-Jordan, *mon père adoptif*, who has taught me much about how the French eat, and think; his wife, Pepita, who showed me for the first time real French home cooking, up close; Jonathan Waxman, a boon companion at the table and obviously a kind of genius, since he agrees with me so often about food and wine (etc.); Roy Brady in particular (for teaching me to taste the wine and not its reputation) and the Saturday Lunch Boys in general—Joe, Sid, Bill, Lloyd, Dan, Norm, Marty, et al. (all those Madeiras! all those '29s and '45s!); Darrell Corti, who has shared his remarkable erudition generously and amiably with me for nearly twenty years; Karen Kelly Miller, who introduced me to real Italian food in Rome, long before it had shown its face in public in America; my friends in Barcelona, especially Agustí and Lluïsa Jausas and Lluís and Lola Cruanyas, who opened a whole new (old) world of food to me, and made it possible for me to write my first real book; and the Viscount Furness, who offered me some of my most memorable early dining experiences and taught me several little lessons about wine that I have never forgotten.

I must also thank several architects of my professional life—Lois Dwan, who introduced me to (and inducted me into) the restaurant-reviewing big time at the *Los Angeles Times*; Ruth Reichl, who has remained a pleasure to work with (and to know) throughout our long editor-writer relationship, no matter which side of it she's been on; and Dorothy Kalins, who encouraged me to write about food and wine in a larger context in *Metropolitan Home,* and helped me find the tone in which to do it. I have elsewhere acknowledged the late Silas Spitzer, who let me write my first restaurant reviews and encouraged me to think and write further about food (see Chapter Nine).

Now on to specifics: For having generously shared their recipes with me for this book, my thanks are due to Alice Waters, Lydia Shire, John Sedlar, Jimmy Schmidt, Gianni Franzi, Mauro Vincenti, David Grinstead, Linda B. Ebert, Steve and Betty Hope, Ronald Clint of Chasen's, and Knox Gelatin, Inc. I owe thanks, too, to Steve Wallace and Charles Perry for answering so many of my questions; to Patrick Healy for the inside information; to Andrew Anspach for telling me the truth about the Blue Bar; to Helen Spitzer, for granting me permission to quote from her late husband's letters; and to Alan Barker and Bruce and Matt Coe, for allowing me to use portions of their own correspondence.

Special thanks are due to Tina Ujlaki for testing a number of the recipes herein, and for fine-tuning virtually all of them; and to Joan Freese for efficiently and accurately researching what must have seemed at times a bewildering assortment of matters for me.

For their guidance and, above all, their patience, I am

grateful to Fran McCullough, Coleen O'Shea, and Barbara Lowenstein.

Finally, I must thank Mr. Food, Morley Jones, Gaston Pinard, and all my fellow members of Les Chevaliers de la Morue, wherever they may be.

About a dozen of the following chapters are based in part on columns that appeared in *Metropolitan Home* and the *Los Angeles Times*. Though I have borrowed some titles from these earlier pieces, and sometimes incorporated portions of my earlier texts herein, the chapters themselves are in effect entirely new.

INTRODUCTION:
EATING AMERICA

I. WHAT IS A TACO, ANYWAY?

"I am looking rather seedy now while holding down my claim,
And my victuals are not always of the best...."
—"THE LITTLE OLD SOD SHANTY" (AMERICAN FOLK SONG)

MERICANS EAT BADLY. OUR FOOD IS OVER-salted, full of sugar, full of fat. Much of it is highly processed to the point of being artificial—filled with emulsifiers, extenders, preservatives, and dyes—and even when it's not, it's often canned or frozen into insipid mush. Our bread is like cardboard, our cheese is like plastic, our fish is two weeks old. We care more for speed and convenience, both in our home kitchens and in our restaurants, than for flavor. Worst of all, we scarcely notice how bad our food is and probably wouldn't mind much if we did notice, because we have no real appreciation for the art and romance of gastronomy.

Americans eat well. We enjoy a variety and a quality of produce, meats, and other foodstuffs all but unparalleled in the world. We're learning to moderate our consumption of salt, sugar, and animal fats, and we're starting to demand (and get) good bread, fresh fish, organically grown fruits and vegetables. Our recent "culinary revolution," inspired by James Beard and Julia Child and led by Alice Waters, Wolfgang Puck, and their colleagues, has raised standards of both cooking and dining in this country dramatically, and promises to turn us finally into a nation of true gastronomes.

Who *cares* how Americans eat? We're all still here, aren't we? We must be doing something right. What more is there to say about it? Food is no big deal. It's just fuel— something you put in your belly when you're hungry. So what if it's processed? So what if it's organic? And what's all this crap about "gastronomy"? Why don't we all just shut up about food and get on with our lives?

There is something to be said for each of these positions. Each is, in a sense and to an extent, quite easy to defend. We eat badly, we eat well, and we probably worry too damned much about which is which.

What we don't do, however, is eat the way we used to. That "we" contains multitudes, of course. There is no single American diet, and no single American attitude toward food, or level of sophistication regarding it. We are a famously diverse people, and the way we eat (and think about eating) both reflects and reinforces our diversity. Still, no matter who we are or what we had for lunch today, our diet has changed significantly over the past twenty years or so.

The most obvious changes, because they're the ones that get written about the most in our magazines and newspapers, are those impelled by fad, or by fad's slower-but-surer cousin, trend. I'm thinking, for instance, of "California cuisine" and "designer pizza," and of the cooking of the "Pacific Rim" or the "New Southwest"—none of which anyone had ever heard of twenty years ago. In those days, too, food that was "blackened" got that way by mistake. (Now you can get blackened catfish in coffee shops.) Tuna came exclusively in cans—and it wasn't "dolphin safe" or packed in spring water, either. The jagged little greens we now refer to jauntily as "field salad" or "*mesclun*"—and buy, prewashed, for twelve bucks a pound—were thrown away as weeds. Salmon caviar was fish bait.

But other changes in our eating habits are more basic, and almost certainly more permanent, than any of our high-profile infatuations with individual ingredients or cuisines. I'm thinking, for example, of the marked increase in our consumption of seafood in recent years—and of the fact that, fad foods aside, our supermarket produce sections now carry more than twice the number of items they did ten years ago. And I'm thinking of the epic internationalization of American cooking—the way in which, on every level, it has so eagerly embraced and adapted the flavors of an entire world.

One day about fifteen years ago, as my father and I were driving down Santa Monica Boulevard in Los Angeles, we happened to pass a Mexican-themed fast-food stand with a banner reading "TACOS 25¢." My father turned to me and asked, "Just what *is* a 'taco,' anyway, son?" At that point in his life, he had lived in southern California for roughly forty years.

My father was not by any means an incurious or provincial man. In his heyday in Hollywood, he probably ate more dinners in restaurants and nightclubs than he did at home. Later in life, he traveled frequently to Asia and the Middle East, making more than twenty trips (as he liked to say) "east of Suez"—and presumably ingesting, of necessity, all manner of exotic and no doubt sometimes daunting dishes. Yet it had somehow never occurred to him, in all his years in southern California, to sample one of that region's most popular and widely available culinary specialties—a food item so typical of L.A.'s casual, Hispanic-flavored, eat-on-the-run culture as to be almost heraldic of the city. Apparently, he had never even wondered what it was before. It simply had no relationship to the life he lived.

If my father were alive today, I think he'd know very well what a taco was. The food not just of Mexico (and of Italy, France, China, and Japan—the basics), but also of Thailand, India, Ethiopia, Morocco, Central America, the Caribbean, Spain and Portugal, and more is represented amply in our cities today, offering us a seemingly endless menu of new culinary possibilities. This is true on the fast-food-and-frozen-dinner level (tacos and pizza have, after all, become as American as apple pie—and even dim sum and falafel have recently applied for citizenship), and it is certainly true in temples of the "new American cuisine." Dining in the present-day equivalents of the restaurants he used to frequent, my father would almost certainly be introduced, perforce, not just to tacos but to sashimi, paella, satay, and lots of other things he likely never tasted (although those tacos might well be filled not with fast-food ground beef but with duck breast, venison, or sea bass—say, just what *is* a taco, anyway?). The melting pot has found its ultimate metaphorical expression in the cooking pot.

I think all this is great. I think we're growing up gastronomically as a nation. We've certainly got more good restaurants than we used to have, more cuisines (both traditional and hybrid) to choose from, more food products with which to construct our meals, more good cookbooks, more good wines. We've also started paying more attention, finally, to the relationship between diet and health—and we're at least beginning to accept the possibility that good flavor and nutrition can go hand in hand.

That's the bright side of the American food story. At the

same time, though, I think many of the apparent changes in our eating habits have been illusory, and even sometimes just plain phony. Whatever claims we may hold down, our victuals are still not always of the best.

If we've got more good restaurants today, we've also got more fast-food chains and "theme" eateries—apparently the theme of good food served well is not sufficient—and more dining "concepts" and contrivances (as if we needed to be *tempted* to eat, somehow, like children who will only take their vitamins if they're shaped like Yogi Bear). For every conscientious chef striving for purity and authenticity in his food, we've got a thousand—*ten* thousand—self-styled mass-feeders (who asked 'em?) cloaking precooked frozen entrees in sugary, salty premixed sauces. And, sure, our supermarkets offer ever-larger choices of fresh fruit and vegetables—but they also stock ever more varieties of frozen diet dinners, sugar-coated cereals, imitation eggs and butter, canned "pasta," and those mysterious powdered products that are said to be able to "help" tuna and ground beef (to do what?).

Almost half the $260 billion that Americans spend annually on food goes for highly processed items, and sales of snack foods (potato chips, etc.) alone have more than doubled in the last ten years. Indeed, the idea of "natural" food is such an anomaly today that our supermarkets have to have a special section for it—a section usually considerably smaller, it might be noted, than those devoted to the sugar-coated cereals and the frozen diet dinners.

Even our fresh fruits and vegetables aren't always what they seem. True, they're beautiful to look at—but do they have any flavor? Any aroma? Walk into the middle of your local supermarket produce section and inhale deeply. What do you smell? The damp, earthy scent of mushrooms and potatoes? The bright perfume of pineapples and melons? The frank, gassy odor of cauliflower or broccoli? Probably not. You're more likely to smell the disinfectant on the floor, or the produce manager's cologne. Meanwhile, our tomatoes are a well-known joke. Our strawberries are watery and pithy. Our garlic is old and dry. Our produce travels well, but it doesn't deliver.

A lot of this is our own fault: All too often, we take what we're given. We're gullible about food. We'll swallow anything. We believe those strawberries taste great because they *look* great. We believe (to appropriate the motto of one brand of precut freezer-bin fish fillets) that "frozen fish is fresher." We believe glossy magazines when they tell us that, for instance, basil is "out" this year and cilantro is "in"—as if the culinary validity of herbs that have been used for thousands of years was somehow affected by the capricious eating habits of a few thousand trend-conscious Americans!

And we're inconsistent: We might make much of bright young chefs and unusual cuisines—but at the same time we've somehow bought the lie that the only way to feed millions of people efficiently is with food that is processed, packaged, degraded. When we clamber onto airplanes, we obediently gobble down our tired, steam-soaked "flight-kitchen" dinners like so many starving sheep—as if *this* eating had nothing to do with the eating we do in restaurants and thus needn't be held to the same standards. And in our hospitals and schools, we accept without protest our canned fruit cocktail and our pressed turkey with instant mashed potatoes, as if this is the best that can be done under the circumstances.

Meanwhile, we pay lip service to unusual, well-written cookbooks, but make best-sellers out of aw-shucks TV chefs, and out of a culinary Barbara Cartland named Martha Stewart (whose evocative good-life reveries might almost have been penned by "Elizabeth Lane," the Barbara Stanwyck character in the original 1945 version of *Christmas in Connecticut*—except that Stewart, unlike Lane, apparently really leads the life she describes). We probably know more than ever about wine, and have access to an ever-greater choice of bottles, but we buy it by label or by "Parker score" (see page 212) instead of by taste. Anyway, our drinking-age young men and women seem to favor pallid beer, or cocktails made with Jell-O. And "health"? Let's face it: For all too many of us, the most significant nutritional event of recent years has been McDonald's debasing of its already sorry excuse for a hamburger with carrageenan, a gelatinous substance extracted from seaweed—*voilà,* the McLean burger.

Whatever tendencies we might have toward gastronomic sophistication as a nation, we ain't no gastronomes yet. Whatever we may like to tell ourselves while we're planting borage in the windowbox or buying our month's supply of Arborio rice and balsamic vinegar or ordering our American-eclectic carpaccio or tajine down at the local trenderia, we're still mostly just going through the motions. We haven't come to terms with food yet. We haven't accepted it as a natural and enjoyable part of normal life.

Something about food is eating us in America today, I think. Something about food unsettles us, makes us nervous. For some strange reason, and in many strange and senseless ways, I think we're afraid of food.

II. FOOD WITHOUT FEAR

"It would seem that for thousands of years man has been eating all the wrong things! He has enjoyed the sense of taste that Nature has endowed him with, and all the time Nature was an ignoramus!"
—PIERRE ANDRIEU, *FINE BOUCHE*

When I say that Americans are afraid of food, I mean that we're afraid to buy it, because we're not sure how to pick it out or what it ought to cost; we're afraid to cook it, because we don't begin to understand the cooking process; we're afraid to eat it, of course, because we've heard about all the awful things it can do to us; we're afraid to utter its very name, for heaven's sake, because we'll probably pronounce it incorrectly.

Above all, we're afraid to *enjoy* food, or at least to let our enjoyment show—because, in this country, people who like food too much are objects of suspicion, likely to be branded by their peers as sissies, gluttons, or elitists, or held in pity and contempt for their obvious "self-destructive" tendencies. Somehow, we've managed to turn the primal act of eating—which ought to be appreciated as a glorious gift to humankind, a daily wonderment—into a sort of necessary evil, or at best a furtive pleasure. We don't *trust* food. We think it's out to get us.

As noted, of course, a large and conspicuous portion of our fear is physical. Food—our very sustenance—is seen increasingly as something deleterious to health, something that threatens life as much as it sustains it. As any reader of the popular press has surely learned in recent years, our lettuces and apples now drip pesticides like venom; our poultry is laced with harmful hormones; the animal fats we eat so freely are pure poison (may as well drink arsenic-spiked lemonade or oleander tea!); raw eggs, even in the form of mayonnaise (or of ice cream!), are breeding grounds for salmonella—and raw oysters on the half shell are little more than bivalved petri dishes growing hepatitis cultures wholesale; caffeine causes cancer (or is it heart disease?), and so does the stuff they use to decaffeinate coffee; wine rots your liver and turns upright citizens into drunken butchers at the wheel.

Food also makes us fat. In this (theoretically) most diverse and individualistic of societies, we end up worshipping supposed ideal body types more reverently than did the most platonic-minded denizens of ancient Greece. We diet desperately and repetitively—becoming more obsessed with food in our avoidance or our measuring of it than we were when we just ate the stuff. In extreme cases, some of us literally starve ourselves to death, or purge our bodies violently, spewing back food gulped down in the first place not for nourishment or pleasure but in a vain attempt to fill an emptiness that, sadly, turns out not to have been attached to our digestive systems at all.

Physical fear of food is as ridiculous as it is sometimes tragic. Foods that people have been eating with impunity for centuries haven't suddenly turned deadly. Of course, it makes sense to limit our consumption of some foods—but maybe that's the whole point, the elegance of the design. Maybe we're not supposed to turn the best foods into commonplaces. Maybe we suffer from them, when suffer we do, because we've taken them for granted, gotten used to having them at whim. Only a fool or a glutton eats a pound of Stilton or a dozen scrambled eggs a day. On the other hand, some "bad" things are just *so good*—for instance, the fat-striated meat and sweet peripheral fat of good *jamón jabugo* or prosciutto from Parma or San Daniele, the juicy cheeseburger with a pile of perfect French fries, the catfish rolled in cornmeal and fried in bacon fat, the fettuccine cloaked with concentrated butter and Parmigiano, the rich vanilla ice cream topped with toasted almonds and warm caramel or chocolate—that I simply cannot believe that we're not meant to enjoy them at least occasionally. (Those dieters who sport bumper stickers reading "*Nothing tastes as good as thin feels*" haven't been eating the right stuff.)

Why are we so susceptible to fear of food? I think there's a lot more to it than mere physical trepidation. I think the problem is fundamental: Somewhere along the line, and for whatever reasons, our innate ability as a nation (as a culture) to understand and appreciate food has been bred right out of us.

Maybe it's our rigid sociopolitical underpinnings— what people tend to call our "puritanical" heritage (though I suspect that the average seventeenth-century Puritan emigré to the New World ate with a good deal more guiltless gusto than does the average urban secretary or construction worker today). Maybe we're too busy making money, making deals, making our own lives, to worry about just making stocks and vinegars and jellies. Maybe growing food ourselves and shopping for it enthusiastically and cooking it at home seem too much like corny old-country pursuits to us—things our grandparents did grudgingly, because they had to, but from which we have been liberated. Maybe the sheer abundance and variety of food available to us in America has overwhelmed us and finally anesthetized us to the keen, bright possibilities of the kitchen and the table. Maybe some of us are simply born incapable of appreciating food, in the same way that some of us are born without good hand-eye coordination or an ear for music.

Whatever the reasons, we're simply not connected with food anymore. We don't know where it comes from, how it gets from there to here, what it looks like whole—and mostly we don't want to know. We don't want to see food in its unfinished (i.e., fresh) state—dirty, bloody, raw, still in pods or shells. We want it washed, prepackaged, ready-to-serve. We don't want to take our time with food, to smell it, taste it, think about it, cook it with love or at least with wit. We just want to grab it, bolt it down, get it over with, hope it doesn't hurt us too much. We have no real investment in it to begin with, and so when we're told that it's not good for us, we don't fight back, we don't defend it. Can't eat Brie anymore or have that second glass of beaujolais? we ask. Who cares? Just pass the cheddar-flavored rice cakes and the kiwi-flavored mineral water.

(I was amused by the popular reaction to the announcement by a group of French researchers, late in 1991, that foie gras and other poultry fat might actually be beneficial to the human cardiovascular system: Everybody scoffed and tittered. A common response was something like "Oh, *sure*, the French *would* say that." Yet similarly, preliminary studies suggesting that this substance or that might be *dangerous* are taken as gospel. It's as if we want to believe the worst.)

I found what I'd call a positively emblematic example of our cultural disconnection from food in, of all places, the *Los Angeles Times* food section, as recently as late 1989: A column called "You Asked About" bore the headline, "Exactly What Is Meant by Phrase 'Leftover Chicken'?" The lead query itself read, "I would like to find out about getting chicken to the form requested in recipes that call for 'leftover chicken.'" The question stunned me. Was this a joke? No, it was apparently a legitimate, serious request for information, and it was answered seriously by the *Times*. ("When a recipe calls for 'leftover chicken,' any mildly seasoned roasted, broiled, baked or poached poultry may be used. . . .")

Obviously, the person who made the request was someone to whom chicken was not a bird, but rather a series of neatly trimmed (and probably skinless, boneless) pieces of anonymous pale flesh, neatly portioned out and wrapped in plastic. If the supermarket didn't sell something called leftover chicken, I suppose, then leftover chicken was beyond this correspondent's ken. (One day soon, supermarkets probably *will* sell something called leftover chicken, precisely to satisfy the obvious demand for such a product.)

Here's another example of how divorced we sometimes are from the reality of food: One evening, over dinner at the Gotham Bar & Grill in New York, I happened to mention to one of my dinner companions that the potatoes in my fish stew—Yukon Golds, perfectly cooked—were some of the most delicious I'd ever tasted. "You mean there are different flavors of potato?" he asked, incredulous. We are a society that accepts without question the need for several dozen flavors of canned soda and forty or fifty kinds of cat food—but it never occurs to many of us that there is more than one kind of potato or apple or salmon, or that there might be any point in having more than one. (In fact, something like 400 varieties of potato were cultivated in the Andes in pre-Columbian times.)

On the positive side, I love this story told by landscape designer and writer Rosalind Creasy (author of *The Complete Book of Edible Landscaping* and *Cooking from the Garden*) in an interview in the Berkeley-based monthly *Bay Food:* A neighbor boy was waiting near Creasy's yard for his father to pick him up. Creasy asked him if he'd like to pull up a carrot while he waited. He looked confused. Could he find a carrot in her yard? she asked. No. That's because they grow underground, she said. "They do?" he asked. Creasy continues: "I showed him where it was and had him pull it out. He was so excited! He runs over to the car. 'Daddy, look at what I have! A carrot!' It's as if I had just given him some fancy toy from the store. He'll remember that carrot forever. Because in that instant, he realized that this stuff comes from the ground."

Even people who cook regularly and even rather well often betray a curious unfamiliarity with the nature of the materials they use, as well as a curious procedural rigidity, as if they're just going through the motions, making food by rote, with no idea of what they're really doing. Thus an outdoor cook who can grill New York steaks to perfection on the Weber has no idea what to do with T-bones. A mother cooking Thanksgiving dinner flies into a tizzy because she's out of powdered sage—even though there's fresh sage growing in the windowbox. A would-be baker rejects a recipe that calls for vegetable oil because all there is in the cupboard is peanut oil—and peanuts aren't really vegetables, are they? Some home cooks are reduced to indecision by recipes that list optional ingredients. "Well," they demand, "do I add the chervil or not?"

Don't misunderstand me: I'm not proposing that we all go sign up at the Cordon Bleu, or that we should all start making everything from scratch, churning our own butter, baking our own bread (even in Europe, it's mostly only show-offs or the poor who bake their own bread today), butchering our own calves. On the other hand, it probably wouldn't hurt if we all knew how to open a wine bottle, strip thyme leaves from their stalk, and maybe clean a fish. More to the point, I think we all ought to remind ourselves now and then that food is or was a living thing, a product of our environment—and that it deserves appreciation and respect as such. I believe, for instance, that when we eat vegetables, we ought to remember that they come from the soil and that the "dirt" we sometimes recoil from and wash down the drain has in fact nourished them and given them their character. I believe that when we drink wine, we ought to be aware of it both as an agricultural product and as a miracle of the benevolent decay known as fermentation. I believe that when we eat meat or fish or fowl, we ought to realize that we are consuming the flesh and blood of a fellow creature, which died to give us strength and pleasure.

I also believe that the way people eat and drink is one of the most vital and authentic things about them as a culture, linking them individually to their ancestral past and their communal present, and connecting them as a people, immediately and intimately, with the earth itself and its seasons and cycles. Thus I believe that betraying our culinary past, and even moreso our culinary instincts—which is precisely what we do when we rely too heavily on processed foods, and shrink from food as if it were poison, and carelessly lose touch with the reality of food—is dead wrong, and very nearly unforgivable; and that a critical concern with food and drink—even a mild obsession with it—is, far from being somehow trivial or unhealthy, both sensible and admirable.

And I believe, above all, that we ought to learn to dine, or even just sit down and eat, not with fear or with the feeling that we're doing something bad, but with the happiness born of appetite and anticipation—with, if possible, sheer, ravenous joy.

RECIPES

Here are six of my favorite recipes, all of them frighteningly full of cream, butter, and other well-known poisons. Eat them entirely at your own risk—and, hey, don't blame me if you die someday.

OYSTER AND SAUSAGE BISQUE

SERVES 4 TO 6

This was an improvisation: Planning to make oyster bisque at my friend Betty's house in New York one night, I suddenly realized that I didn't have enough oysters. The fish market was closed, but I remembered that, in Bordeaux, oysters are often accompanied by little chipolata sausages, and found not chipolatas but good homemade Italian sausage at a butcher shop nearby. I think the combination works quite nicely.

4 tablespoons (¹/₂ stick) unsalted butter
Extra-virgin olive oil
3 to 4 shallots, peeled and minced
¹/₂ celery rib, minced
1 tablespoon tomato paste
¹/₂ pound mild Italian sausage, removed from casings and chopped or crumbled
2 tablespoons flour
3 cups half-and-half
1 pint freshly shucked small oysters (20 to 25), liquor reserved
Salt and freshly ground black pepper

In a large saucepan, over medium heat, melt butter to which a few drops of oil have been added. Add shallots and celery and cook until very soft. Add tomato paste and stir well, then add sausage. Cook for about 5 minutes, then dust contents of pan with flour, stir again, and add half-and-half.

Bring to a boil, then reduce heat to medium and cook, stirring frequently, until mixture has thickened. Add oysters and their liquor and salt and pepper to taste. Cook for 3 to 4 minutes more and serve.

CREAM OF BRUSSELS SPROUT SOUP

SERVES 4

I've found that this is a good way to get people to eat their damned Brussels sprouts.

2 tablespoons butter
Extra-virgin olive oil
4 scallions, trimmed and minced
2 garlic cloves, peeled and minced
1 pound Brussels sprouts, washed, trimmed, and halved
   lengthwise
2 to 3 ounces prosciutto, shredded
3 cups rich chicken, duck, or turkey stock
1 cup half-and-half
2 tablespoons crème fraîche or sour cream
Salt and white pepper

In a large saucepan, melt butter to which a few drops of oil have been added. Add scallions, garlic, and Brussels sprouts and cook over low heat for 10 to 15 minutes.

Meanwhile, separate shredded prosciutto into strands. In a skillet, sauté them in a small quantity of oil over medium-high heat until beginning to brown. Remove and drain on paper towels.

Add just enough stock to cover vegetable mixture, and allow to simmer uncovered for 15 minutes or until liquid is reduced by about half. Add remaining stock and half-and-half, cover, and simmer for 15 minutes more.

Allow soup to cool to room temperature, then purée it (in two batches if necessary) in a blender or food processor until smooth. Return soup to original pot and reheat on low heat. Whisk in *crème fraîche* or sour cream and season with salt and white pepper to taste just before serving.

Ladle soup into bowls and garnish with fried prosciutto.

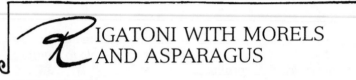

$\mathcal{R}$IGATONI WITH MORELS AND ASPARAGUS

SERVES 4 TO 6

The combination of fresh morels, asparagus, and Parmigiano Reggiano is one of my favorite blends of flavor. Up jumped spring!

1 pound fresh morels*
1 pound fresh asparagus
Salt
Extra-virgin olive oil
4 tablespoons (½ stick) unsalted butter
½ cup good-quality dry red wine
1 tomato, peeled, seeded, and finely chopped
½ cup heavy cream
1 pound rigatoni pasta
Freshly grated Parmigiano Reggiano
Freshly ground black pepper

*This dish is incomparably better made with fresh morels, but dried ones may be substituted if necessary. Soak 3 to 4 ounces dried morels in warm (not hot) water for 20 to 30 minutes, changing the water once, drain, then proceed as with fresh morels.

Trim morel stems slightly if they appear woody (do not remove too much), then rinse morels carefully in cool water. If they seem particularly sandy, clean them gently with a mushroom or pastry brush, then rinse again. Cut them into quarters and set aside.

Snap or cut off fibrous lower stems of asparagus spears, then cut asparagus into 1½″ to 2″ lengths. Blanch for about 3 minutes in boiling, salted water, then drain and rinse in cold water. Set aside.

Bring a large pot of salted water, to which a bit of olive oil has been added, to a boil.

Meanwhile, melt butter in a saucepan. Add morels and cook over low heat for about 5 minutes, stirring frequently, then add red wine to pan and increase heat. Cook for 2 to 3 minutes more, or until wine has reduced completely. Add tomato and cream, stir well, add salt to taste, and remove pan from heat.

When water is boiling, cook pasta to taste. Just before it finishes cooking, add asparagus to morels and reheat.

Drain pasta well, then toss thoroughly in a large bowl with a handful of Parmigiano Reggiano. Add morel mixture and toss thoroughly again. Add plenty of pepper and serve at once with additional Parmigiano on the side.

FRIED SAND DABS WITH BACON AND THYME

SERVES 6

This idea is based very loosely on a dish of sweetbreads in a cream sauce flavored with pearl onions, bacon, and fresh thyme that Jonathan Waxman used to serve at his late, lamented Jams in New York City.

1/2 pound thinly sliced bacon
1 teaspoon sweet paprika
Leaves from 8 to 10 sprigs fresh thyme
Salt and freshly ground black pepper
1 cup coarse yellow cornmeal
2 1/2 to 3 pounds sand dab fillets (3 to 4 per person) or small, whole lemon or gray sole
1 cup half-and-half or whole milk
2 tablespoons very cold salted butter, sliced into as many slices as there are sand dabs
4 scallions, trimmed and finely chopped

Fry bacon over medium-low heat until brown and crisp in 1 very large or 2 smaller skillets. Drain on paper towels, reserving rendered fat in pan.

Mix paprika, thyme, salt, and plenty of pepper into cornmeal. Dip sand dabs in half-and-half or milk, then dredge thoroughly in cornmeal. Fry in batches in bacon fat over medium-high heat until golden brown, about 2 minutes per side.

Divide sand dabs evenly between 6 warm plates, place 1 slice butter in the center of each fillet, crumble bacon evenly over fish, and scatter with scallions.

GRILLED CHICKEN BREASTS WITH CREAMED CORN

SERVES 4

And this idea is based very loosely on a dish of scallops with corn, bacon, and red peppers created by Leonard Schwartz at 72 Market Street in Venice (California) some years ago.

Juice of ¹/₂ lemon
¹/₄ cup extra-virgin olive oil
2 garlic cloves, peeled and minced
1 teaspoon herbes de Provence
Salt and freshly ground black pepper
4 large skinless, boneless chicken breast halves
5–6 ears fresh corn, shucked and cleaned
¹/₄ pound slab bacon in one piece, cut into ¹/₂" cubes
6–8 whole scallions, trimmed and coarsely chopped
¹/₂ cup heavy cream
4 sprigs fresh parsley, minced

Mix lemon juice, olive oil, garlic, *herbes de Provence,* and salt and pepper together well in a large bowl. Add chicken breasts and marinate at room temperature for about 30 minutes, turning occasionally.

Drop ears of corn into ample boiling salted water, cook for 3 minutes, then rinse with cold water. Set aside to cool.

Fry bacon over medium heat until light brown, then drain off about 2 tablespoons bacon drippings, reduce heat to low, and add scallions. Cook until softened, stirring occasionally, then remove from heat.

Remove chicken breasts from marinade and grill them (on a barbecue or gas grill) over high heat for 5 to 7 minutes on each side, or until done, basting with remaining marinade.

Meanwhile, cut corn from cobs with a sharp knife, and

purée about half of it in a blender or food processor. Add the cream and blend for 1 second.

Add creamed corn and remaining corn to the bacon and scallions and heat through, adding salt and pepper to taste.

Spoon the corn onto 4 warm plates and top with chicken breasts. Scatter minced parsley over corn.

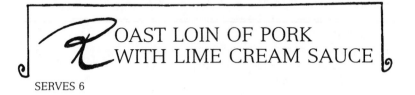

ROAST LOIN OF PORK WITH LIME CREAM SAUCE

SERVES 6

1 boneless pork loin (approximately 3 pounds)
4 limes
1 12-ounce jar lime marmalade
Salt and cracked or very coarsely ground black pepper
Extra-virgin olive oil
1/2 cup dry white wine
1 cup cream

Puncture pork loin well with a fork on all sides, 20 or 30 times in all, then place in a nonreactive dish just large enough to hold it.

Grate zest off the limes on the finest holes of a grater, then halve the limes and squeeze their juice into a small saucepan. Add the grated zest and the marmalade. Add salt and pepper to taste. Cook gently over a low flame, stirring well, until marmalade has melted.

Pour marinade over pork, cover with foil, and allow to marinate overnight in the refrigerator, turning it once or twice. Remove pork from refrigerator about an hour before cooking.

Preheat oven to 350°.

Coat the bottom of a small covered metal roasting pan with olive oil, then place pork in pan, conserving marinade. Roast pork, covered, for 1 hour and 15 minutes, basting once or twice with marinade. Uncover pan, raise heat to 450°, and continue cooking 10 minutes longer.

Remove pork to cutting board and allow to rest. Meanwhile, deglaze pan with wine over high heat, stirring well to scrape browned bits off bottom of pan. Add remaining marinade to roasting pan and cook over high heat on top of the stove, stirring constantly, until mixture is thick and syrupy or until alcohol has evaporated. Remove pan from heat and stir in cream, mixing well. Adjust seasoning if necessary.

Slice pork thinly and serve, topped with sauce.

PART I

*Gourmets and How
We Got That Way*

"I love a hearty eater,
but I do despise a goormy."

—JOSEPH MITCHELL, *OLD MR. FLOOD*

1

GOURMET WITH GARNISH

"Maslama b. Abd al-Malik said to Alyun, king of the Byzantines:
'Who do you count the most foolish among you?' And he replied:
'One who fills his stomach with whatever he finds.' "
—IBN 'ABD RABBIHI, "AL-'IQD AL-FARID"

". . . I mind my belly very studiously, and very carefully; for I look upon
it, that he who does not mind his belly, will hardly mind any thing else."
—SAMUEL JOHNSON, AUGUST 5TH, 1763,
QUOTED IN *THE LIFE OF SAMUEL JOHNSON L.L.D.*, BY JAMES BOSWELL

*T*HERE IS NO SUCH THING AS GOURMET FOOD, and the distinction between so-called gourmet food and everyday fare is thus a phony one. The genuine goodness or worth of any dish or culinary raw material has little or nothing to do with its price or rarity or "refinement"—and I think that the perpetuation of what might be called the "gourmet cliché" is ultimately unfair both to those who produce food and those who (on whatever level) enjoy it. I also think it's probably as responsible as anything for the suspicion and sense of disconnection with which we so often consider food today.

About a dozen years ago, passing the butcher case in an L.A. supermarket, I encountered the phrase "Gourmet with Garnish." The words were emblazoned boldly on stickers attached to packages of assorted high-priced meat and poultry items—filet mignon, rack of lamb, boneless chicken breasts, and so on. The implication of the phrase, as best I could interpret it, was that if a customer were to purchase an item so marked, cook it up, and then embellish it with garniture of some kind (what—parsley? lemon wedges? slices of black truffle?), it would deserve the sobriquet "gourmet." The phrase has haunted me ever since, because I find it a particularly terse and vivid expression of a particularly unfortunate idea—the cliché incarnate.

I reject the notion utterly. Food is good or bad, stale or fresh, satisfying or deceiving. Elaborate names and ambitious price tags don't automatically make food worthier or more refined, any more than popular availability devalues it. Some ingredients, inevitably, are rarer and more expensive than others, but that doesn't mean that they're intrinsically better or that they will bring more real sensual pleasure to the person who consumes them. Fine chefs are to be respected and admired—but some delicate, elaborate creation on which they've labored for hours won't necessarily please the palate more than a hunk of good cheese and a piece of just-baked bread. A perfect string bean is worth more than a gummy chunk of canned pâté flecked with bits of bland black truffle; fresh-caught codfish properly roasted is superior to frozen lobster boiled to rubber. There are places in the world where pheasant is a commonplace and chicken is a delicacy; which one, then, is "gourmet"? And, incidentally, garniture decorates food; it does not somehow ennoble it.

When someone says something like "Mom's a great cook, but of course she doesn't cook 'gourmet'" or "I don't feel like eating anything 'gourmet' tonight," they're using the word to mean "fancy" or "fussy"—to imply exotic raw materials, complicated cooking methods, frills. They're describing a kind of food they probably think they ought to like but probably don't. Or maybe they have in mind the "gourmet" section of their supermarket, stocked with fancy-label sardines, salad dressings, and preserves at three times the price of the virtually identical ones in other sections of the market. At best, they're describing something outside their normal purview, something weird; at worst, they're describing something they think they don't deserve—something they lack the knowledge or experience or breeding to appreciate.

In an installment of the Brant Parker/Johnny Hart comic strip "The Wizard of Id" a few years back, the wizard's wife presents him with his dinner. Inspecting it skeptically, he asks what it is. "Gourmet meatloaf," she replies. He asks how meatloaf can be "gourmet." "I put snails in it," she replies. And there you have it. Add snails—an oddball ingredient, not eaten by the common man (at least in America, or apparently in Id)—to meatloaf and the meatloaf becomes . . . well, *gourmet with garnish!*

This view of "gourmet food" gives us one more reason to be *afraid* of food, or at least some kinds of it. By labeling certain dishes or ingredients "gourmet," we put them at a distance, on a shelf—out of reach of everyday experience—and thus come to think of them as daunting or inaccessible. We needlessly limit our repertory of consumption—at the same time, at least subconsciously, perhaps resenting or distrusting those of our fellow citizens who eat snails quite happily.

The opposite also sometimes happens: Instead of avoiding "gourmet" foods, sometimes we're drawn to them, eating them even if we don't particularly want them, even if they're not particularly good. This happens all the time at cocktail buffets, where the waterlogged, bland shrimp disappears faster than the fresh, bright crudités; and on airplanes, where most travelers given the choice will pick (say) overdone, chewy "filet mignon" over at least edible lasagna. And why? Because raw vegetables are refrigerator snack food and noodles are for Sunday nights at home, but shrimp and steak are, well, you know what. Thus we end up eating (as it were) our ideas about food, or our expectations of it, rather than just food itself.

That's not what gourmets do. And if I don't believe in gourmet food, I most certainly do believe in gourmets themselves. America is full of them. I'm one, and proud of it. You're probably one yourself. A gourmet is not, by my definition, a studied epicure, a food snob. A gourmet is not someone who eats only fine French food and turns up his nose at hot dogs and apple pie. A gourmet is not a stuffed-shirt or an upper-class twit or a hoity-toity self-styled aristocrat—at least not necessarily, though I suppose such people can be gourmets, too. A gourmet is simply a person who cares about what he eats.

I sat next to a gourmet one morning several years ago in a coffee shop in West Los Angeles. He was an average-looking man, eating an average-looking breakfast—bacon and eggs and thin white toast washed down with thin black coffee. Nothing particularly "gourmet" there. But he revealed his gourmet nature by a fragment of his conversation, which I couldn't help but overhear: "You know," he suddenly announced to the woman he was sitting with, "I never eat breakfast out if I can help it, because nobody knows how to make bacon and eggs the way I like 'em. And you know, when I cook bacon, I know how to do it so it doesn't curl up, and I don't weight it down with anything, either."

I call this man a gourmet because, on some level and for at least one meal a day, he paid attention to his food, expressed his preferences, knew what he liked and how to get it. *The Oxford English Dictionary*—after noting that the word "gourmet" derives originally from the Old French word *gromet* or *groumet,* meaning a servant, valet, shop-boy, or wine-merchant's assistant—defines the term simply as "A connoisseur in the delicacies of the table." Fair enough: Any good food is a delicacy, and anyone who likes good food and seeks it out is a connoisseur, at least in my book.

You don't have to have a snootful of arcane food knowledge to be a gourmet, that is. You don't have to know which fork to use or how to tell the difference at a sniff between Bordeaux and Burgundy. You just have to eat what you want to eat, and like it. If you've ever sent your lamb chops back because they were too well done, or driven just a little farther than you had to to see a movie because the popcorn was better at that theater than at this one, or even taken the trouble and the time to get that fast-food hamburger with exactly the kinds and proportions of condiments you savor the most, then you're a gourmet in my book—or at least have tendencies in the gourmet direction.

And why not? Why can't a gourmet be just some ordinary Joe or Jane who likes good grub, who can cook bacon without curling it, maybe, or who knows a good hamburger from a sorry shrimp? Why can't we all be gourmets, and proud of it—confident, hungry, and to hell with the garnish?

RECIPES

I was sorely tempted to make up a recipe for meatloaf with snails here, just for the fun of it—but instead I'll just offer three dishes I thought were pretty darned "gourmet" back in the mid-1960s. Along with a simple green salad, they add up to a hearty, deliciously reactionary dinner—reactionary even to the point of requiring the energy-squandering use of two ovens simultaneously.

STEVE HOPE BREAD

SERVES 6 TO 8

Steve Hope was my boss for a time when I worked as a film inspector at ABC-TV in Hollywood in the early 1960s. He used to bring this bread to work sometimes, and I liked it well enough to ask him for the recipe—which in fact was his wife Betty's.

Hope now has his own film-editing company, I learned when I tracked him down recently to ask his permission to use the recipe, and he remembers me well. This, I assume, is because I was always getting in trouble for one thing or another at ABC. Like staying out too long for lunch.

1 long loaf sourdough bread
¹/₂ teaspoon garlic powder
1 pinch each dried thyme and dried basil
2 pinches dried rosemary
1 teaspoon each dried oregano, marjoram, summer savory,
    sweet red bell pepper flakes, sweet green bell pepper
    flakes, onion flakes, parsley, chives*
2 sticks salted butter, at room temperature

Preheat oven to 250°.

Carefully slice bread into thirds lengthwise.

Blend all remaining ingredients together well, then spread evenly on all cut surfaces of bread and reassemble loaf.

Wrap loosely in aluminum foil and bake on cookie sheet for 30 minutes. Serve at room temperature.

---

* Red and green bell pepper flakes are hard to find these days, and may be omitted if necessary. Would this bread taste as good with fresh herbs instead of dried ones? Sure. Probably better. But it wouldn't be Steve Hope Bread.

GREEK LAMB BAKED IN FOIL

SERVES 6

I don't remember where this recipe came from originally, but I know that I've added ingredients to it over the years, and that I used to cook it sometimes in an attempt to impress girls I had invited over to dinner. It rarely worked.

Extra-virgin olive oil
6 8-ounce lamb steaks (cut from leg or shoulder)
1 teaspoon dried oregano
6 garlic cloves, peeled and thinly sliced
6 bay leaves
6 slices feta cheese, about 2" × 3" and ¹/₃" thick
6 slices kefalotyri *or* kasseri *cheese, about 2" × 3" and*
  ¹/₃" thick
6 baby carrots, peeled, trimmed, and halved lengthwise
6 slices of leek, white part only, about ¹/₂" thick
6 large celery leaves
Juice of 1 lemon
Salt and freshly ground black pepper

Preheat oven to 350°.

Lay 6 sheets of heavy-duty aluminum foil, about 12" × 12" each, on flat work surface and brush very lightly on one side with olive oil.

Place 1 lamb steak in the middle of each sheet, sprinkle with oregano, distributing it evenly between the steaks, and then divide all other ingredients except lemon juice, salt, and pepper evenly and arrange them on top of steaks in matching patterns. (Be sure that garlic touches meat directly.)

Sprinkle lemon juice evenly over vegetable arrangements, add salt and pepper to taste, then fold each piece of foil into a packet, leaving a bit of room at the top, and crimp edges to seal.

Place packets side by side in a large baking dish and bake in the middle of preheated oven for 1 hour. To serve, carefully cut packets open (be careful of escaping steam), drain off fat if necessary, and slide lamb steaks and vegetables onto plates.

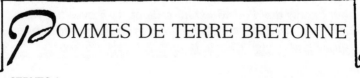

$\mathcal{P}$OMMES DE TERRE BRETONNE

SERVES 6

I don't remember where this recipe came from, either, but I think it must have been the first putatively French dish I ever essayed.

8 to 10 slices bacon
6 large white or red potatoes, well scrubbed and thinly sliced
¹/₄ pound (1 stick) unsalted butter, melted
Salt and freshly ground black pepper
3 onions, peeled and thinly sliced
2 cups rich beef stock

Preheat oven to 425°.

Blanch bacon slices in ample boiling water for about 10 minutes. Remove, rinse well in cold water, and dry thoroughly with paper towels.

Line a large casserole with bacon slices, then place a layer of potatoes on top of bacon. Drizzle with butter and season lightly with salt and pepper. Place a layer of onion slices on top of potatoes, then top with a layer of potatoes. Add butter and seasonings as before. Repeat process until onions and potatoes are used up, ending with a layer of potatoes. Pour remaining butter, if any, over final layer of potatoes, then add beef stock to casserole. Cover and bake for about 1 hour, testing for doneness. Uncover and bake for about 5 minutes more, to brown top lightly.

2

ROOTS

"What we have inherited from our fathers
and mothers is not all that walks in us."
—HENRIK IBSEN, *GHOSTS*

HEREVER I MAY HAVE ACQUIRED MY DISPO-
sition toward gourmandise, it was not at my mother's
(or father's) knee. I do owe to my parents the strong
beginnings of my love for restaurants, because they ate
out a lot and often took me along. But they used restaurants more for social than for gastronomic reasons. When
they dined at Romanoff's, Chasen's, Scandia, or some
other sophisticated Los Angeles restaurant of the era, they
ordered relatively unsophisticated fare—vichyssoise,
shrimp cocktail, well-done beef, maybe chicken in some
innocuous sauce. They may have had a cocktail or two

before dinner, but with their food, I shudder to report, they mostly drank skim milk.

At home, things were even worse. The guiding spirits in my mother's kitchen were not Julia Child or James Beard, or even Fannie Farmer or Mrs. Rombauer. They were Mary Kitchen, Dinty Moore, and the Jolly Green Giant. Mom's idea of prep work was opening cans and thawing freezer packages. What my mother made best for dinner, to paraphrase the old joke, was reservations.

A food-business trade magazine once asked me if I had any favorite old recipes of my mother's. I replied that I certainly did not, and that, in fact, if any of my mother's old recipes were to turn up, I'd burn them immediately. I know, I know. That wasn't very nice. But I was the one (along with my sister Merry) who had to eat the tuna-and-cream-of-mushroom-soup over toasted English muffins and the Chef Boyardee spaghetti gussied up with canned corn, canned olives, and cocktail franks (gourmet with garnish?), not to mention the endless canned stews and frozen pot pies. The closest thing to real food my mother ever made was a kind of pot roast, invariably sweltered into grayness, and accompanied by canned new potatoes and fresh(!) carrots cooked for hours in the pan juices underneath the meat. (These were actually quite delicious, with leathery surfaces and an unlikely sweetness that I still recall fondly today.)

If indeed my mother couldn't cook, though, it turns out that I wasn't being strictly accurate when I told that food magazine that I didn't have any of her recipes. Not long ago, I came across a sort of scrapbook of recipes she had culled from assorted magazines and newspapers in the late 1940s and early 1950s—the one concrete culinary legacy I have from her.

That many of the recipes, which carry such bylines as Marian Manners, Cleo Kerley, and of course "Prudence Penny (Reg. U.S. Pat. Off.)," date from the immediate postwar years is plain from some of the accompanying introductions. "Naturally sweet," reads one, "raisins are a tremendous help when it comes to making desserts these days, when sugar still is scarce." Another exults, "Now that ham has no [rationing] points you'll be serving it whenever you can buy it!" And my favorite: "Fats and oils are still on the shortage list and are badly needed for the starving people of Europe and Asia. However, that need not affect our summer salad schedule. . . ."

Certain themes recur frequently in the recipes my mother chose to save. There are, for example, numerous formulae for yams and sweet potatoes, almost all of them involving marshmallows, and also for corn dishes—many of them either fritters of some sort or corn cooked loose and accompanied by "frizzled" ham or Spam. There are lots of desserts and pastries, very few fish dishes, an inordinate number of salads and salad dressings (which I find curious because I don't remember ever having seen my parents eat raw greens), and quite a few straightforward preparations of meat—meat loaf, Swiss steak, ham with raisin sauce, and so on. There is also what must have been the recipe my mother used for her pot roast. It calls for browning a four-pound hunk of chuck for thirty minutes in "fat" and then pot-roasting it for four more hours. No wonder it was gray.

Some of the recipes have been slightly emended in my mother's hand—the onion, green pepper, and cloves excised from a recipe for "varsity baked beans," for instance, and "bacon fat" substituted for the generic "shortening" here and there. (Mom was a great believer in bacon fat as a frying medium, and there was always a coffee can on the back of the stove for drippings. I share her predilection.)

In any case I certainly didn't develop my own tastes in food in general—and my sense of food's profound importance beyond its mere nutritional value—in imitation of my parents. But I don't think I developed them out of rebellion, either, because I don't recall that there was ever any great urgency attached to my feelings about food, one way or the other, when I still lived at home.

So where did I come from, then, gastronomically speaking? I wonder sometimes if it might have had something to do with my Roman Catholic upbringing. Food and wine figure symbolically and ceremonially in many religions, of course, but they are central to Catholicism. The great defining mystery of the faith is the transubstantiation of bread and wine (not, you will note, of oat bran and mineral water) into the body and blood of Christ, echoing an event that first took place at the dinner table, during the Last Supper. Christ's first miracle, by which he chose to introduce himself to public life, was the turning of water into wine at the marriage feast in Cana—particularly good wine, to boot. (Though how could it have been otherwise?) A number of the Apostles were even in the food business, on the fishing end of things. And the altarpiece in the church we attended while I was growing up, I remember vividly, was a mosaic still life involving bread, fish, lamb, and grapes—which, symbolic values aside, are the fixings of a pretty good dinner, a fact I remember remarking on at the time.

In any case, whether or not I was encouraged by the gastronomic trappings of Catholicism, I know for sure that I experienced a seminal event in my development as an eater—my first small gastronomic epiphany, if you will— while I was still in the care of the good nuns at St. Paul the Apostle grammar school in West Los Angeles. One fine lunchtime in coolish weather, when I was in the sixth or seventh grade, the school cafeteria served us little round cardboard cartons full of a mysterious substance called chili con carne. I had never tasted anything like it. It was spicy and exotic and complex and somehow almost *dangerous* in some unfamiliar way. Where had this stuff been all my life? I wondered. That, in fact, is more or less what I asked my mother when I got home that day. She was horrified. "Chili con carne?" she asked with a shudder, rather as if I'd said that I had just tried sky diving or smoking opium. "Oh, for heaven's sake. You don't like *that*."

And I realized at that very moment, for the first time I think, that she didn't know *what* I liked when it came to food, and quite possibly didn't care—but that *I* did know, and did care, and was probably pretty much going to have to feed myself from that day on, at least figuratively. And thus, I suppose, a gourmet was born.

RECIPES

Here are two recipes, both for pie, that appear in my mother's scrapbook.

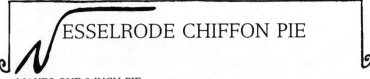

ESSELRODE CHIFFON PIE

MAKES ONE 9-INCH PIE

Count Karl Robert Nesselrode (1780–1862) was a Russian diplomat, famous for having negotiated the Treaty of Paris after the Crimean War. I'm not sure what his connection with chestnuts was, but in classical French cooking, anything with his name on it involves chestnut purée. This decidedly American recipe is innocent of chestnuts, but otherwise seems to be based on a French dessert called pouding Nesselrode *or Nesselrode pudding, which includes, besides the purée, candied orange peel, candied cherries, raisins, and currants. It is also one of the silliest desserts I can imagine, and I love it.*

In my mother's scrapbook, the recipe appears in an ad for Knox Gelatine, headlined "AMERICA'S NEW FAVORITE—A real 'dress-up' dessert." When I wrote to Knox, now part of the Thomas J. Lipton company, to ask for permission to use the recipe, the manager of the Lipton test kitchens sent me another version of the formula, with a note that it had been developed in 1955. I would bet that the recipe in my mother's book is at least a few years older than that. The following is basically "America's new favorite," with a few particulars borrowed from the 1955 recipe.

1 cup milk
1 cup heavy cream
3 egg yolks
³/₄ cup sugar
¹/₂ teaspoon salt
1 envelope Knox Unflavored Gelatine
3 tablespoons rum or sherry*
3 egg whites, lightly beaten
1 tablespoon chopped maraschino cherries
1 baked 9″ pie shell
¹/₄ cup shaved milk chocolate

Combine milk and cream in a mixing bowl, then lightly beat in egg yolks, ¹/₄ cup sugar, and salt.

Transfer mixture to a bain-marie and cook, stirring constantly, until it coats spoon (about 7 minutes). Stir in gelatin and continue stirring until it dissolves completely, about 5 minutes.

Allow mixture to cool, then stir in rum or sherry. Chill until it begins to thicken.

Add remaining sugar to egg whites and beat until stiff, then fold egg whites and cherries into thickened custard.

Fill pie shell with mixture and sprinkle with shaved chocolate. Chill before serving.

---

* The recipe in my mother's scrapbook offers the alternative of 2 teaspoons of rum flavoring. Over my dead body.

$\mathcal{R}$ AISIN PIE

MAKES ONE 9-INCH PIE

I do remember this pie from my childhood, and I remember that I loved it mightily—though I can't recall if my mother actually used to make the pie herself or entrusted the task to our housekeeper. This recipe is adapted from a newspaper recipe of uncertain provenance, probably c. 1947–1949.

2 cups raisins (about 8 ounces)
1½ cups water
3 tablespoons flour
1 cup and 1 tablespoon sugar
2 tablespoons fresh lemon juice
1 tablespoon grated lemon rind
¼ pound (1 stick) unsalted butter
1 cup chopped walnuts (optional)
1 unbaked 9" pie shell

Preheat oven to 450°.

Combine all ingredients except walnuts and a table-spoon of the sugar (and pie shell) in a large saucepan and cook over low heat, stirring constantly, for about 10 minutes or until mixture becomes thick and syrupy. Stir in walnuts and remove from heat.

Pour mixture into pie shell and bake for 10 minutes. Reduce heat to 350° and bake for another 20 minutes or until rim of pastry is golden brown.

Remove from oven to cool. When pie pan is still slightly warm to the touch, sprinkle remaining sugar evenly over top of pie.

3

THE UNBEATABLE SWEETNESS
OF FRYING

"Onions are excellent company."
—ROBERT FARRAR CAPON, *THE SUPPER OF THE LAMB*

*C*HIEF AMONG MY MOTHER'S FOOD PREJU-
dices was her intense and unequivocal dislike for garlic,
onions, and all the rest of (as Mrs. Beeton once put it) "the
alliaceous tribe"—all the way down to the subtle, humble
chive. (She would have sooner put ground glass in her
baked potato than those little snips of green.) According to
Waverly Root in his book *Food*, an ancient Turkish legend
holds that when Satan was cast out of heaven and fetched
up on earth, garlic sprouted where he first placed his left
foot and onions where he placed his right. The identifica-

tion of these vegetables with Satan would have made terrific sense to Mom. I love the things myself.

The onion is a scrappy little creature. When you take your knife to it, trimming off its wiry root-end and its papery, twisted topknot, then peel back its fine-veined skin and chop it or slice it, it fights back strenuously. Off into the air, up toward your eyes and nose, it exhales a volatile disulfide compound called lacrimator (literally "tearmaker"), which dissolves in the fluids of the eye to form sulfuric acid, stinging you, provoking you to weep. Even in defeat, as it lies there on the cutting board in pieces, it continues to fight back, to pour forth its fumes, as if hoping you'll come close enough to get your throat burned and your nostrils stung. If you were to bite into it at this point, it would bite back.

But once you introduce those shards of onion to hot oil or butter, the most amazing transformation takes place: The onion gives up almost immediately, losing heart, abandoning its chemical weaponry. As heat permeates it, its lacrimator dissipates; its volatile compounds are transmuted—some of them, according to Harold McGee in his authoritative *On Food and Cooking,* apparently converted into a complex molecule as much as fifty to seventy times sweeter than a molecule of table sugar. The onion is converted; your adversary is reborn as an amiable culinary ally.

This simple process has almost mythic importance to me—for the simple reason that I first started to understand cooking, however tentatively, the first time I ever fried onions myself. I remember the circumstances well: The year was 1967, and I had an English girlfriend. She was small, brunette, attractively sarcastic—herself rather scrappy—and one night, inspired by what must have been my first tentative stirrings of domesticity, I decided to cook dinner for her.

The dish I chose to prepare was *thon au cari,* fresh tuna steaks in a simple, French-style curry sauce. I was attracted to the dish because the recipe looked quite simple, because I liked curry, and because I relished the idea of cooking with an offbeat ingredient, fresh tuna, which was in those days almost wholly unknown in this country (and which turned out to be, I remember, very difficult to locate). Where did I get the recipe? A good question. The English girl had come equipped with an unconventional little cookbook called *Où est le Garlic?*, a collection of elementary cooking lessons in comic-strip form by author Len Deighton (better known now, of course, for his masterful spy novels), originally published in the London Sunday newspaper *The Observer*. For some years, it was my vivid recollection that I had found *thon au cari* in its pages.

I got the recipe somewhere, in any case, and I did make the dish. The recipe began—as, I subsequently learned, do so many recipes in so many cuisines—with the simple instruction (I paraphrase) "Sauté sliced onions in butter until golden." I thus peeled the onions (awkwardly, and with the appropriate welling up of tears), sliced them reasonably thinly, and introduced them to the pan. . . .

From the instant they hit the butter, sputtered a bit, then settled down to turning limp and clear, I was hooked. I felt as I imagine a budding naturalist must feel watching his first time-lapse film of a flower blossoming. There, before my very eyes, some glorious alchemy was taking place, a primal alteration of basic form. Cool and crisp became warm and tender; acridity turned into sweet perfume. So *this* was what cooking was all about, I remember thinking—not just heating something up, but transforming it elementally, evoking the delicious secrets it has locked in its atomic structure. (I owe to the aforementioned Harold McGee, too, the observation that, historically, cooking provided mankind with "the initial realization that we can transform natural materials by means of heat and that the results are consistent, predictable, and often useful." Cooking might then very well be considered the mother of the sciences.)

I like to think that I've subsequently become something of an expert in the alchemical treatment of onions and its relatives. I can roast whole heads of garlic deftly into caramel and cream, deep-fry little rings of leeks to perfect crispness, cosset minced shallots in butter until they grow as sweet as raisins. But frying onions remains my favorite such process—quite possibly my favorite part of cooking, period.

One of the things that most attracted me to the food of the Spanish region of Catalonia, in fact, and encouraged me to write a book on the subject, was its extensive use of the *sofregit*, a marmaladelike confection of cooked-down onions that grows positively dark with sweetness during its long, slow preparation. Catalan author Manuel Vázquez Montalbán goes so far as to propose that a good *sofregit* should possess "the strange and mysterious color that . . . the brushstrokes of the great master Titian obtain." Me, I'm usually happy if I can get my onions to a pale Turneresque umber. It reminds me of the English girl. Mom didn't like her, either.

RECIPES

THON AU CARI

SERVES 2

This is my approximate reconstruction of the recipe I cannot now locate. (Unlike the other recipes in this book, incidentally, this one is written for two servings only—for sentimental reasons.)

1 tablespoon extra-virgin olive oil
2 tablespoons unsalted butter
2 tuna steaks, about 8 to 10 ounces each
2 onions, thinly sliced
2 teaspoons curry powder
1 tablespoon fresh-squeezed lemon juice
$1/2$ cup dry white wine
$1/2$ cup crème fraîche *or heavy cream*
1 teaspoon tomato paste
Salt and freshly ground black pepper

Heat oil and butter in a medium-sized skillet. Add tuna steaks and fry over medium heat until lightly browned on both sides. Remove from pan and set aside. Cover loosely with foil.

Sauté onions over low heat in same pan (adding more oil and butter if necessary) until softened but not brown. Stir in curry powder and lemon juice. Raise heat to high and deglaze pan with white wine. Simmer, stirring constantly, until liquid has reduced by about one-third. Lower heat, stir in *crème fraîche* or cream and return tuna steaks to pan. Cover pan and cook for about 5 minutes or until tuna is warmed through.

Place tuna on plates. Quickly stir in tomato paste and stir until well dissolved. Add salt and pepper to taste.

Pour sauce over tuna, dividing onions equally between the plates.

CATALAN CHILI

SERVES 6

In describing the sofregit *and another basic Catalan "sauce" called the* picada *(a paste of ground nuts, chocolate, garlic, fried bread, and other ingredients) in my book* Catalan Cuisine, *I suggested that both might be used with some success in certain non-Catalan dishes. "Like what?" asked a friend of mine recently. Like this, for instance.*

1 tablespoon lard or bacon fat
Extra-virgin olive oil
2 pounds lean pork, finely chopped or coarsely ground
1 pound mild pork sausage (preferably Spanish-style
   botifarra or Italian sausage without fennel seeds),
   removed from casings and chopped
2 teaspoons ground cumin
1 tablespoon mild paprika
1 teaspoon cayenne or spicy paprika
1 teaspoon ground turmeric
1/2 teaspoon ground cinnamon
Salt and freshly ground black pepper
4 to 5 cups rich beef stock
2 onions, minced
1 teaspoon dried oregano
1 teaspoon dried red chili flakes (optional)
3 tomatoes, peeled, seeded, and chopped
4 garlic cloves, peeled and minced
10 to 15 almonds or hazelnuts (or a combination of both),
   lightly toasted

1 *small slice fried sourdough bread**
2 *ounces cooking chocolate (Ibarra brand, e.g.), grated*
2 *sprigs parsley, minced*

In a large heavy skillet, melt the lard and approximately 2 tablespoons of olive oil. Brown pork and sausage in the hot fat. Transfer the meat to a Dutch oven or stewpot, and add cumin, paprika, cayenne, turmeric, cinnamon, and salt and pepper. Stir well. Deglaze the skillet with 3 cups stock and add to the Dutch oven or stewpot. Simmer, partially covered, for about 3 hours, or until meat is almost falling apart. (Add more stock as necessary; the chili should be thick and moist but not soupy.)

Meanwhile, in a medium skillet, make the *sofregit* by cooking onions over lowest possible heat in about half an inch of olive oil, stirring occasionally, for about 1 hour. Add oregano and chili flakes (if desired), then continue cooking for another 1½ hours, or until onions are very soft and dark golden brown. Stir in tomatoes and cook for 10 minutes longer.

While onions are cooking, make a *picada* by crushing minced garlic in a mortar with a bit of salt, then pound in the nuts, fried bread, and chocolate until very well mixed. Add parsley and barely enough olive oil to cover the *picada,* then work in oil to form a thick paste. (All ingredients should be amalgamated completely and nuts should be thoroughly crushed.)

About 30 minutes before chili is done, stir onion mixture into it. Adjust seasoning. Remove cover and continue cooking, skimming excess fat off surface if necessary. About 5 minutes before serving, stir in *picada.*

* *Quickly fry a piece of good French bread, with crusts trimmed off, in olive oil until lightly browned on both sides.*

Here are three other onion-based recipes of which I'm quite fond:

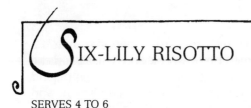

SIX-LILY RISOTTO

SERVES 4 TO 6

Notwithstanding the fact that a notorious Berkeley-based organization of garlic enthusiasts calls itself The Lovers of the Stinking Rose, garlic and its relatives of course aren't roses at all, but Liliaceae—members of the lily family. Thus the rather poetic name of this dish, which uses six different members of the clan. The black sesame seeds, which have practically no discernible flavor when used in this modest quantity, constitute a rather sophomoric gastro-literary joke, best appreciated by admirers of John Ruskin.

1 head garlic
Extra-virgin olive oil
1 pound pearl onions, peeled*
4 tablespoons (¹/₂ stick) butter
5 to 6 shallots, peeled and minced
2 leeks, white parts only, well washed and very thinly sliced
5 to 6 cups chicken stock†
2 cups Arborio rice
1 cup freshly grated Parmigiano Reggiano
4 scallions, trimmed and minced
Salt and freshly ground black pepper
1 bunch chives, minced
2 tablespoons black sesame seeds

To peel pearl onions, plunge into boiling water for about 15 seconds, rinse, cool, then slice off the root ends only and slip onions out of their skins.
† It is impossible to predict the exact amount of liquid the rice will absorb, as this varies with the age and brand of the rice, the cooking temperature, and the cook's philosophy of risotto (soupy or dry, al dente or tender). If you run out of stock before the risotto is completely cooked, a bit of hot water won't hurt it.

Preheat oven to 350°.

Rub whole garlic head well with a bit of oil, wrap tightly in aluminum foil, and bake for about 30 minutes.

Heat a spoonful of olive oil in a medium-sized skillet. Sauté pearl onions over low heat, stirring occasionally, and allow them to cook until they are added to the risotto.

At the same time, melt butter with a few drops of oil in a large, high-sided skillet, then sauté shallots and leeks over very low heat for about 10 minutes, stirring frequently.

While shallots and leeks are cooking, bring stock to a boil, then reduce to a simmer.

When garlic is cooked, slice off the top of the head, and squeeze garlic against a cutting board with the blade of a knife to extrude purée. Set aside.

Add raw rice to shallots and leeks, stir well until all grains are coated with butter and oil, and continue cooking for 2 to 3 minutes. Add about 1 cup of stock to rice and continue stirring until it is almost completely absorbed. Continue this process until rice is almost cooked and there is only about 1 cup of stock remaining, about 25 minutes.

Stir cheese, scallions, pearl onions, garlic purée, and a little of the remaining stock into the rice, season to taste, and continue cooking until risotto is thick and creamy but not overcooked or mushy.

Serve *absolutely* immediately in individual shallow bowls, with chives and sesame seeds scattered atop each serving.*

* Risotto should be not only served immediately but eaten *immediately*. And never ever serve risotto in a big bowl such as you might use for pasta. In the time it takes to dish the risotto up, the portion at the bottom of the bowl will almost certainly turn to mush.

SWEET ONION SOUP

SERVES 6

Though this soup can be made with ordinary Spanish or Bermuda onions, it's particularly good with mild, sweet ones—Walla Walla Sweets from Washington State, Vidalias from Georgia, 1015s from Texas, Osos from Peru (a recent import), or the currently ubiquitous Maui onions from Hawaii. Be careful with the last-named, though. According to the Maui Farmers Co-Op Exchange, which markets about 65 percent of all Maui onions, the only ones that are truly mild and sweet in character are those from the island's Kula highlands; onions grown in the nearby flatlands and not labeled Kula are likely to be more pungent. There is also at least one brand of so-called Maui onions on the market that are not grown on Maui at all, but in Southern California. These are nowhere near as sweet as a good Kula Maui.

8 sweet onions, very thinly sliced
1 tablespoon extra-virgin olive oil
$^1/_2$ teaspoon paprika
2 tablespoons butter
2 tablespoons flour
2 cups milk, heated to just below boiling
2 tablespoons freshly grated Parmigiano Reggiano
Salt and finely ground white pepper
6 cups beef stock, warmed
3 scallions, finely chopped

In a large skillet, sweat onions in olive oil over very low heat for about 1 hour, stirring occasionally. Stir in paprika and cook about 10 minutes longer.

After adding paprika to onions, melt butter in a medium saucepan, whisk in the flour, and cook, stirring constantly, until flour has turned golden—about 3 minutes.

Remove saucepan from heat and add milk slowly and steadily, whisking vigorously to make a thick sauce. Stir in cheese. Add salt and white pepper to taste. Set aside.

Purée about half the onions with half the beef stock in a food processor or blender, then pour into a large soup pot. Add remaining stock and whisk in sauce.

Add remaining onions to soup, stir well, and simmer about 10 minutes. Sprinkle with scallions just before serving.

$\mathcal{U}$NUSUAL WONTONS

SERVES 6 TO 8

2 large red or Bermuda onions, peeled and finely chopped
Extra-virgin olive oil
3 ripe mangoes, peeled, pitted, and chopped
Freshly ground black pepper
6 to 8 shallots, peeled and very thinly sliced
2 teaspoons curry powder
2 medium white potatoes, peeled and halved
1 cup crème fraîche or sour cream
1 bunch cilantro, stems discarded, leaves coarsely chopped
2 cups plain (unflavored) yogurt
2 ripe tomatoes, peeled, seeded, and chopped
Tabasco sauce
Salt
48 round (gyoza) or square (wonton) wrappers, refrigerated
    (but thawed if frozen)
Peanut oil

In a large skillet, sweat onions in olive oil over lowest possible heat, stirring frequently, for 2 to 3 hours or until very soft, golden brown, and marmaladelike. Add mangoes and continue cooking for about 10 minutes. Season very generously with pepper, remove from heat, and set aside to cool.

Meanwhile, in another skillet, sauté shallots in olive oil, also over lowest possible heat, for about 30 minutes. Add curry powder, stir in well, and continue cooking for 5 more minutes. Remove from heat and set aside to cool.

While onions and shallots are cooking, bring salted water to a boil and cook potatoes until done (about 20 minutes). Drain and mash with 2 tablespoons of *crème fraîche* or sour cream, then mix in cilantro thoroughly. Set aside to cool.

Divide yogurt evenly between two bowls and mix half the remaining *crème fraîche* or sour cream into each one. Stir shallots and a little of their cooking oil into one bowl. Stir tomatoes into the other and season with a few drops of Tabasco sauce. Salt both mixtures to taste, then refrigerate.

Remove gyoza or wonton wrappers from refrigerator, cover with a damp, clean cloth to keep them from drying out, then begin filling half of them with onion and mango mixture and half of them with potato mixture. To do this, place a small amount of filling in the middle of each wrapper, then fold over (gyoza wrappers into half-moon shapes, wonton wrappers into triangles) and crimp edges lightly.

Heat peanut oil to 375°, then fry gyozas or wontons in small batches until golden brown, draining on paper towels as done. Serve with chilled dipping sauces on the side.

4

COOKING BY EAR

"Learn to cook!"
—JULIA CHILD, *FROM JULIA CHILD'S KITCHEN*

*I*T SEEMS SELF-EVIDENT TO ME THAT WHEN the Creator made it necessary for every one of us to eat, He must simultaneously have given every one of us the ability to fix ourselves a little something now and then. I believe, in other words, that anyone can cook—maybe not as well as Fredy Girardet, or even Dinah Shore, but well enough. People who "can't" cook, I suspect, are people who don't want to cook.

Not wanting to cook, of course, is anybody's privilege. I just have a hard time understanding why so many people should desire to invoke it. I understand not wanting to be *forced* to cook. Cooking isn't necessarily hard, but it can certainly be arduous, and even tedious. But there are so many different kinds of cooking, and so many different ways to go about it, that there must be *something* about the act of making food that would appeal to almost anybody who gave it a chance.

Popular food culture in the United States today, unfortunately, is madly winnowing down the possibilities, reducing cooking to a few automatic, soulless motions: Drop bag into boiling water. Remove tray from carton. Just add 1 cup low-fat milk. Just thaw and eat. We are more at home with toaster ovens than with roasting pans, more concerned with shortcuts than with shortcake. We have very nearly abdicated our native sense of flavor, texture, and aroma—and why? For the sake of "convenience." Because we want our food fast and easy. Because we've got more important things to do. (Like what?)

Well, sure, our food is fast and easy these days. But is it good? Does it bring real pleasure to the palate, real nourishment to the human engine? *Family Circle* publishes a magazine-sized booklet called "Speed Cooking," whose cover promises that it will reveal "250 Ways to Get Out of the Kitchen Fast." But what's the hurry? What is it about the contemporary American kitchen—so bright and clean and well equipped—that people find so uncomfortable or unwelcoming? *Reader's Digest,* which has based its existence on helping people get out of the *library* fast, has a book called *Cook Now Serve Later,* subtitled *More Time with the Family Less in the Kitchen.* Why on earth should family and kitchen be mutually exclusive?

There's plenty of room for family (and friends) in most kitchens—even if they have to take turns—and plenty for them to do if they want to help. And even if there isn't, and they don't, the end product of the cook's labors is (or should be) enjoyed communally, at table. Sharing what you've cooked with others is one of the most intimate, authentic expressions of friendship, and even of love, that one human being can offer to the other. (The word "companion," remember, derives from the Latin *cum,* "with," and *panis,* "bread.") Is it, then, something to be avoided whenever possible, or gotten over with in record time?

Maybe speed shouldn't be our goal in cooking. Maybe it's time to reevaluate—revalue—cooking as a pursuit. Processed and precooked foods are a fact of life in America (and much of the rest of the world), and most of us resort to them at least occasionally. But every time we use them we rob cooking of its soul, reducing it to the mere act of heating things up and dishing them out. No wonder people don't find cooking fun. Even machines can do it.

One afternoon, my wife, who seldom cooks, decided to make a bourbon cake, using a friend's recipe. Following the directions, she started heating sugar, water, and butter together slowly on the stove. "It's great the way it gets thicker and changes color," she remarked as she stirred the mixture. The next step was to pour a tot of bourbon into the pan, off the heat. She did so. SSSSSSSSSSZZZZZZZZZZ! The pan hissed and sputtered and welled up, foaming like some mad scientist's secret formula. My wife jumped back, startled, but then started smiling. "That's *amazing,*" she said, in genuine delight.

Well, sure. Cooking *is* amazing. It's also important: It's life-sustaining, and something to be proud of when done well. In its ritual aspects, and in the way it transmutes raw materials, it has almost a religious (or at least sacramental) aspect. It reconnects us with the physical world, symbolizing the passing seasons with its seasonally changing products, reminding us of our place in the ecology. (A good cook never wastes, and never takes his resources for granted.)

I spend a lot of time in the kitchen myself. I make dinner almost every night at home. I invite friends over sometimes and put things on the table in front of them that they mostly seem to eat up reasonably happily. I cook at other people's houses sometimes, too, and I have on occasion overheard my hosts bragging mildly about my abilities to their own guests. People even ask me for my recipes from time to time.

Treading that vermicelli-thin line between modesty and its false cousin, though, I'm never quite sure how to respond when people ask me if I'm a good cook. I would certainly never call myself a chef, or anything close to it. But "good cook"? I don't know. I'm not a good cook in the sense of a dedicated amateur of the culinary arts, who studies, codifies, reproduces things consistently. I just riff in the kitchen. I cook by ear. I like to play with fire, and with knives. I've never made a *beurre blanc,* much less a *pâte feuilleté* in my life, and probably never will. My culinary imagination far outstrips my practical abilities. I think about food a lot, and I often have ideas for dishes that I know full well I'll never realize, but that doesn't particularly bother me. The thinking alone is enough for me most of the time.

You can learn to cook, after a fashion, by studying cookbooks and following their instructions faithfully; you can learn to cook by taking lessons, or, if you're really serious about it, by apprenticing at a restaurant or catering company. Or you can learn to cook—at least by ear—by simply doing it a lot. That method has its advantages: You can proceed at your own pace and follow your instincts, and you can concentrate on the foods that interest you, instead of those on somebody else's menu or curriculum. There are also disadvantages to the learn-by-doing method, though: The principal one is that you'll almost certainly make an awful lot of mistakes. That's fine if you're just fooling around at the stove some afternoon by yourself, but less fine if you're making dinner for your family (or, worse, dinner guests).

My early experiments with onion-frying aside, I started really learning to cook (by doing) myself when I got married for the first time. Because I worked at home and my wife worked at an office—and because I enjoyed cooking more than she did—I was the one who made dinner almost every night that we stayed home. I never used recipes. I never cooked to themes. I'd just try stuff out. Every once in a while, I'd come up with something vaguely brilliant—good enough that my wife would ask me to write down exactly what I'd done so that I could reproduce it. More often, we'd simply eat what I'd cooked without comment, me probably wondering what would have happened if I'd used tarragon instead of rosemary and she probably wondering if tomorrow we shouldn't maybe bring home a pizza for a change. And sometimes what I cooked was so terrible that we simply threw it out and headed for the nearest Thai place.

And, of course, in keeping with the cliché, I learned more from my failures than I did from my successes. I learned, for instance, that yogurt tends to curdle when you stir it into hot liquid (though not always—someday I've got to track that one down), that garlic turns bitter if you let it burn, that imitation Parmigiano clumps into stringy wads instead of melting smoothly into a sauce.

I learned that spinach, leeks, mushrooms, and clams nearly always have a bit more sand in them somewhere. I also learned that butter browns very quickly, but that a few drops of oil in it will slow the process down, and that a bit of tomato paste stirred into a sauce will thicken it and add a hint of acidity and sweetness without turning it red.

And I learned unforgettably one day that one should never, ever, flambé alcohol into a pan full of hot olive oil and lard. (Luckily, I wasn't leaning over to inhale the aromas of the dish at the time. I did look kind of funny without eyelashes for a few weeks, though.)

I'm still learning, of course, and have still got a lot to learn. Here's an example both of the way I make food up sometimes and the way I learn about it when I do: Not long ago, my neighborhood market offered a "special purchase" of red bell peppers. These weren't the long, glossy, cosmetically perfect (but often rather bland) red peppers commonly sold in Southern California supermarkets. These were smaller, rounder, about half the price, and so fragrant I could smell them from ten feet away. They were irresistible, and I bought three pounds of them in an instant, without even thinking what I might do with them. They were the kind of peppers I might stuff with salt cod mousse, Spanish-style, or maybe turn into soup. But we were having friends over to dinner that night, and I had already bought vegetables for a first-course salad, and a leg of lamb to grill as a main course. . . .

Okay, I thought when I got home, I'll stuff at least some of the peppers and serve them with the lamb. I looked around for something to stuff them with. I found goat cheese, shallots, and fresh thyme, which seemed like a reasonable start. I sliced the shallots finely and sautéed them in olive oil, added thyme to the pan, and then poured the contents of the pan, oil included, into a bowl with the goat cheese. I mashed it up with a fork, then whisked some cream into it and set it aside.

Next, I cored the peppers and parboiled them, then drained them and dried them thoroughly inside and out. When I went to fill them, though, I found that the goat cheese mixture was too runny; it leaked. I had the bright idea of adding bread crumbs to absorb some of the moisture, which I did generously. Then I tasted the filling. The bread crumbs were gritty, grainy. The effect was most unpleasant. I nearly threw the mixture out and started over.

For some reason, though, I didn't. I went on to something else, and then came back forty minutes later and tasted it again. The bread crumbs had absorbed the moisture, softened, and thickened the mixture nicely. I stuffed the peppers with it and, just before I took the lamb off the grill, baked them briefly at a high heat. They were, it was commonly agreed, quite wonderful. I'd gotten lucky—and added a dish to my repertoire. And I'd learned something about bread crumbs, among other things, in the process. No big deal, of course, but all part of the blend.

Here's another, rather more complicated example of how I sometimes think up dishes: One winter Saturday in 1983, I had some wine-trade friends of mine over for lunch. I planned to grill plump moulard duck breasts like steaks, in the Bordeaux fashion, and as a first course I wanted to make something equally straightforward, but also something at least vaguely wintry in spirit—and something I could make up ahead of time. Browsing through some of my cookbooks, I came across a recipe that sounded perfect in *The Four Seasons Cookbook* by Charlotte Adams (the original cookbook from that august New York restaurant): Sweet Potato Vichyssoise, which was basically sweet potatoes puréed with beef stock and cream. It turned out to be a very simple soup to make and was a great success with my guests.

Three or four years later, in a restaurant in Atlanta, I was served a classic leek-and-potato vichyssoise, which was thick and creamy but undersalted. As I seasoned it, I found myself wondering, for some reason, how it would taste topped with a bit of good caviar. (Don't some chefs serve caviar on roasted potato slices, after all?) A few months after that, planning a dinner at my friend Betty's house in New York, I thought I might make the Four Seasons' sweet potato vichyssoise again. Then I remembered the caviar, and thought I might try it with *this* soup. It worked. The pearlescent gray of Petrossian sevruga played beautifully against the faint salmon-pink color of the soup, and the soup's smooth sweetness framed the salty snap of the caviar exquisitely.

Another dinner, back in Los Angeles, not long afterward: Sweet potato vichyssoise again. With caviar? Well, no. The woman at whose home I was cooking didn't like the stuff. All right, then, I thought, I'll do the same sort of thing with one of caviar's partners in luxury—smoked salmon, cut into very thin strips and scattered across the top of the soup. It turned out very well, too, though I did miss the textural contrast caviar would have added.

Bringing things full circle, about two years after that meal, I again cooked lunch for my wine-trade friends—and again the sweet potato vichyssoise seemed like a good dish to serve. This group loves caviar, but in this case the budget wouldn't cover it. I had the idea of trying smoked salmon again, but with a bit of salmon caviar added? Unfortunately, the member of our company who was assigned to obtain the smoked salmon misunderstood and came back with a little piece of fresh salmon fillet instead. Why not? I thought. Thus, the dish became sweet potato vichyssoise with salmon caviar and little cubes of lightly poached fresh salmon. Yet again the combination worked.

The next time I make the soup, maybe I'll use salmon caviar, smoked salmon, *and* fresh salmon (see the following recipe). The time after that, I might go back to plain sevruga. And the time after that—who knows? Maybe I'll try making regular vichyssoise, and not put anything special in it at all. Except enough salt.

RECIPES

SWEET POTATO VICHYSSOISE WITH THREE KINDS OF SALMON

SERVES 6

1 *onion, coarsely chopped*
2 *leeks, white part only, coarsely chopped*
2 *tablespoons unsalted butter*
1 *tablespoon corn or canola oil*
1¹/₂ *pounds sweet potatoes, peeled and sliced*

2 quarts rich beef stock
Salt and white pepper
Half-and-half (optional)
$^1/_4$ pound salmon fillet, cut into $^1/_2$" cubes
1 to 2 slices good-quality smoked salmon, cut into very thin
    strips
2 to 3 ounces salmon roe (salmon caviar)
1 bunch chives, minced

Sweat onion and leeks in butter and oil in a large pot until
soft, then add sweet potatoes, stirring well. Add all but
$^1/_2$ cup of the stock, bring to a boil, then simmer, covered,
for about 40 minutes or until sweet potatoes are very soft.

Cool soup to room temperature, then purée in blender
or food processor and season to taste. Chill in refrigerator
for at least 3 hours. If too thick to pour fluidly when cold,
thin with a small amount of half-and-half.

About 15 minutes before serving, poach salmon cubes
briefly in a small pan in remaining beef stock. Remove
gently from liquid and drain on paper towels, blotting
carefully to remove white residue.

Divide salmon cubes, smoked salmon, and salmon roe
evenly between six chilled, wide, flat soup bowls (not
cups), preferably white, arranging them in an attractive
pattern. Scatter chives evenly over the six bowls, including rims.

Serve by placing bowls on table without soup, then
ladle soup or pour soup from a pitcher into them.

ꟿNSALATA DI FRITTO MISTO

SERVES 6

This is another dish I made up for a Saturday lunch for my wine-trade friends. "Fritto misto is an Italian mixed grill," wrote the saucy Molly Castle back in 1935 in her Round the World with an Appetite *(see page 196), "but it is as different from the English mixed grill as the Italian and English methods of lovemaking. Fritto misto is light, airy, unexpected, and its intentions are not strictly honourable." A classic* fritto misto *might include as many as 12 or 14 different ingredients—for instance, chicken livers, calf's brain, sweetbreads, frogs' legs, strips of veal scalloppini, tiny meatballs, zucchini, eggplant, apples, artichoke hearts, chestnuts, mushrooms, potatoes, even amarettini cookies— all dipped in batter and deep-fried, then jumbled up together on a platter. I love* fritto misto, *but, frankly, making the real thing is an arduous task. (Each item must be fried separately, and most of them require significant preparation.) On the Saturday in question, then, I improvised a stripped-down (and untraditional) version of the dish, using only four ingredients—shiitake mushrooms, Brussels sprouts, sage leaves, and thin slices of chicken sausage. I must immodestly admit that it was delicious—and that my last-minute notion of serving it atop a tangle of bitterish salad greens to help cut the richness of all this fried food was a good one. (The idea of using a splash of gin in salad dressing instead of vinegar or lemon juice, incidentally, I owe to the late Jock Livingston—founder, with his wife, Micaela, of the legendary Ports in West Hollywood.)*

1 *pound chicken or turkey sausages*
2 *quarts corn, canola, or grapeseed oil*
1 *cup sifted flour*
2 *cups light dry white wine (such as Pinot Grigio)*

2 bunches sage leaves, stalks and stems discarded, rinsed
   and thoroughly dried
1 pound Brussels sprouts, trimmed and halved lengthwise,
   rinsed and thoroughly dried
1 pound shiitake or other fresh mushrooms, stems trimmed
   and thoroughly washed and dried
$^1/_2$ pound assorted cleaned field greens (mâche, curly endive,
   arugula, radicchio, dandelion greens, baby lettuces, etc.)
Extra-virgin olive oil
Gin
Salt
1 bunch Italian parsley, stems discarded, leaves finely
   chopped
$^1/_2$ lemon

Poach sausages for 15 to 20 minutes in water to cover, then
remove from pot, drain, and pat dry. Set sausages aside to
cool.

Meanwhile, heat oil in a pot with at least a 3-gallon
capacity.

While oil is heating, place flour in a large mixing bowl,
then add wine slowly, stirring constantly with a whisk,
until a smooth batter is formed. To test for consistency, dip
a sage leaf into batter. Batter should adhere to leaf, coating
it thoroughly, but should remain translucent. If consistency isn't right, add more flour or wine as necessary.

When oil begins to make a light popping sound, stir
batter once, then, working as quickly as possible, dip
Brussels sprouts into batter and fry until golden brown,
lifting out of pot when done with a slotted metal spoon.
Drain Brussels sprouts on paper towels as they are done.*

Repeat the process with mushrooms and sage leaves,
allowing oil to reheat a minute or two between batches.

Slice cooled sausages on the bias into pieces about $^1/_2''$
thick, then repeat the battering and frying process with
them.

---

* Items can be fried in a deep-fryer, if available.

When all items are fried, toss salad greens in a large bowl with a small quantity of olive oil and a small splash of gin. Distribute them evenly among six plates.

Either arrange fried foods over greens in an attractive pattern or toss them together lightly in a bowl and serve ingredients mixed together. Salt the *fritto misto,* then sprinkle each serving with parsley and a few drops of strained lemon juice.

Here's a dinner of more or less original dishes that I might make for friends:

ORANGE AND FENNEL SALAD WITH FETA CHEESE

SERVES 4 TO 6

4 *medium fennel bulbs, trimmed*
1 *large navel orange, peeled, with white membrane removed*
6 *ounces feta cheese**
2 *tablespoons extra-virgin olive oil*
2 *teaspoons fresh lemon juice*
Salt (optional) and freshly ground black pepper
4 *branches of fennel leaves and/or fennel flowers*

With a very sharp knife, slice fennel bulbs crosswise into paper-thin slices, then cut slices into quarters. Slice and quarter orange similarly.

Put fennel and orange slices in a salad bowl, then crumble in feta cheese and add olive oil and lemon juice. Toss thoroughly, then add salt to taste (if desired) and grind in plenty of black pepper. Toss again and serve on salad plates garnished with fennel leaves and/or flowers.

* I prefer Bulgarian or Greek feta, available at specialty cheese stores and delis, to the French, Danish, and American fetas more commonly sold in supermarkets.

CRABMEAT-AND-MASHED-POTATO ENCHILADAS IN SWEET RED PEPPER SAUCE

SERVES 4 TO 6

5 *large red bell peppers*
1 *red or Bermuda onion, minced*
3 *garlic cloves, peeled and finely chopped*
Olive oil
³/₄ *pound Idaho potatoes, peeled and cut into eighths*
Salt
³/₄ *cup* crème fraîche *or* crema mexicana *(Mexican-style sour cream)*
1 *pound fresh lump crabmeat*
4 *scallions, trimmed and finely chopped*
Juice of ¹/₂ *lemon*
Salt and freshly ground black pepper
1 *cup heavy cream*
Spicy paprika
12 *8″ to 10″ flour tortillas*
1 *pound fresh peas, shelled, or 1 cup frozen peas*
3 *ounces firm young blue cheese (e.g., Cabrales, Danish Blue, or Maytag Blue)*

Char peppers on gas grill, over gas flame on range, or in preheated broiler, turning occasionally, until black on all sides. Allow to cool slightly, then core and halve peppers, remove ribs and remaining seeds, scrape off skin, and set aside.

In a small saucepan, sweat onion and garlic in olive oil over medium-low heat until onion is very soft, then drain.

Meanwhile, place potatoes in a saucepan with cold salted water to cover. Bring to a boil over high heat and continue boiling until potatoes are done (about 20 minutes). Drain, allow to cool slightly, and mash well in a large bowl. Add *crème fraîche* or *crema mexicana* and mix well, then fold in crabmeat, scallions, and lemon juice.

Bring cream to a simmer in a saucepan. Meanwhile, purée peppers with softened onion and garlic in a blender or food processor. Stir purée into hot cream and return to a simmer, then remove from the heat and season with salt, pepper, and paprika to taste.

In a medium skillet, heat ¼″ of olive oil over high heat until very hot but not smoking. Using tongs, dip tortillas one by one in oil and fry for a few seconds on each side. Drain tortillas and stack them between paper towels. Add more oil to skillet and reduce heat slightly if oil begins to smoke.

Preheat oven to 350°. Lightly oil a 9″ × 11″ baking dish. Brush both sides of each tortilla with red pepper sauce and spread about ¼ cup of crab mixture in a line down the center of each. Roll up tortillas and place seam side down in the baking dish. Spoon remaining red pepper sauce over tortillas, cover loosely with foil, and bake for about 15 minutes.

Meanwhile, cook the peas *al dente* in boiling salted water. Drain and set aside.

Remove foil from enchiladas, crumble blue cheese on top, and continue baking, uncovered, until cheese is just melted. Serve enchiladas scattered with peas.

*M*ELON ICE CREAM WITH BLUEBERRIES AND CANDIED WALNUTS

SERVES 6 TO 8 (MAKES 1 QUART)

2 to 3 cups coarsely chopped very ripe melon (e.g.,
cantaloupe, honeydew, crenshaw)
2 eggs
²/₃ cup granulated sugar
2 cups heavy cream
1 lime
1 cup candied walnuts*
2 cups fresh blueberries

Purée melon in a food processor or blender.

In a large mixing bowl, beat eggs and sugar together until thick and creamy. Add cream and puréed melon and continue beating until mixture takes on the light color of the melon.

Process in an ice cream maker according to manufacturer's instructions.

Freeze 1 to 2 hours before serving.

To serve, place a scoop of ice cream in each of 6 or 8 bowls and squeeze a few drops of lime juice on top. Divide walnut pieces evenly among the bowls, sticking them into the ice cream, then scatter blueberries over each serving.

---

* *Use commercially prepared candied walnuts, available at specialty stores and some Chinese markets. Or toss walnut halves with 2 tablespoons sugar and toast lightly in the broiler.*

5

THAT WAS NO CUISINART,
THAT WAS MY KNIFE

"The great mechanical impulses of the age,
of which most of us are so proud, are a mere passing fever,
half-speculative, half-childish."
—JOHN RUSKIN, *MODERN PAINTERS*

HEN I READ, A FEW YEARS BACK, THAT CUIsinarts, Inc.—the company that introduced the French-style electric food processor to America—had filed for Chapter 11 bankruptcy protection, I had mixed feelings. On one hand, I was sorry to hear of the company's misfortunes, because the Cuisinart is a genuine icon of the American culinary revolution—no mere appliance, but the very engine of our aspirations as contemporary preparers of good food. On the other hand, I also felt somewhat vindicated: I *knew* those darned gadgets wouldn't sell! I thought to myself.

Of course, the American public has snapped up about a zillion Cuisinarts thus far, and I'm sure they're still selling by the carload even as we speak. (Cuisinarts, Inc., hasn't gone out of business; it is just, as they say, under new management.) But, hey. Chapter 11. That's symbolic. End of an era, right? Time to move that thing off the kitchen counter. Time to stick it up there on that back shelf in the garage, next to the eight-track tape player and the CB radio and the Simpsons lunchboxes.

Now, I must quickly add that I know the Cuisinart to be an excellent product. It is well made and does what it is supposed to do. My objection to it—and to food processors in general—is more philosophical than practical: It seems to me that machines of this sort, though ostensibly allies of gastronomy and boons to the serious cook, in fact insulate us from food, or at least from the preparation of same. Food processors turn what ought to be a slightly messy, tactile pleasure into a neat, mechanical procedure. They make mincemeat out of culinary sensuality, replacing the compelling crunch of celery under the knife with the click of a plastic feeder-tube screwing into place— obscuring the scent of fresh-minced garlic with the faint odor of a however-many-horsepower motor whirring hotly on and off. (I called Cuisinarts, Inc., to ask what the machine's exact horsepower was—and was informed that this was a trade secret.)

When I've written in the past about how much I enjoy the nuts-and-bolts (or perhaps I should say soup-to-nuts) manual labor involved in cooking, I get letters saying things like, "You're obviously a lazy bachelor, because if you had six kids like we do, you'd welcome all the mechanical help you could get in the kitchen," or "Have you ever canned sixty jars of green tomato pickle relish? I did once by hand, and never did it again until I got a Cuisinart."

Well, fair enough. I'm not a lazy bachelor, but I'm a reasonably lazy married man, with only one daughter and one wife. But I can tell you one thing: If I did have six kids, they'd be helping in the kitchen as soon as they were old enough to know which end of a knife to hold. I'll tell you another thing, too: I wouldn't can sixty jars of green tomato pickle relish in the first place, unless I were planning on going into the green tomato pickle relish business. How much of it can you use in a year's time, anyway? How much of it can you give away? And if you have so many green tomatoes at the end of the season every year that you have to make vast quantities of pickle relish with them—well, say, have you ever stopped to think that maybe you've been sticking too many tomato plants in the ground?

The truth is that I am in general opposed to almost any machine that does things to food mechanically. I do sometimes use a standard two-speed Waring blender, I must admit, but that's just because I can't seem to find my hand-cranked food mill. Beyond that, I suppose you could call me a culinary Luddite, though of course I don't go around smashing other people's appliances. I just don't have much room in my kitchen, physically or otherwise, for so-called labor-saving contraptions that take food literally out of my hands.

Here are some other things I don't have in my kitchen:

A "professional" range. The complexity and technological sophistication with which kitchens are outfitted these days often far outpaces the skills or legitimate needs of the people who own them. I think people who install so-called professional kitchens and then use them to cook one dish out of *The Silver Palate Cookbook* every other Saturday are like people who show up for their first tennis lesson carrying $300 racquets. Form precedes content in such cases—and often, in my experience, precludes it. (P.S. Have you ever seen a French home kitchen? The French, after all, practically invented home cooking, and they tend to rustle up their own grub in little rooms the size of walk-in closets, on stoves the size of trash compactors.)

A microwave oven. Noted chefs and food writers galore have embraced the microwave in recent years. (This doesn't hurt; microwaves don't get hot on the outside.) At a microwave industry conference in Chicago in 1990, industry leaders even predicted that by the year 2000, American homes would commonly contain not just one microwave apiece but several—perhaps one for every room in the house. Not *chez moi.* I have no use for the things at all. For one thing, I never quite got over Paul Brodeur's book *The Zapping of America,* which I can assure you will put you off microwaves pretty quickly. For another thing, I think microwaves are soulless. You can't smell food cooking in a microwave—at least not very well; you can't fuss with what you're making, giving it a stir, turning the heat up or down a bit, adding some of this or some of that. Microwaves reduce the act of preparing food to predetermined "power" and "time" settings. What's the point? Where's the fun? Where's the *cooking*? If all I want is to get food on my table in a hurry, I'll swing by El Pollo Loco on the way home.

An automatic dishwasher. I was brought up to believe that you ought to finish whatever you start, and I think an automatic dishwasher's job is basically to complete a task somebody else has already begun. You can't just stick all your pots and pans and plates and glasses into the thing, complete with mashed-potato smears and coffee grounds and sticky bits of chicken skin and all. You've got to *rinse* everything first. And the truth is that there's usually not much more than a swipe or two of the sponge between rinsing and actually *washing*. Okay, okay. I know that some new dishwashers are supposedly able to handle unrinsed dishes. One brand even claims to be capable of disposing of an entire birthday cake, if one should somehow get shut up in the thing ("Someone left a cake out in the dishwasher"?)—a claim I saw verified on television, I must report with mixed emotions, by an initially skeptical consumer-advocate type. But even with one of these things, you've still got to scrape off the big pieces of non–birthday-cake-like food—the sparerib bones and clumps of congealed spaghetti and woody ends of asparagus stalks—and that *still* seems like half the job to me.

Anyway, whether you have to rinse the dishes first or not, once you get the appliance loaded, that great philosophical trick question always comes up: Is the dishwasher *full* or not? Careful with your answer. Yes? Okay. Turn it on. About five minutes later, you'll discover that you forgot to clear the dining room table and there's loads more to do, and you can't even *rinse* the dishes you've just discovered (to get them ready for the dishwasher) because while the machine is running it's sapping all the water pressure. No? Okay. Let the dirty dishes sit there, shut up inside the thing. Tomorrow morning you'll realize that precisely the glass or bowl or spatula you've got to have right this minute is sitting there, still dirty, and you have to pull it out and wash it by hand *anyway*—only now all the little bits of grease and gravy that you missed when you "just rinsed" the item earlier have fossilized and won't come off.

There's another reason why I don't have an automatic dishwasher: I happen to love to wash dishes. Call me crazy. Call me weird. Call me every woman's dream. (Yes, as noted earlier, I'm married; and no, there is no waiting list.) But the plain truth is that there is probably no series of actions that can be performed in a kitchen—while the children are still up, at any rate—that I find more agreeable than swabbing plates and scalding glasses and scrubbing saucepans and then leaving them all upended in a rack to dry in God's own air. Maybe it's my sense of order. Maybe it's something about completing the cooking process, closing the circle, shutting the dinner-making machinery finally down. Which in my case, of course, doesn't mean unplugging the Cuisinart.

RECIPES

Here are three recipes, all of them for salads, that involve a great deal of peeling, chopping, and such—the kind of thing that makes cooking so much fun for me. Maybe you can make these with a Cuisinart instead of a knife, but I wouldn't know.

$\mathcal{U}$NDERGROUND SALAD

SERVES 4

2 large carrots, peeled
2 medium-sized parsnips, peeled
1 turnip, peeled
1 rutabaga, peeled
1 celery rib
1/4 cup mayonnaise
1/4 cup sour cream
1 bunch chives, minced
Salt and freshly ground black pepper

Have ready a large bowl of ice water.

Dice carrots, parsnips, turnip, rutabaga, and celery into cubes approximately 1/2" square, keeping them separate.

In a large pot of salted water, boil carrots for about 5 minutes, then add parsnips, turnip, and rutabaga. Continue boiling for 5 minutes more, then drain vegetables and plunge immediately into ice water. Drain again and spread out to cool and dry on paper towels placed on a cutting board or large cookie sheet. (Do not place vegetables in a bowl, as they will continue to cook and become mushy at the bottom.)

When vegetables have cooled to room temperature, place in a large salad bowl and add celery.

In a small bowl, mix mayonnaise and sour cream together thoroughly, then stir in chives.

Toss vegetables gently but thoroughly with mayonnaise mixture, then add salt and pepper to taste.

SCALLOP COLE SLAW

SERVES 6

1 pound bay scallops
¹/₂ head red cabbage, shredded
¹/₄ large head green cabbage, shredded
2 large carrots, shredded
1 head radicchio, shredded
1 cup mayonnaise
2 tablespoons mustard seeds
2 tablespoons roasted sesame seeds*
Salt and freshly ground black pepper
2 tablespoons soy sauce, preferably aged tamari
Juice of ¹/₂ lemon

Drain scallops in a colander, then pat dry with paper towels.

Mix cabbages, carrots, and radicchio together in a salad bowl. Stir in mayonnaise, mustard seeds, sesame seeds, and salt and pepper to taste, then toss very thoroughly. Divide salad evenly among six plates.

Put soy sauce and lemon juice in a nonstick skillet over high heat. When liquid begins to bubble, add scallops and

---

* Available at Asian groceries and in some supermarket "Oriental" food sections.

cook, stirring constantly, for about 2 minutes. Quickly transfer scallops, with slotted spoon, to the tops of the salads.

*C*OOKED AND RAW VEGETABLE SALAD

SERVES 6 TO 8

6 to 8 shallots, peeled and thinly sliced
Extra-virgin olive oil
4 bell peppers, 2 red and 2 yellow if possible
1 cup shelled fresh fava beans*
1 cup shelled fresh peas
¹/₂ pound fresh haricots verts or yellow wax beans (or a
*   combination of the two), trimmed and cut into ¹/₂" to 1"*
*   lengths*
¹/₂ cup lightly toasted pine nuts
1 bunch watercress, chopped, roots and thick stems
*   discarded*
3 to 4 bunches mâche, trimmed
Leaves from 2 bunches celery
2 carrots, shredded
2 to 3 small celery ribs (preferably white hearts), sliced
*   paper-thin*
1 bulb fennel, trimmed and finely chopped
1 cup coarsely chopped fresh basil leaves
1 cup coarsely chopped fresh Italian parsley leaves
4 scallions, finely chopped
2 medium green tomatoes, finely chopped (optional)

* If fresh fava beans are unavailable, double the quantity of peas or omit altogether. Frozen fava beans, thawed and cooked according to instructions on package, are an acceptable substitute if necessary, but dried fava beans or lima beans (even fresh ones) are not.

$^1/_4$ *pound prosciutto di Parma or other good-quality*
   prosciutto-style ham, cut into thin strips 1" to 2" long
Juice of $^1/_2$ lemon
$^1/_2$ *cup freshly grated Parmigiano Reggiano*
Salt and freshly ground black pepper

In a small skillet, sauté shallots in a little olive oil over low heat, stirring occasionally, until soft and dark brown (but not burned). Drain on paper towels.

Meanwhile, prepare other vegetables:

Char peppers on gas grill, over gas flame on range, or in preheated broiler, turning occasionally, until black on all sides. Allow to cool slightly, then core and halve peppers, remove ribs and remaining seeds, and scrape off skin. Cut peppers into thin strips, chop into small confettilike squares, and set aside.

Blanch fava beans for 1 minute in salted boiling water, then drain and rinse immediately in cold water. Slip favas out of skins and separate into halves. Set aside.

Blanch peas for 1 minute in salted boiling water, then drain and rinse immediately in cold water. Set aside.

Cook *haricots verts* or wax beans for 2 to 3 minutes in salted boiling water, then drain, rinse immediately in cold water, and set aside.

When all vegetables have reached room temperature, pat them dry, then combine all ingredients up to but not including lemon juice in a large salad bowl and toss together well. Moisten salad generously with olive oil, add lemon juice, and toss again. Add cheese, season to taste with salt and pepper, and toss a third time.

6
I CAN'T BELIEVE
YOU ORDERED THUMPER

"Well, if it looks just like chicken,
and it tastes just like chicken,
WHY DON'T THEY JUST GIVE ME THE GODDAMN CHICKEN?"
—BOBCAT GOLDTHWAIT, IN PERFORMANCE

ABBIT IS GOOD EATING: IT'S LOW IN fat and calories; it's reasonably priced (less than $3 a pound as I write this); it has a mild, clean, pleasant flavor; it's all white meat. You can do almost anything with rabbit. You can make pâté or *rillettes* out of it. You can braise it in mustard sauce, roast it with prunes, grill it with olive oil and fresh herbs, stew it with red wine or sherry, deep-fry it in a cornmeal crust. You can turn it into pasta sauce. You can stuff the loin or saddle of a rabbit with goat cheese or Swiss chard or the rabbit's own innards, or slice it thinly and fan it out on plates napped with almost

any sauce you'd care to think of. You can make ice cream with it.

No, no. Just kidding about that last one. . . .

Zoologically speaking, the rabbit is a short-tailed, long-legged lagomorph of the order Rodentia—a burrowing, gnawing mammal with two pairs of incisors in its upper jaw, one behind the other. It likes to use these incisors to nibble at various kinds of plant life, wild and cultivated both. Its appreciation of the latter, together with its notorious fecundity, has earned it classification as a pest in agricultural communities. Even so innocuous a lagomorph as Beatrix Potter's Peter Rabbit was a crop-chewer. When he got into Mr. McGregor's garden, you will remember, "First he ate some lettuces and some French beans; and then he ate some radishes. And then, feeling sick, he went to look for some parsley." (When Peter's father had tried the same trick somewhat earlier, McGregor's wife had baked him into a pie. What dedicated gardener could blame her?)

The rabbit's association with Easter, and thus with springtime, the season of growth and renewal, apparently proceeds from its aforementioned fecundity. Rabbits can produce as many as seven litters a year, with as many as eight—I kind of hate to put this in, especially since I'm talking about eating the little critters, but what baby rabbits are properly called is kits or kittens—per litter. Rabbits, in other words, go like bunnies. (Hugh Hefner didn't choose no chipmunk as his Playboy symbol.)

For reasons that may or may not be related to the apparent frequency of its sexual encounters, the rabbit is also widely considered to be a symbol of good luck, thus the custom of wishing someone "Rabbits, rabbits" on the first day of each new month, or of carrying a lucky rabbit's foot—a talisman that, as has been widely observed, is apparently good luck to everybody but the rabbit who owned it originally.

Rabbit is widely eaten in Europe, in both its wild and its

domestic forms. It is particularly popular in France, where *lapin à la moutarde,* rabbit in mustard sauce, is a bistro standard. Rabbit is eaten in America, too—it has enjoyed something of a vogue in recent years in restaurants of a contemporary persuasion—but it is not eaten by everyone. There is a great deal of resistance to eating rabbit in some quarters, in fact. This resistance is obviously not based on rabbit's flavor or consistency: The all-white meat of domestic rabbits really does look and taste just like chicken. It is difficult indeed to imagine that anyone would find it unpleasant on its gustatory merits alone. But, then, food taste is not entirely gustatory.

As far as I can tell, there are three basic categories of resistance to rabbit consumption:

The aristocratic. Because it reproduces with such enthusiasm, and is relatively easy to trap or shoot in the wild, rabbit has for centuries been considered poor people's food. It is a great favorite in the rural South, for instance, where it has been called "white-trash chicken." Certain self-styled epicures, then, scorn it as beneath them, inappropriate to the delicacy of their palates. Waverly Root, in fact, once proposed that rabbit "can serve as a touchstone to separate food snobs from those earthy creatures who really like to eat."

The satiated. Others refuse to eat rabbit simply because they've had their fill of it. My ex–father-in-law, for instance, though quite adventuresome gastronomically, refused categorically to consume rabbit, on the grounds that he had been forced to eat it almost daily as a child during the Depression.

The sentimental. Most Americans who won't eat rabbit, though, refuse because of something I call the Thumper Factor. Thumper, as you may recall, was the bright-eyed, chipper little lagomorph in *Bambi*—the one with the over-sized and hyperactive back foot. How could anyone who ever saw that cinematic classic (the anti–rabbit-eating faction inquires) even *consider* dishing up a serving of

Thumper's real-life counterpart on a plate? (*Bambi* fans, it will not surprise you to learn, don't eat much venison, either.) And if cartoons don't move you, then how about the genuine article—those teeny, tiny snow-white bunnies Mom used to bring home for Easter, for you to fuss over all day long and feed rabbit kibble and little shreds of lettuce—at least until you got tired of them and let them starve to death, or set them loose to get run over by a truck or gobbled up by the neighbor's dog (who had not seen *Bambi*)? The Thumper Factor is based on the fact that we are reluctant, as a culture, to eat anything we can also pet.

My wife has eaten rabbit once and only once, to the best of my knowledge—a Catalan dish of stuffed rabbit loin with apple *allioli,* which she pronounced delicious. But she told me the next morning that she had kept waking up all night thinking that furry little animals were hopping out of her mouth. That story belongs in the Thumper Factor Hall of Fame.

I incurred the wrath of the Thumperites several years ago when I wrote a brief appreciation of rabbit as food for *Metropolitan Home.* In need of a quick, flip finish to the piece, and having earlier mentioned *Bambi,* I closed the piece thus: "So what's the big deal about bunnies? Why *not* eat the little critters? Leave 'em alone and some forest fire will just get 'em anyway. And then they'll be overcooked."

Well, now, let me tell you that I got some response to that. Angry letters fairly poured into the magazine—letters that were not, for the most part, models of rhetorical restraint. Mention was made of the fact that animals die so that people like me "can fill their no doubt fat insipid unfeeling bellies feeling so smug and satisfied with themselves." I was accused of "irrational and incomplete thinking." I was called "repulsive," "sarcastic," "self-centered," and even—the unkindest cut of all—"unfunny." If I read one letter correctly, I was even accused of some vague complicity in the fact that "animals horrifyingly die in forest fires."

I deserved it. My finish was a cheap shot. I admit it. And I should have long since figured out that people who base their philosophical beliefs, and their beliefs about the way the natural world works, on *Bambi* probably don't have the same kind of sense of humor I do. It was probably a good thing that I didn't write about eating venison, too. Although, come to think of it, I'd as soon be hung for a hind than hung for a hare.

RECIPES

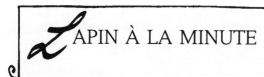

APIN À LA MINUTE

SERVES 4

The first time I made lapin à la minute, at a friend's house, it was very good. My friend liked it so much, in fact, that he invited me back to cook it again—this time for some guests, among them Michel Richard. At the time, Richard was merely the best pastry chef in Los Angeles. Today, at his own Citrus in Hollywood, he is quite possibly the best chef, period. In any case, and for whatever reason, when I made the dish for Richard, et al., it was a disaster. I burned the shallots, scorched the rabbit, and filled the kitchen (and probably the dining room) with the unpleasant odor of overheated oil—with Richard looking on the whole time. He was polite enough not to comment as he saw what I was doing. He was even polite enough to eat some of the rabbit. We both survived the experience. The first time I dined at Citrus, though, I remembered the evening, and felt very silly. The next day, I made lapin à la minute at home until I got it right again.

3 tablespoons unsalted butter
2 tablespoons extra-virgin olive oil
Salt and freshly ground black pepper
1 rabbit, cut into 10 pieces
4 shallots, peeled and minced
1 cup light red wine
2 teaspoons fresh lemon juice
6 to 8 sprigs parsley, minced

In a large cast iron skillet or other deep and heavy pan, heat butter and olive oil until the mixture starts to brown.

Meanwhile, salt and pepper all surfaces of rabbit generously. Sauté rabbit pieces quickly in the hot butter and oil, turning occasionally with tongs, until golden brown on all sides. Reduce heat to medium and stir in shallots. Cook for about 5 minutes more, continuing to turn rabbit pieces.

Deglaze pan over high heat with wine, then reduce heat and simmer, stirring constantly, until liquid reduces to a thick, concentrated sauce. Stir in lemon juice, then serve rabbit with parsley sprinkled on top.

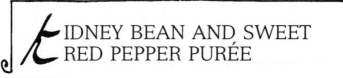

KIDNEY BEAN AND SWEET RED PEPPER PURÉE

SERVES 4

This is a quick, easy, and appropriate accompaniment to the preceding dish.

2 cans of kidney beans (15 to 16 ounces each)
2 red bell peppers, cored, seeded, and finely chopped
2 scallions, trimmed and finely chopped
2 garlic cloves, peeled and finely chopped
1/4 teaspoon paprika or cayenne
Salt (optional)

Place all ingredients except salt, including liquid from canned beans, in a saucepan. Bring to a boil, then reduce heat and simmer, uncovered, for 10 to 15 minutes. Purée mixture in blender or food processor, then return to pan and continue cooking over very low heat, stirring frequently, until thickened. Add salt to taste (but be careful: canned beans are usually sufficiently salty to begin with). Allow to sit for about 5 minutes, stir again, then serve.

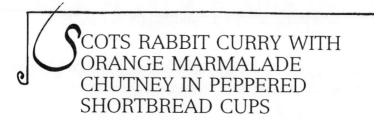

SCOTS RABBIT CURRY WITH ORANGE MARMALADE CHUTNEY IN PEPPERED SHORTBREAD CUPS

SERVES 4 TO 6

I made this dish up as sort of a joke—albeit a joke with a point. In the fall of 1990, I prowled around Scotland for a time at the behest of the now-defunct British edition of Metropolitan Home, *looking for good contemporary Scottish cooking. I found a great deal of more-than-competent French food, but disappointingly little that I thought made smart use of both local raw materials and traditional Scottish recipes. I was looking for, say, a Scottish Larry Forgione or Mark Miller, I guess, and didn't find one. Just for fun, then, I invented a few recipes of the sort I imagined some young Scottish equivalent of those chefs might have come up with. This was one of them.*

It might be noted that curry is an old Scottish tradition—Scots have been eating curry for longer than Americans have been eating hamburger—and that the curry portion of the recipe below is closely adapted from The Scots Kitchen *(1929) by F. Marian McNeill. McNeill in turn borrowed it from a book published in Edinburgh in 1826,* The Cook and Housewife's Manual *by "Mrs. Margaret Dods"—who was in fact one Mrs. Isobel Christian Johnston. (The original Dods was a character—a no-nonsense innkeeper—in the Sir Walter Scott novel* St. Ronan's Well, *and Scott apparently helped Mrs. Johnston with her cookbook.)*

Orange marmalade is a Scottish specialty, of course, said to have been invented by one Janet Keiller of Dundee in the early eighteenth century, as a way of utilizing the cargo of unfortunately bitter oranges her husband, James, had purchased from a storm-bound ship. As for the peppered shortbread, well, I simply made it up, but I was encouraged to do so by a reference I found somewhere or other in my researches on Scottish food to the fact that shortbread was originally not very sweet.

CHUTNEY
1 10-ounce jar good-quality Scottish orange marmalade (not bitter)
¹/₂ teaspoon salt
¹/₄ teaspoon dried red chili flakes (more or less to taste)
¹/₂ ounce fresh ginger root, peeled and minced
2 garlic cloves, peeled and minced (more or less to taste)
Juice of ¹/₂ lemon
2 tablespoons lightly toasted pine nuts

Gently melt marmalade in a small saucepan over low heat, stirring constantly, until liquefied. Put into blender or food processor with salt, chili flakes, ginger root, garlic, and lemon juice and process until well mixed. Stir in pine nuts.

Allow chutney to cool to room temperature, then refrigerate in covered container for at least 4 hours. About 2 hours before beginning curry, remove from refrigerator and bring to room temperature.

PEPPERED SHORTBREAD CUPS
1 cup unbleached flour
1 teaspoon sugar

1 teaspoon freshly ground black pepper
5 tablespoons unsalted butter, softened to room temperature

Preheat oven to 350°.

Mix flour, sugar, and pepper together thoroughly. Work butter into flour mixture with your hands; dough should be crumbly, but will hold together when squeezed.

Divide the dough evenly among 6 standard-sized ungreased muffin cups and press it evenly on the bottoms and up the sides of the cups. Prick the bottoms with a fork.

Bake for 22 to 25 minutes or until pale brown all over.

Allow shortbread to cool, then remove from molds. Shortly before serving, fill each cup generously with room-temperature chutney.

SCOTS RABBIT CURRY
1 3- to 4-pound rabbit, cut into 8 or 12 pieces
Flour for dredging
Salt and freshly ground black pepper
3 tablespoons corn or other vegetable oil
1 tablespoon unsalted butter
1 onion, minced
1 celery rib, minced
8 white mushrooms, quartered
1 tablespoon curry powder
$1/2$ teaspoon turmeric
$1/8$ teaspoon cayenne
2 teaspoons flour
2 cups chicken stock
6 ounces slab bacon, cut into $1/2''$ cubes

Dredge rabbit pieces in flour seasoned with salt and pepper to taste. In a large skillet over medium heat, heat the oil and butter. Add the rabbit and turn frequently until pieces are golden brown on all sides. Remove from pan with slotted spoon or tongs and set aside to drain on paper towels.

Add onion, celery, and mushrooms to pan and continue

cooking until vegetables are soft. Dust mixture with curry powder, turmeric, cayenne, and 2 teaspoons flour. Stir well so that vegetables are well coated. Continue cooking until spices are fragrant, 3 to 4 minutes, then raise heat to high and add chicken stock.

Meanwhile, in another skillet, fry bacon until lightly browned, then drain on paper towels.

To finish sauce, lower heat to medium and simmer, stirring occasionally, until slightly thickened. Return rabbit to sauce and cook, turning pieces frequently, for about 5 minutes longer. Stir in bacon and add salt to taste.

Serve over plain boiled white rice, accompanied by orange marmalade chutney in a peppered shortbread cup.

7

WE EAT WHAT WE WANT

*J*ATE BEAR ONCE, IN THE 1970s, AT A RUSSIAN
restaurant in Helsinki. I remember it as rich and slightly
sweet, not unlike wild boar. I'd eat it again. My wife, on the
other hand, has never eaten bear (or for that matter boar),
and almost certainly never will. The whole idea of consuming wild game distresses her—both the slaughtering-
of-big-eyed-innocents aspect of the thing and the flavor of
game meat's (usually) dark, strong flesh. She doesn't like
the dark meat of chicken or turkey, either. (I've already
described her feelings about rabbit.)

My professional colleagues and eat-anything friends

sometimes find it ironic that I should have married a woman who won't even eat a chicken leg, and console me for having to cater to her whims. The truth is, though, that my wife's food prejudices don't bother me a bit. Oh, I do think she's probably missing out on some flavors she might enjoy by eschewing whole classes of food, and I do feel somewhat limited in what I can make for dinner (I must know 300 things to do with a chicken breast by now), but beyond that, I'm actually proud of her gastronomic limitations, and think they speak quite well for her. I say that because I firmly believe that folks should eat what they damned well want to eat and leave the rest alone.

What surprises me more than the fact that some people won't eat some foods, in fact, is that so many people will eat foods they don't much like because they're afraid that not eating them will be taken as a sign of inexperience or unsophistication. My friend Betty told me a story that illustrates this phenomenon vividly: She once went out to dinner at a French restaurant in New York with her old high school boyfriend, who had grown into a collegiate man of the world. As befits that role, he ordered sweet-breads. The stout Breton waitress shook her head ruefully and replied that the kitchen was out of sweetbreads. Then I'll have the kidneys, he said. The waitress disappeared, and then quickly returned to inform the young man that the kitchen was out of kidneys, too. Well, then, he said, calf's brains. The chef, it turned out, had just served his last order of *cervelles*. At that point, Betty recalls, her friend said to her sotto voce, "Thank goodness! Now I can have *steack frites.*"

Although I suppose there are people in the world who will eat almost anything, I simply don't believe that there's such a thing as somebody who genuinely likes everything equally. There is certainly no such thing as a true gourmet without at least some food preferences and prejudices—logical or not. It has always seemed to me, in fact, that the very mark of a gourmet—of a critical, appreciative eater—

is not omnivorousness at all, but discrimination, discernment, the ability to say, without embarrassment or guilt, "I'll have the *steack frites*" (if that's the item on the menu that most appeals to him).

Many famous chefs and food authorities have well-known dislikes. Marcella Hazan is said to hate cinnamon. Alice Waters scorns watermelon, and isn't very fond of broccoli. Ruth Reichl can't abide honey. John Thorne fails to see the charms of celery. The noted Spanish author and gastronome Nèstor Luján drew chuckles at a conference on the exchange of food products between the Old and New Worlds in 1991 when he noted that "Europe was slow to accept tomatoes; I still don't like them."

One thing a good many Americans don't like is organ meats. There are a number of perfectly understandable reasons for this. For one thing, they tend to have funny textures: Brains are squishy, tripe is rubbery, lungs are gristly. Then, too, we know that organ meats are often the repositories of unpleasant fluids—urine, bile, and so on—hardly appetizing stuff. Another problem with organ meats for some people, I suspect, is that we call many of them by names that seem to anthropomorphize them, thus at least subliminally suggesting cannibalism. (Human beings don't have sirloins, chops, or tri-tips—at least not by those names. We do, on the other hand, have livers, kidneys, and hearts.) Probably most of all, though, we don't like organ meats because we don't *have* to like them. We're a wealthy society as a whole, and a wasteful one, perfectly capable of carving the filet mignon out of a beef carcass and feeding the rest to our pets.

I like most organ meats just fine myself. I have not—to anticipate a question wiseacres sometimes pose when I talk about eating offal—ever tasted monkey brains scooped warm out of the animal's skull, and I hope I never shall. I have, however, eaten deep-fried sheep's blood, marinated cow's udder, sautéed bull's testicles, and the spinal marrow of calves, among other unusual animal parts, and found all of them quite agreeable. I think the Peruvian specialty called *anticuchos*—bits of marinated beef heart, skewered and grilled—is one of the most delicious cow-derived dishes I've ever tasted. I'm very fond of sweetbreads. I like liver very much, too—the fattened livers of ducks and geese, chicken livers, calf's (and cow's) liver, even the livers of lambs and pigs. (Calf's liver was the only form of organ meat my mother would eat. She used to get me to eat it as a child, she once confessed, by describing it to me as "liver steak," with the emphasis on the latter word.)

On the other hand, I would never dream of ordering kidneys—though I'll consume them (unenthusiastically) if they're given to me. I've had only two tripe dishes in my life that I genuinely liked well enough to want second helpings—little bits of it tossed with *penne* pasta, shredded savoy cabbage, and onions and gratinéed with bread crumbs and Parmigiano, which Paul Bertolli prepared one night at Chez Panisse in Berkeley (the recipe appears in *The Chez Panisse Cookbook*); and the classic long-cooked *tripes à la niçoise*, sweet and tender, at La Merenda in Nice—also flavored with Parmigiano, incidentally. (Are tripe and Parmigiano perhaps a little-known classic food affinity?) I find brains tolerable, but detest them in the form they are most often served—with black butter and capers—and only really like them crisply fried.

My wife, it will not surprise you to learn, won't eat organ meats in any shape or form. I believe that she had serious second thoughts about the wisdom of marrying me, in fact—just an hour or so too late—when at our wedding banquet, which I had planned, one of the courses turned out to be a magnificent appetizer of marinated veal tongue with Roman beans.

My own lack of enthusiasm for certain organ meats, or certain preparations of them, aside, there are all kinds of other things that I don't particularly care for. For some unknown reason, for instance, I don't particularly like pickles made from cucumbers, whether sweet or sour,

Kosher or dill. Now, I do like pickled peppers, pickled carrots, pickled cauliflower, pickled herring, pickled watermelon rind—even pickled pigs' feet. But not *pickle* pickles. If their juice leaks onto my sandwich or I find tiny bits of them lurking in my tuna salad, my lunch is all but ruined. Why this should be so, I cannot imagine.

Another thing I don't much like is mustard as a condiment. Mustard seed, yes. Mustard sauce on rabbit or chicken or whatever, sure. Mustard mixed into a classic vinaigrette dressing, okay—as long as it's not too strong. But mustard itself spread on hot dogs or cheese sandwiches or alongside baked ham or boiled beef, absolutely not. The very thought makes my taste buds shudder.

I am also an ovaphobe. I have in recent years grown quite fond of dry, tortelike frittatas and Spanish-style omelettes (rather to the disbelief, incidentally, of those who have known me at earlier periods of my life, when I would often refuse to remain in the same room with an egg in any recognizable form), but that's as far as I'm willing to go. French omelettes, scrambled eggs, hard-boiled eggs, egg drop soup . . . no, thanks.

My aversion to eggs has got me into trouble more than once. I was very nearly booted out of St. John's Military Academy in the fifth grade, for instance, for steadfastly refusing to sample the poached eggs we were served for lunch one Lenten day. Even worse was the time Ruth Reichl took me to lunch at M. F. K. Fisher's home in Sonoma—the only time I ever met Fisher, whose books I so admire and enjoy—and the centerpiece of the light lunch she had prepared turned out to be, yes, a bowl of hard-boiled local yellow farm eggs. (I muttered some excuse about an allergy and ate lots of bread instead. I don't think she was very impressed with me.) On the other hand, I like to think that my aversion to eggs has had at least one beneficial side effect: Against all odds, I have never had a problem with my cholesterol. And I can proudly say that I eat what I want.

RECIPES

Here are some dishes you shouldn't even consider eating if you don't really want to.

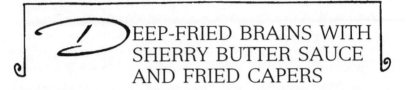

DEEP-FRIED BRAINS WITH SHERRY BUTTER SAUCE AND FRIED CAPERS

SERVES 4

One rainy April evening in 1986, Alice Waters, Jonathan Waxman, Mark Miller, Bradley Ogden, and Lydia Shire crowded into the tiny, ill-equipped kitchen of the Cafè de l'Acadèmia on a cobblestoned side street in the Barri Gotíc in Barcelona to improvise a dinner for about forty of the Catalan capital's most prominent restaurateurs, winemakers, and journalists. Assisting the five chefs in the kitchen were two food writers from Los Angeles, Ruth Reichl and Charles Perry. I was there, too—but I was outside, in the rain, trying to roast several dozen sweet red peppers on a sputtering charcoal grill. The rest of the group had put me out there on purpose. It was their way of getting back at me for having gotten them into this mess in the first place. The story of what we were all doing there—and of what we all did during the faintly delirious week we spent in Barcelona together, eating and drinking and just in general trying to devour as much of the city as we could—is a long and fairly complicated one, whose telling I must defer until another occasion. For now, though, I might just note that of all the dishes prepared by this illustrious crew, I think the one that most delighted and surprised our guests (the common view in Spain being that Americans don't eat offal, much less know how to cook it) was Lydia Shire's appetizer of deep-fried lamb's brains. Today, at her superb Boston restaurant, Biba, Shire serves a rather more elegant version of this dish, based on a flan of brains and marrow. This, though, is the way she made the dish in Barcelona.

8 ounces lamb's or calf's brains
1½ quarts court bouillon*
Salt and freshly ground black pepper
Flour
2 eggs, beaten
1 cup fresh bread crumbs
1 bunch fresh parsley
3 shallots, peeled and finely chopped
Olive oil
½ cup dry sherry
3 tablespoons sherry vinegar
1 tablespoon Pommery mustard
8 tablespoons (1 stick) unsalted butter, cut into 8 pieces
½ cup large capers, rinsed and dried

Soak brains in cold water for 5 to 10 minutes, pull off any loose pieces of membrane, and rinse well. Bring court bouillon to boil, then reduce to simmer, add brains, and poach for about 15 minutes.

Cut brains into pieces slightly bigger than bite-sized, then add salt and pepper to taste. Dust brains with flour, dip into beaten egg, and roll in bread crumbs into which 2 to 3 sprigs of finely chopped parsley have been mixed.

Sauté shallots in a bit of olive oil in a medium skillet until soft, then deglaze pan with sherry. Stir in sherry vinegar and mustard, then whisk in a little more than half the butter. Season to taste. Cover pan to keep sauce warm.

Meanwhile, fry capers and remaining whole sprigs of parsley in remaining butter until the capers open and get crispy. Drain on paper towels and salt to taste.

Fry brains until golden brown in an ample quantity of olive oil heated to about 375°. To serve, put a spoonful of sauce on each plate, add brains, and sprinkle fried capers and parsley on top.

* Use any standard court bouillon recipe, or, to 1½ quarts water, add a carrot and a rib of celery (both cut into 1" pieces), ½ cup dry white wine, half an onion (cut into wedges), 1 teaspoon whole black peppercorns, 2 bay leaves, a quarter of a lemon, and a few parsley stems.

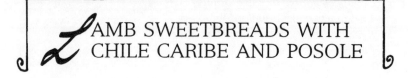

LAMB SWEETBREADS WITH CHILE CARIBE AND POSOLE

SERVES 6

I first tasted lamb sweetbreads in the early 1980s at St. Estèphe, the pioneering contemporary-Southwestern restaurant in Manhattan Beach, just south of Los Angeles. Chef John Sedlar used to serve them there in a New Mexican chile sauce with hominy (posole), in pretty little copper cassolettes, and they were memorably good. I once tried to create a lamb sweetbread dish of my own—something with tomatillos and pearl onions, if I recall correctly. Assuming that the sweetbreads had to be blanched and peeled like veal sweetbreads, I spent at least two hours scrupulously picking bits of tissue off a couple of pounds of them, pretty much reducing them to rubble in the process. (The dish turned out to be edible but hardly brilliant.) When I chanced to mention this misadventure to a French chef of my acquaintance shortly thereafter, he laughed heartily and said, "But you don't peel lamb sweetbreads! They'll fall apart!" Sedlar agrees, but says that he does peel off the larger pieces of membrane, which are easily removed. Beyond that, he counsels, there's no point in getting obsessive about it. Here is his recipe.

1   cup dried posole (hominy)
6   ounces slab bacon, sliced about 1" thick
4   garlic cloves, peeled
¹/₂ small onion, peeled and chopped
2   sprigs fresh oregano
1¹/₂ pounds lamb sweetbreads*
12 dried large New Mexico red chiles, cores and seeds
     removed

---

* *Though hardly a common inhabitant of the supermarket butcher cases, lamb sweetbreads can usually be ordered from any serious butcher.*

$^{1}/_{2}$ *cup toasted pine nuts*
Peanut, corn, or extra-virgin olive oil
$^{1}/_{2}$ *teaspoon each salt and white pepper, or to taste*

Rinse posole well, then let soak overnight in cold water in a large bowl. The next day, drain posole and rinse again, then place in a pot with bacon, garlic, onion, and oregano. Cover with 4 quarts of water and bring to a boil over low to medium heat, skimming occasionally. Simmer posole until puffed and tender, about 3$^{1}/_{2}$ hours. Add more water if necessary to keep posole covered. Drain posole, remove and discard bacon, garlic, and oregano, and set posole aside.

About half an hour before posole is done, bring 2 quarts of salted water to a boil in a medium saucepan. Reduce heat to medium, carefully slide sweetbreads into water, and poach for 20 minutes. Have ready a large bowl of ice water. When sweetbreads are cooked, drain carefully and plunge them into water to stop cooking. Drain again. Remove any pieces of clear membrane that pull off easily, and cut sweetbreads into pieces about 1$^{1}/_{2}$″ square. Set aside.

While sweetbreads are poaching, preheat oven to 425°. When oven is preheated, place chiles on an ungreased broiler tray or cookie sheet and roast until crisp and very dry but not blackened (about 5 to 10 minutes), turning them several times. (Watch chiles closely, as they will blacken quickly once they're sufficiently dried.) Purée chiles in a blender or food processor with pine nuts, 2 tablespoons oil, and salt and pepper to taste.

Stir sweetbreads and puréed chiles together in a large bowl so that sweetbreads are coated evenly. In a large skillet, sauté sweetbreads in a small amount of oil over medium-high heat until crisp, turning them as necessary. Drain on paper towels.

Warm posole over a bain-marie if necessary, then divide evenly among 6 deep bowls. Top with equal amounts of sweetbread mixture.

SPICY SALT COD STEW

SERVES 4

Though not as daunting as organ meats, salt cod is still regarded with suspicion by the majority of Americans, who seem to think that it is inevitably chewy and, of course, salty as hell. Neither is true if it is properly prepared.

1 pound salt cod
3 onions, coarsely chopped
Extra-virgin olive oil
1 teaspoon spicy paprika or cayenne
Juice of ½ lemon
1 green and 1 red bell pepper, cored, seeded, and cut into
  strips
1 fresh serrano or jalapeño chile, with ribs and seeds
  removed, finely chopped*
2 to 3 garlic cloves, peeled and finely chopped
1 pound potatoes, peeled and cut into 1½" cubes
½ bottle dry white wine
Salt and freshly ground black pepper

Soak salt cod in a large bowl of water, in the refrigerator, for about 48 hours, changing the water 2 or 3 times a day.

Drain salt cod, cut or pull off skin and remove any bones, then chop into pieces 1½" to 2" square. Set aside.

In a large skillet or stew pot, sauté onions in a little olive oil over lowest possible heat for 1 to 1½ hours, stirring occasionally. Add paprika or cayenne and lemon juice, stir well, and continue cooking for another 15 or 20 minutes. Add bell peppers, chile, and garlic, and cook for 15 or 20 minutes longer, stirring occasionally.

Handle chiles carefully, and wash hands very thoroughly with soap and hot water after touching them.

Add potatoes and wine to pot, turn heat to high, and bring to a boil. Reduce heat, add salt cod, cover, and simmer for 15 to 20 minutes. Add pepper to taste and salt if necessary (do not add salt without first tasting stew).

Serve with warm country-style bread.

PART II

Waiter, There's a
Flaw in My Soup

"I am nothing if not critical."
—WILLIAM SHAKESPEARE, *OTHELLO*

8

RESTAURANT CRITICS NEVER
HAVE A NICE DAY

"Ninda abaku nam khebtar." ("*Only when he
has eaten the food let him give his verdict on it.*")
—SUMERIAN PROVERB, C. 4600–3600 B.C.

EING A RESTAURANT CRITIC IS SORT OF
like being put out to stud: There's no denying that the
basic activity is highly pleasurable, but when you have to
do it when and with whom somebody else tells you, it
loses a lot of its appeal.

I used to be a restaurant critic, but I gave it up. I still
write about restaurants, certainly, and sometimes offer
critical opinions of them. But I no longer review them
formally, dining the now-traditional three times or more at
each establishment, taking copious notes, appraising
them in detail. That kind of thing is no fun at all. Trust me:
It's a terrible job.

I realize full well, of course, that there are people who would sack and pillage for the chance to be a restaurant critic. What a *scam*, they think. Imagine being able to go out to dinner *all the time*, at somebody else's expense. Imagine getting paid to eat. . . .

No. Imagine getting paid to eat something you probably don't want, at a restaurant you probably wouldn't be caught dead in if the choice were up to you, on a night when you're probably dog-tired and not particularly hungry anyway (and certainly not for your third deep-dish pizza of the week), and then having to make intelligible and (one hopes) intelligent notes, mental or otherwise, about the whole experience—forever analyzing, forever making judgments, not just on the food but on virtually every aspect of the restaurant-going experience, from the valet parking to the background music to the barkeep's knack with a cocktail shaker. Oh boy. What fun. What sensual abandon. If that's eating, then Masters and Johnson are Romeo and Juliet.

I wrote my first restaurant review in September 1970: It was a report, not for publication, on Dan Tana's in West Hollywood—and it both began and ended my brief career as an "eater" for the Holiday Dining Awards (see the next chapter). My second restaurant review, and the first actually to show up in print, was an assessment of Musso & Frank's Grill in Hollywood, which appeared in the October 14, 1971, edition of *Los Angeles Flyer*—a short-lived local supplement to *Rolling Stone*. Since writing those two reviews, I reckon that I must have eaten something like 2,000 meals in a professional capacity (and, believe me, in this job you *need* a professional capacity). The depressing thing is how few of these meals I have really enjoyed.

I'm probably betraying a trade secret here, but the fact is that most restaurant critics prefer good restaurants to bad ones. Restaurateurs stung by unfavorable reviews often accuse reviewers of promiscuous fault-finding, of exaggerating minor flaws in order to justify their biting witticisms. In my experience, the opposite is true: Critics—at least the ones I know—tend to approach each new eating place hopefully, hungrily and wide-eyed, sometimes actually downplaying what they perceive as minor failings if their dining experience is in general pleasant.

Why, then, are restaurant reviews so often negative? For a very simple reason: There are a lot of genuinely lousy restaurants out there.

Here's a typical scenario: The critic anonymously approaches some instantly trendy, loudly ballyhooed new establishment, hoping for the best. Then he and his party are made to wait at the bar for forty-five minutes, eventually seated on uncomfortable chairs at a table near the kitchen, ignored by the serving staff for a good fifteen minutes more, brought the wrong cocktails, offered a hackneyed menu supplemented with a spoken list of grotesquely "creative" specials, told that the kitchen is out of most of what the group finally decides upon, given a wine list full of pretentious and overpriced selections (again with much of the good stuff missing), and forced to watch in silence as some so-called "waitperson" waves the wine around in the air gouging at the cork with a poorly designed corkscrew. Then the group is served an assortment of overcooked, underseasoned victuals—and, probably before it's been asked for, presented with a check that totals eighty or ninety bucks per person. This sort of scenario gets played out far more frequently, I can assure you, than someone who does not sample new restaurants regularly might suspect.

Sure critics write unfavorable reviews, packed with all the biting witticisms they can muster—and then with great pleasure see them published in Friday's paper for several hundred thousand of the restaurant's potential customers to read. That's one of the *good* things about being a restaurant critic: You can get even for the kind of crap lousy restaurants put you through—simultaneously (and this is really the whole point) getting even on behalf of all the other people to whom the same has happened, but who don't have the same effective recourse you do.

But that's not fair! exclaims the restaurateur in question. This is a tough business! The chef was sick! We were breaking in a new manager! We can't have a decent wine list because all the good wines are too expensive! Our prices are high because we buy only the best ingredients! We work hard for our money! What right does some self-styled critic have to come in and say nasty things about us and ruin our business?

Veteran New York restaurateur Alan Stillman (whose restaurants, which include Smith & Wollensky, the Post House, and the Manhattan Ocean Club, I happen to like very much) once asked in a letter to the trade publication *Nation's Restaurant News*, "What happens to the guy who has sunk his last $150,000 into a restaurant, and some critic comes along and virtually closes the place down with one review a month after it opens?"

In the first place, outside perhaps of New York City—a provincial town at heart, with one legendarily authoritative newspaper and a notorious herd mentality when it comes to restaurants (and also, incidentally, theatre)—I simply don't believe that a single bad review can close a genuinely good eating place. (Bad reviews and failing business are usually symptoms of the same disease: Something seriously wrong with a restaurant, front or back or both.) Beyond that, though, as I wrote to *NRN* in reply to Stillman's letter, what he asks is not the appropriate question from the critic's point of view. The appropriate question from the critic's point of view is, "What happens to the guy who works hard all week and then sinks a couple of days' take-home pay into a special dinner with a special friend, only to buy himself mediocre food and rude, incompetent service?" (Some restaurateurs have suggested that restaurant critics should be licensed. I think that's a reasonable enough idea—just as soon as chefs and restaurant owners are licensed, too.)

The restaurant business is a notoriously high-risk endeavor, and anyone who opens a restaurant ought to realize what a gamble it is—ought to have assessed both the possible rewards and the opportunities for failure that this most difficult of industries provides in such abundance. The restaurant customer, on the other hand, shouldn't have to gamble. He has a right to expect certain things, certain value for money spent. Nobody begs a restaurateur to open a restaurant; nobody promises success. Once he opens, though, a restaurateur does beg the customer (through advertising, posted menus, whatever) to come in and spend money. If critics should somehow be held accountable for financial losses incurred by restaurateurs whose places they unfavorably review—as more than one restaurant owner has suggested—then why shouldn't restaurateurs be held responsible, too, for the financial losses incurred by customers who have not had their implied contract with the restaurant fulfilled?

Sometimes disgruntled restaurant owners go further than just writing letters to trade publications. One famous foe of restaurant critics in general is Nick Nickolas, proprietor of the Nick's Fishmarket restaurants in Chicago, Rosemont (Illinois), and Boca Raton. "The critics don't know what they're talking about," he once told *NRN*. "They're trying to be cute and we've got to fight back." His own tactics for doing so, he continued, were to "call and tell the critic how I feel and I'm not polite. Then I write to the editor and then I yank my ads. And I tell my friends to cancel their ads and subscriptions." (That Nickolas is a man used to getting his way, incidentally, is suggested by his use of the word "tell" in that last sentence.)

Other restaurateurs ban critics from their restaurants, though usually just one specific critic per restaurant, because if they banned them all, they'd never get reviewed, and interestingly enough it's only when critics say negative things about a place that restaurateurs call their honesty or ability into question.

Some restaurateurs actually sue critics—for instance Michael Chow, who filed a successful lawsuit against the Gault Millau company's *The Best of New York* guide in 1983 after that publication panned Mr. Chow New York. One of the guide's criticisms was that the restaurant's Chinese-style pancake wrappers were "as thick as a finger." Incredibly, Chow's lawyers were permitted to bring the restaurant's noodle chef into the courtroom for a pancake-making demonstration (as if the pancakes he made in the courtroom necessarily had anything to do with the ones he made on the night the restaurant was reviewed!), and Chow was awarded a $20,005 judgment. (The verdict was overturned in 1985 on the grounds that "expressions of opinion are constitutionally protected.")

Another restaurateur who sued a restaurant critic and won was Sal Hochman of the Caves Restaurant in Fort Lauderdale, who earned $23,000 in damages in the late 1970s after an unfavorable (and, he contended, inaccurate) review of his establishment appeared in a local entertainment publication called *Good Times*. According to *Nation's Restaurant News*, "Hochman said [the critic] got a bad steak because the regular broiler chef had gone home early and the substitute prepared the meal." This is a pretty ingenuous excuse. First of all, if Hochman knew a steak prepared by a substitute chef was going to be inferior, shouldn't he have warned his diners—or perhaps offered them a "substitute" price? Anyway, if Hochman had taken his car in for a tune-up and got it back running badly, would he have been mollified, I wonder, if told that "the regular mechanic had gone home early and the substitute worked on the car"? I doubt it. I'll bet he would have been damned mad, with good reason—the same good reason that a customer who was served a substitute cook's inferior steak should have been, restaurant critic or not.

Restaurateurs aren't the only ones who criticize restaurant critics, of course. The general public frequently betrays disdain for critics, on the grounds that they are obviously food snobs or freeloaders or both. When a fellow member of my weekly tennis clinic learned that I wrote professionally about food, he asked, in a not particularly admiring tone, "Does that mean that you're one of those guys who goes into restaurants and everybody stands up straight and brings you great food all night?" Ah, would that it were so.

It becomes increasingly difficult for a critic to maintain anonymity when reviewing restaurants regularly in the same community over a long period of time. The busboy who knew your name ten years ago because he went to school with your girlfriend's cousin has become a captain; the chef recognizes you because somebody pointed you out at that charity food festival last week; at the least, the very way you order dinner brands you as a specialist. When I was a working critic, nonetheless, I did my best to seem like just an average diner—but that was as much for my own peace of mind as for any reasons of objectivity. I hate being fussed over in restaurants, offered special wines or dishes, complimented effusively on past writing, and the like, whether I'm working or not.

What I quickly learned when restaurateurs did start recognizing me, though, was that—annoyance factors aside—it usually didn't make a bit of difference. Most restaurants that serve mediocre food don't do so deliberately. They just don't know any better. Based on their price structure, their management philosophies, and the talents of their staff, they do more or less the best they can. The idea that a place serves slop to the ordinary Joe and then pulls the good stuff out of the larder when Mimi Sheraton walks in simply isn't true. They couldn't if they wanted to.

Chefs can, of course, dish up larger portions to VIPs, arrange the plates with more care, perhaps oversee preparation themselves instead of trusting a subordinate—and certainly the best waiter can be assigned to a recognized critic's table. But any critic worth his salt spots these transparent cosmetic measures immediately, and good critics pay attention to what's going on at the tables around them. Thus a restaurant that assigns all its best resources to the critic might actually damage its chances of a good review, because the critic will meanwhile be "reviewing" the dining experiences of the rest of the customers.

I might add that sometimes, I suspect, recognized restaurant critics actually get *worse* treatment than other diners, either because the staff is nervous or because some hotshot chef or manager wants to make some kind of "point" by not catering to the press. It has become something of a joke between my colleague Ruth Reichl and myself, in fact, that when we go out to eat together, we almost never get a good meal—even in places where we're both known, and even in ones that we've enjoyed separately in the past.

There's one other thing the general public doesn't like about restaurant critics: Sometimes they give bad reviews to popular favorites. Not long ago, I came out of retirement as a critic for a few weeks to review several old-fashioned, long-lived L.A. restaurants for the *Los Angeles Times*—places that had been open twenty years or more and that just seemed to keep going, oblivious of fad or fashion. I liked some of these establishments (one of them, sentimentally, was Dan Tana's), but found myself greatly disappointed by two of them—two that I had wanted very much to like. In reviewing these two, I took special care to sample a particularly wide range of dishes, to record my objections to the ones I didn't like in great detail, to praise the ones I did like, and to offer what I thought was constructive criticism—the kind of thing, I thought, that in an ideal world the restaurateurs in question should have thanked me for. I never heard from them.

But in both cases I heard from many of their loyal customers. They were not happy. They were not shy about expressing their unhappiness. I was called "malicious," "cruel," "stupid," "ignorant," "cretinous," "a liar." One of my more intelligent correspondents—smart enough not to sign his name—denounced me in derogatory terms referring to what he imagined to be both my religion and my sexual preference. Several readers merely wrote to the editors of the *Times* demanding that I be fired.

They needn't have bothered. I'm back out to pasture now anyway, far from the critic's paddock, far from the wrath of restaurateurs who would rather blame a bad review for their troubles than investigate the possibility that they really might be doing something wrong; far from the ire of restaurant patrons whose own judgments of a place I have somehow impugned by not agreeing with them. I like it here in, as it were, another field. Here, I can assure you, the grass really is greener. And here, nobody tells me what to cover.

RECIPES

When I was reviewing restaurants regularly, people used to ask me if I ever stayed home for dinner. "As often as possible," I'd reply. The next question, of course, was inevitably, "What do you eat when you do stay home?" The obvious answer was that I ate all sorts of different things—but sometimes, if a check had just come in and I was feeling particularly self-indulgent, I'd fix myself something simple but elegant, like one or more of the following.

CAVIAR COUNTRY-STYLE

SERVES 4

*This is an elaboration on the way I was once served caviar
by English-born, Paris-based restaurateur/wine merchant
Mark Williamson and his wife, Dominique, in the apartment
they then occupied on the Ile St-Louis. They simply heaped
the caviar on slabs of toasted Poilâne bread spread lightly
with* crème fraîche. *I loved the combination of the rustic
and the sophisticated—and took it a short step further.*

*4 large slices French- or Italian-style country bread from a
    round boule-type loaf, cut about 1" thick
¹/₂ cup fresh ricotta cheese
2 tablespoons minced chives
Fresh lemon juice
Freshly ground black pepper (optional)
Sevruga or Beluga caviar (as much as possible)*

Toast bread lightly, preferably on a wood-fired grill.

In a small bowl, mash ricotta with chives, a bit of lemon
juice, and black pepper to taste if desired. Spread mixture
on one side of the toast, then cut toast into three or four
pieces.

Divide caviar evenly among toast pieces, spreading on
very lightly so as not to crush the eggs.

IGURIAN-STYLE STUFFED MUSSELS

SERVES 4

I got this recipe from Gianni Franzi, who owns the popular trattoria that bears his name in the storybook-pretty village of Vernazza in the Cinque Terre, on the Italian Riviera.

1 onion, minced
1 carrot, minced
2 garlic cloves, minced
Olive oil
2 pounds (35 to 40) fresh small mussels, cleaned*
1 slice French- or Italian-style bread, crusts trimmed and
     discarded, soaked in milk for 10 minutes
2 slices mortadella, minced
3 to 4 sprigs parsley, minced
2 tablespoons freshly grated Parmigiano Reggiano
Pinch of nutmeg
Salt

Preheat oven to 400°.

In a skillet over medium heat, sauté onion, carrot, and garlic in a little oil until they begin to brown.

Meanwhile, with an oyster knife, sever the muscle at the back of each mussel and pry open the shell. Cut each mussel out of its shell and set aside, reserving one half-shell for each mussel.

Chop raw mussels coarsely and mix them in a large bowl with the onion mixture and all other ingredients. Add salt to taste.

---

* To clean mussels, discard any that may be open, then scrub exteriors well with a stiff brush under cold running water. Pull off stringy beards if necessary, then cover with cold water in a large pot for at least 1 hour. Repeat process, rinsing well after final soaking.

Generously fill each half-shell with mussel mixture, then place stuffed mussels side by side in a large baking dish. Bake for about 15 minutes.

 *J*OE BRODSKY'S DEEP-FRIED STEAK

SERVES 4

Driving through Spain some years ago, my friend Joe Brodsky, a Los Angeles businessman and lover of wine and food, found himself around lunchtime in a town whose name and precise location he cannot remember. He noticed a line of people standing outside a small restaurant, so he did the logical thing: He joined the queue. The restaurant's specialty, he found out once he got in, was deep-fried steak. He tried it, loved it, and figured out how to reproduce it at home. The first time I tried it at his house, I fell in love with it, too. This is, simply, a great way to cook steak. The very hot oil seals the meat instantly, keeping it wonderfully juicy inside; being literally surrounded by heat, it cooks evenly throughout; the chocolate-brown crust that forms on the meat's exterior is wonderfully good; and the meat absorbs little if any of the oil.

1 gallon corn, canola, or grapeseed oil
4 New York steaks, 1¼" to 1½" thick
Salt and freshly ground black pepper

Heat oil almost to the smoking point in a deep-fryer or large stockpot with at least a 3-gallon capacity. (Test the oil's temperature by carefully putting the end of a wooden toothpick into it. If it turns dark brown at once, the oil is hot enough.)

With long tongs, wearing a glove or oven mitt and keeping your face away from the pot, carefully place 2 steaks at a time into oil. (Oil will foam up.) Cook for exactly 7 minutes. Remove with tongs, drain on paper towels, and keep warm while remaining steaks cook. Just before serving, salt and pepper steaks to taste.

(A pat of plain or *maître d'hôtel* butter allowed to melt on top of each steak adds a nice gloss to the meat, but isn't necessary.)

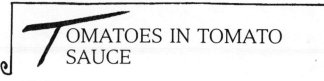

*T*OMATOES IN TOMATO SAUCE

SERVES 4

This side dish makes a great accompaniment to the afore-mentioned deep-fried steak.

1 can oil-packed anchovies
2 pounds very ripe tomatoes
1 tablespoon unsalted butter
Extra-virgin olive oil
4 garlic cloves, peeled and finely chopped
1 small red (Bermuda) onion, minced
1 pinch cayenne pepper
Salt
1 bunch basil, leaves only, rinsed, dried, and coarsely chopped

Drain anchovies over a large nonreactive skillet to reserve packing oil. Separate anchovies into filets and chop finely.

Peel and seed half the tomatoes and chop them coarsely.

Add butter and a small amount of olive oil to pan with anchovy oil. Add chopped tomatoes, half the chopped anchovies, garlic, onion, and cayenne and cook over low heat, covered, for 45 minutes, stirring frequently.

Allow tomato mixture to cool slightly, then carefully purée in a blender or food processor and return to pan. Reheat sauce over low heat, continuing to stir frequently.

As sauce is reheating, halve remaining tomatoes and gently squeeze out the seeds. Chop the unpeeled tomatoes coarsely. Add tomatoes and remaining anchovies to sauce. Add salt if necessary.

Cook tomatoes in sauce until sauce thickens, about 6 to 8 minutes, continuing to stir. Remove from heat and stir in basil.

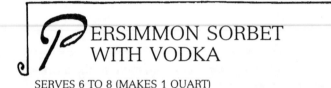

*P*ERSIMMON SORBET WITH VODKA

SERVES 6 TO 8 (MAKES 1 QUART)

2 *cups very ripe persimmon meat (3 to 4 persimmons)*
¹/₂ cup sugar
²/₃ cup ice water
2 *egg whites*
Chilled vodka

Purée persimmons and sugar together in a blender, then cook mixture in a nonreactive saucepan over medium heat, stirring constantly, for about 2 minutes. Add water slowly, continuing to stir, and cook for 3 to 4 minutes longer. Remove mixture from heat and allow to cool to room temperature. Refrigerate, covered, for at least 3 hours.

Remove mixture from refrigerator. Beat egg whites until stiff, then fold into mixture, incorporating thoroughly. Process in ice cream maker according to manufacturer's directions.

Splash a bit of very well-chilled vodka on each portion of sorbet just before serving.

9

SILAS AND ME

"The old order changeth, yielding place to new."
—ALFRED LORD TENNYSON, "THE PASSING OF ARTHUR"

I KNOW EXACTLY WHEN I STARTED TO BE-
come a professional writer about food: August 1, 1970.
That was the date of my first letter to Silas Spitzer.

At the time, Spitzer was food and restaurant editor of
Holiday, America's premier travel magazine. A well-
known New York-based gastronome, he had joined *Holiday* in 1946 as a food writer. In 1952, with the help of two
other legendary bon vivants, columnist and railroad buff
Lucius Beebe and author/artist Ludwig Bemelmans, he,
and then-*Holiday* food editor Elizabeth Woody had
launched the *Holiday* Restaurant Awards. The awards
took up one page of the magazine's July issue that year,

and listed some forty-nine establishments nationwide, adding a few words of description for each. ("Minneapolis: Charlie's Café Exceptionale. . . . Famous for appetizer tray; expensive." That's the whole entry. The ellipses are theirs.)

When Caskie Stinnett took over editorship of *Holiday* in 1960, he hired Spitzer as full-time food and restaurant editor, and the awards were substantially expanded to become an important annual feature of the publication. At their height, they were probably the closest thing America has ever had to a comprehensive and independent national restaurant guide—an American *Guide Michelin* (or at least *Guide Gault Millau*).

The 1970 edition of the awards took up sixteen pages, and offered capsule reviews of some 140 restaurants in the U.S., Mexico, and Canada, as well as brief acknowledgments of some ninety more. In introducing the awards that year, editor Stinnett wrote, "Although [they] . . . are selected under the careful supervision of Silas Spitzer, . . . a number of anonymous scouts, called 'eaters' by the editorial staff, are involved in the selections." He then quoted Spitzer's criteria for these scouts at some length. Though Spitzer patently wasn't soliciting "eater" applications, and though *Holiday* scouts were not paid (only reimbursed for their test meals), I was just young enough (twenty-five) and just confident enough about my own budding taste and experience in food to sit down and write him a letter offering my own services in that regard. And in sealing the envelope, I suppose that in a way I sealed my fate.

My letter initiated a reasonably intense correspondence between Spitzer and me, which lasted for almost exactly a year—and it was during this period, as Spitzer complimented and encouraged me, that I began to seriously imagine, for the first time, that perhaps I might one day be able to write about food and get paid for it. His letters thus have some sentimental (if that's the word) value to me. Quite beyond that, though, I find them fascinating documents today—for what they say about American tastes in general, about the culinary and economic state of restaurants in America in the early 1970s, about the operating standards and then the deterioration of the *Holiday* Awards, and of course about the influential but now little-remembered Spitzer himself.

Replying almost at once to my letter, Spitzer invited me to submit three or four restaurant reports if I wished, but stressed that these would be on a trial basis only, and that I would not be reimbursed for my meals.

I wrote back agreeing to his terms.

By return mail, Spitzer outlined his criteria in more depth: "*Holiday* [is] interested only in good food, *great* food preferably, and appropriately selected wines of honest quality. This may seem to be easy to achieve, but in fact America is terribly uninterested. Only a tiny minority *wants* and *likes* to eat well. The great majority would not recognize good or great food if they tasted it. We are involved with other things; business, wars, wall-to-wall superficial ease, etc. Much of the so-called connoisseurship in America is really pretentiousness. . . ."

His reviewing standards were precise: "Remember: food comes first. . . . Next comes the feeling of the place; whether you are greeted well and made to feel at home; then the spontaneity, sincerity and efficiency of the service. Any side observations after that are up to you; I am personally much affected by the sort of people who come to eat, the smells, the taste displayed in decor, and the presence or absence of that awful quality of fake foreignness which disgraces so many of our aspiring eateries."

On September 27, after having written three trial reports of which Spitzer approved, I mailed in my first official review as a *Holiday* "eater"—on Dan Tana's in West Hollywood. A few days later I got a letter from Spitzer, dated the twenty-eighth, which crossed mine in the mail: "Because of events which have transpired recently," he wrote, "I am asking you, as of now, to postpone any further plans to dine out for the *Holiday* Restaurant Awards." My career as an eater had come to a screeching halt.

What had happened was that the Curtis Publishing Company, which owned *Holiday,* had put the magazine up for sale. "I do not think we will lose the *Holiday* Awards," wrote Spitzer in his next letter. "It is bound to be continued, but apparently the form may change. From present hints, the list will expand, perhaps include popular restaurants of a kind I do not consider up to our former exigent standards. If so, I may depart."

Shortly thereafter, the magazine was indeed sold, and its publishing headquarters moved from New York to Indianapolis. The effect on the awards was immediate and dramatic: In a letter dated December 15, Spitzer wrote, "The fact is that the *Holiday* Awards will never be quite the same again. The new owners [of the magazine] . . . will try to continue them without using scouts in various national areas, as developed by me over the past ten or twelve years. They will try to get their information from various 'regional editors' and newspaper dittos. They do not intend to pay for this information in the former method of reimbursement for all meals and reports. . . . I will be kept as 'consultant,' meaning I will be expected to contribute prestige (?) and perhaps be final arbiter on selection of awards, etc."

By mid-January, though he remained associated with the new *Holiday,* Spitzer was saying, "Sic transit gloria mundi, eheu fugaces, goodby and God bless you!" to the magazine as he knew it. "I am not quite saying goodby, however," he added, "to you or to others of my erstwhile 'eaters' who served so nobly when *Holiday* was still reasonably healthy. . . . There may still be a chance to gather the remnants of our former staff and in some way or other return to some form of restaurant guidance. All it needs is a sponsor. I am struggling manfully to find one. You would be surprised—or would you?—to discover how few are genuinely interested today in the improvement of our restaurant situation, or the restoration of American standards of eating and drinking to a civilized world rank. We are in an economic state of squeeze and alarm; and in America that is what counts—money, or the lack of it, or the possibility that it may grow scarcer and that we may lose some particle of our swollen state of complacent materialism."

There was more on restaurant economics—words that might well have been written in the early 1990s—in Spitzer's letter of June 1: "[A]ll restaurants are suffering from a drop in business, mainly because of the fading away of expense account patronage, and the usual trend to quick economies which a period such as the present one evokes. Some are trying to bridge the profit gap with economies of their own: cutting down the crew, adopting substitutions in basic materials, reducing the scope of menus, going for frosted instead of fresh vegetables and otherwise lowering standards. Most are struggling hard, however, to maintain quality without cutting into it by resorting to measures described. Restaurants feel [the] economic squeeze before most enterprises, and their reaction is predictable."

A month or so later, Spitzer wrote to comment on the recent appearance of what were to be the last *Holiday* Restaurant Awards with which he was associated: "The publishers have given an inordinately prominent place to the 1971 ratings," he wrote. "They have also prefaced them with an absurdly over-written piece of toilet-flush prose by some unknown on the 'staff,' extolling my personal prowess as an unrelenting critic of restaurants, food and wine, before whose presence owners shrink, chefs tremble and entire crews hang breathless upon my first thrust of knife and fork and resulting expression of approval or condemnation. This in spite of the obvious fact that for twenty years I have eaten, like all my correspondents, anonymously, modestly and without display of any sort. Otherwise how could I judge with any honesty? The fact that my face and presence eventually became known to most top-rated restaurants, and many lesser ones, is what forced me to call a halt in my personal visitation, except when prompted by simple hunger and the necessity to eat."

Regarding his hopes to find a new home for his awards, he continued: "The possibility of instituting an Awards-type feature in some other magazine has been offered to *Saturday Review* and *Esquire,* not personally but through intermediaries, and no great enthusiasm for the idea has been expressed. Same result, or non-result, when the proposal has been made to industrial or business corporations like Chanel, General Motors, etc. Facing this hiatus in my life, I exist in my pleasant country retreat without much work and basking in a certain serenity."

The last letter I received from Spitzer was dated August 14, 1971. In it, he bemoaned the closing of Café Chauveron, "The best restaurant in New York—which may mean the nation." The establishment's proprietor, Roger Chauveron, he added, "knew food and wine of the kind which Curnonsky described as 'tasting of what they are' better than almost any man I ever knew." In closing, he noted offhandedly, "Incidentally, I heard yesterday that I have been accepted for the post of Food Editor at *Travel & Leisure* [magazine], at a very generous stipend. . . ."

I wrote back to Spitzer on August 20, but I never heard from him again. His new job must have taken up much of his time—and he was not in good health.

For my part, I went off to Europe in the fall of 1971, and upon my return lost myself in the excesses of the early-1970s L.A. record business. If I ever wrote to him again, I haven't kept a copy of my letter.

Spitzer had, in any case, already offered me a kind of valedictory, not in his last letter but in his penultimate one: "As you grow old," he wrote, "appetite for the new and original weakens. It does not seem as important as it used to. The presence of the Final Act of the bum show a man puts up for too many years overwhelms almost every other element of growth or change. I am not pessimistic, merely realistic. Life is as sweet as ever, but opportunities to enjoy it at the full grow less every day. . . . [But] as one gets nearer to the inevitable exit curtain, the importance of gastronomy and the pleasures of the table never diminish. I am not sorry that they took up so much of my life. And I hope they will continue to dominate it even in lessened scope or intensity. Is there any other sensual gratification that is more consistently rewarding, or that lasts longer? Only an unreformed and unrepentant old hedonist like me can make that statement and feel no shame."

He concluded, "Please write me whenever the mood strikes. I am still hopeful that we will some day share a good dinner at some place where life retains its fitful former glow. . . ."

We never did, of course. Silas Spitzer died on April 28th, 1973.

10
WHY SEAN CAN'T COOK

"Spécialités, c'est le blague."
—M. CAILLON OF RESTAURANT CAILLON, PARIS, QUOTED
IN *WHERE PARIS DINES* BY JULIAN STREET

ON MONDAY, SEPTEMBER 2, 1985, AT AP-proximately 8:40 in the evening, it occurred to me quite suddenly and finally that the much-vaunted imagination and originality of the "New American Cuisine" had gone too far. I was sitting in a restaurant in a beach community in southern California at the time, listening to a waitress recite the evening's numerous and elaborate specials. Having had, by this time, a great deal of previous experience with contemporary Californian cooking, some of it pretty loopy, I didn't blink when she mentioned the salad of sliced chicken breast, fresh pears, and radicchio in pear-liqueur vinaigrette. I winced only imperceptibly when she described the filet of beef *en croûte* stuffed with alternating bands of goat cheese and spinach, mushrooms and roasted garlic, and ratatouille, and served with a sauce of walnuts and sun-dried tomatoes. But then she got to the grilled Chilean sea bass with pineapple-horseradish *beurre blanc....*

Okay, I thought. That's it. Finito. Ix-nay on the California creativity. Pull the plug on the New American Cuisine. Time for something else—Cambodian cooking, maybe, or a Neapolitan revival. Time, for that matter, for the reassuring folk authenticity of a Big Mac or a Del Taco Big Del Burrito.

I must quickly add that I don't mean to single out for criticism the chef of this particular restaurant, whoever he or she might have been. (The place has since closed.) Chilean sea bass with pineapple-horseradish *beurre blanc* made (makes) perfect sense in its trendy, up-to-date, contemporary American context. I see it not as an isolated inanity, but as a sort of innocent symptom—or symbol— of a basic weakness in the genre as a whole: its self-satisfied immaturity.*

The immaturity I speak of isn't just a matter of *outré* combinations of ingredients. It isn't just a matter of pineapple-horseradish *beurre blanc,* or the roasted loin of lamb on top of blueberry fettuccine with shiitake mushrooms and raspberry sauce (or was that raspberry fettuccine with shiitake mushrooms and blueberry sauce?) served so proudly by one L.A. bistro, or (to quote Mimi Sheraton) the "meaty lobster-and-crab cakes accented by

* After scorning this dish in my column in the Los Angeles Times, I received an angry letter from one young chef (not from the restaurant in question). "[Andrews] has a lot of nerve," he wrote. "He should be thanking all the chefs in town for giving him something to write about. If it wasn't for us, he would be reviewing red-boothed steak houses in some beach rag for the rest of his life. If he is so bored with California cuisine, why doesn't he move to another state?" The chef who wrote the letter, you might be interested to learn, is himself now cooking Mexican-inspired food in Chicago. And I go to red-boothed steak houses every chance I get.

ginger-and-clove-scented strawberry chutney" and "salad of warm, crisply fried calamari nested on raw spinach and sunny with dates and orange sections" offered by a trendy eatery in Miami, or even the "blancmange from goats' milk yogurt with blood oranges and lemon grass wine jelly on passion fruit" proposed at a hotel restaurant in Arizona. Dishes of this sort are restauration comedy—as impossible to criticize as they are to parody (or for that matter, probably, to eat).

No, I'm concerned with more basic problems: To begin with, I think we've come too far too fast. We (and I speak here of chefs, restaurateurs, critics, and lay diners alike) were so giddy at our liberation from the old ways—from the martinet Frenchmen who acted as if they virtually owned fine cooking in America (and made us believe they did), from the entrenched clichés of the "continental" kitchen, from the obstinate sameness of even our most exotic "ethnic" menus—that we went a little crazy. Like kids from a strict home suddenly set free at college, we wanted to try everything at once. We devoured the possibilities. We made innovation a cardinal virtue, rejecting anything that tasted of yesterday's dinner—throwing out the *baba* with the *bain-marie*. But rushing headlong into a culinary New Age, we forgot to pack the basics—the solid grounding of tradition, the common sense, the stylistic salt and pepper. We glorified the new, the original, the improvised, so much that we forgot food's primary duty—which is not to stump or to dazzle or to *épater*, but to nourish and bring sensory pleasure.

Don't misunderstand me. Lots of wonderful things have happened in our kitchens in the past ten or fifteen years, and a great deal of genuine culinary genius has appeared around the country. And, easy jokes about its wacky combinations of ingredients notwithstanding, I think much of what is good in American cuisine today comes directly or indirectly from California. (The seminal figures here are, of course, Alice Waters and Wolfgang

Puck, who have together exercised an influence on American restaurants, and attitudes about food, that is almost impossible to overestimate.)

But at the same time, I don't think, to put it bluntly, that the majority of today's young American chefs have any damned sense of food. Whatever their motives for choosing the chef's trade in the first place, and whatever the particulars of their training and experience, all too many of them seem to me to lack the most basic notions of balance, harmony, subtlety, *flavor*. They aren't ready to run their own kitchens, much less their own restaurants.

I eat out a lot, all over the country, and time after time after time, even at the most highly rated places, I encounter food that is misconceived, pretentious, and incompetently executed. I can't help thinking that we've spoiled our broth with too many cooks—that in our hunger for ever more and different restaurants, we have granted too many too-tall toques to beardless heads. In my opinion, probably half the young American "chefs" and "executive chefs" in the country today still ought to be chopping vegetables, and at least half of the rest still ought to be sous-chefs. We need fewer "creative" chefs and more young men and women who actually taste food before serving it, and who know not only how to think straight about cooking but how to turn those thoughts into a reasonable meal.

Creativity is all very well and good, but it has no place in a serious restaurant kitchen at 9 P.M. on a Saturday night. To borrow a line from Len Deighton in his *ABC of French Food,* I am "not opposed to experiment but do not wish to be experimented upon!"

If many of our chefs lack what might be called conceptual maturity, they often lack plain old-fashioned technique as well. What often happens, I think, is a kind of progressive attenuation of skill and experience: Let's say that Sean has studied at the Culinary Institute of America or some other reputable cooking school, apprenticed with

Michel and Alain and Gérard for a few weeks each over in France, and then logged a couple of years as the sous-chef to a noted young American chef of the "first generation"—Wolf Miller, let's call him.

At some point, Sean thinks he's ready to go out on his own, finds some backers, and opens Sean's: A Bar & Grill. His own sous-chef, Tyler, whom he brings with him from Wolf's place, is talented and learns fast, but has never been to the C.I.A. or worked in France.

A couple of years down the road, Tyler starts getting bored and feels that he has absorbed Sean's lessons well, so he goes off and starts his own place. His cousin's boyfriend Carter used to work for a catering company and has always wanted to try his hand at restaurant cooking, so Tyler brings him on board. Carter has a knack, and though he has neither formal training, a French apprenticeship, a tour of duty with Wolf, nor even time logged with Sean, he quickly becomes Tyler's sous-chef. A year or so later, a good customer of Tyler's decides to put a little restaurant into the mini-mall he's just bought, and hires Carter as his chef. . . .

Now, it goes without saying that Wolf Miller is a good chef. It seems that Sean is pretty good, too. Tyler, well, has undeniable abilities. But Carter? Sure, maybe he can make some dishes perfectly well. But where's his depth, his experience, his proven staying power? Somewhere along the line, something has been lost.

Hotelier Bill Wilkinson likes to tell the story of "the first strawberry." He has a friend, it seems, who runs a small family business that makes ice cream toppings. As other similar companies have gone out of business over the years, this one has thrived, and Wilkinson once asked his friend for the secret of his success.

"When all the soda fountains started disappearing," the man replied, "the companies that didn't go out of business were bought up by the large food companies. Then the experts would come in and say, 'How many strawberries do you put in a number-ten can of strawberry topping?' They'd say 220. 'Well, just put in 219 from now on,' the experts would reply. 'Nobody will know the difference.' Next year, they'd come around again. This time they'd say, 'Well, nobody noticed that it was only 219 strawberries the last time, so let's make it 215 strawberries this year.' And the next thing you know, half the strawberries were gone from every number-ten can. You want to know the secret of my success? I never took out the first strawberry."

On their way to becoming professional chefs in America today, I think too many young men and women take out too many strawberries. They scoff at the old French system of *fonds de cuisine* and the traditional Gallic division of labor and hierarchy in the kitchen (which they are either too lazy or too smug to master), and denigrate "old-fashioned, heavy" French cooking or what they mistakenly identify as "southern Italian" food (neither of which they could reproduce if their careers depended on it—and neither of which they have most likely even tasted in its genuine form). They skip cavalierly over their apprenticeships. (A long weekend at a noted restaurant teaches them all they've got to learn from *that* particular chef, thank you very much.) They don't bother learning things they don't see an immediate use for, rejecting the very notion, for instance, that cleaning a fish a hundred times might teach them anything about the creature that they couldn't learn the first time (and, incidentally, might teach them self-discipline, too—a useful quality for a chef to have, and one greatly lacking in our professional kitchens today).

How many of our young culinary hotshots, for instance, can cut a lamb up into its constituent parts, or turn a raw pig's foot or calf's stomach into something savory? How many can make *pâte feuilleté, pâte à choux,* and *pâte sablée* with equal confidence? "But we don't *need* to know those things," some chefs would reply. "That's not the way we cook anymore." So much the worse, I'd say. But let's forget butchery and bakery for a moment: The fact is that not one American chef in a hundred today, young or old, understands pasta—much less risotto—though nearly everyone puts both on the menu. (Pasta is the New American substitute for *pâte feuilleté*—an all-purpose farinaceous "carrier" for a multitude of ingredients. Of course, it's much easier to make than *pâte feuilleté*—and use of the pre-made variety is perfectly acceptable.) Not one in fifty can roast a whole fish properly or fry potatoes right, though they all probably know ninety-nine amusing things to do with balsamic vinegar (an ingredient that their predecessors managed very well without, incidentally). They're great at the sizzle, but they can't cook the steak.

One of the reasons so many young chefs scorn truly simple food is simply that it's beyond them. They dismiss, say, *sole meunière* as a boring old cliché without knowing how to execute a perfect *sole meunière*. They stress originality in their cooking because the truly "original" resists comparison. It's easier to cover up your mistakes when you make blueberry fettuccine or lemon grass wine jelly (because nobody knows what this stuff is supposed to taste like in the first place) than it is when you make just plain meat and potatoes. And, hey, what am I going to say about Chilean sea bass with pineapple-horseradish *beurre blanc*? "It isn't as good tonight as it was the last time I had it—and, anyway, Sean makes it better"?

11

DOWN WITH THREE-STAR
RESTAURANTS

"Michelin stars are awarded for the standard of meals served."
—*GUIDE MICHELIN*, VARIOUS EDITIONS

NE CHILLY EVENING IN EARLY AUTUMN IN
the mid-1980s, I sat down in the dining room of a world-
famous restaurant in Burgundy. I'd been on the autoroute
all day, and I was hungry. I didn't want some delicate,
sophisticated *menu dégustation*, either. I wanted solid, re-
storative provender—something Burgundian, maybe
even something Brobdingnagian. Fortunately, the menu
offered a number of selections that seemed to qualify, and
I eventually chose a ragout of boneless frogs' legs and
what was described as a *pièce de boeuf au poivre blanc*—a
filet of beef with white peppercorn sauce. This I ordered,
as I usually order beef in France, *saignant*—rare.

The frogs' legs were superb—fresh, perfectly cooked, immensely satisfying. Then came the steak, a beautiful hunk of the region's famous Charolais beef, charred and glistening with its peppery sauce. I sliced into it. I could scarcely believe my eyes. My dear departed mother, who would eat meat only if it had been cooked into serious grayness, would have loved it. No, I exaggerate. There was a faint rosy glow in the very center of the steak. She would have cut that bit out.

The meat, in other words, was scandalously overdone. I did the obvious thing: I beckoned the waiter to my table and, apologetically, asked him if he would please replace my steak with one cooked as I had ordered it. He looked stunned. His expression suggested that this was not at all the kind of restaurant at which the patrons sent back food. Indeed, he actually left the steak in front of me while he went to get the chef's permission to remove it.

Eventually he returned, and without a word took the steak away. After a rather (perhaps punitively) long interval, he returned with a new piece of meat. I cut it open. The faint rosy glow was slightly bigger. Mom would have still found lots to eat. I ate it myself—I couldn't just keep sending back steaks all night—and it turned out to be delicious. But it would have been much better rare.

Later, when the restaurant's legendary chef-proprietor came out to tour the dining room, he stopped to chat at every table—except mine. Mine, he simply strolled past with a haughty smirk that seemed to say, "Why does a barbarian like you bother coming to my great restaurant in the first place?" I gave him a haughty smirk right back. Mine said: "So who cooked the steak, maestro? The dishwasher?"

The chef's name was Pierre Troisgros, and the restaurant was, of course, his own three-star eatery in Roanne, one of the most influential French restaurants of our era.

When I recounted my experience at Troisgros to my friends in Paris, they were shocked—and not at the restaurant. "But you can't go to Troisgros and have steak!" one of them exclaimed. Another said, "That's what you get for ordering like an American." Nonsense. To begin with, there were at least three beef dishes on the Troisgros menu, Charolais beef being one of Burgundy's most famous gastronomic resources, so it could be argued that beef was something of a house specialty. Beyond that, any single item on the menu at a three-star restaurant— whether house specialty or not—ought to be superb. And beyond *that*, if there hadn't been a steak on the menu but if I had asked for one and the kitchen had agreed to serve it, *that* steak should have been superb as well. Plainly and simply, and for whatever reasons, Troisgros dropped the ball.*

I don't mean to imply that Troisgros isn't an excellent restaurant, or that Pierre Troisgros himself isn't a highly skilled chef. I'm just reporting an indisputable fact: On one evening in the mid-1980s, I was unable to get a piece of meat cooked properly, *in two tries*, at a veritable temple of gastronomy, a place that nearly everybody would agree is one of the top ten or fifteen restaurants in the best food country in the world. And for that, to my mind, there is no excuse.

Are you surprised that I should have had such an experience at a three-star restaurant? You shouldn't be. Stuff like this goes on at three-stars all the time. By "three-star restaurants," of course, I mean those that have been awarded three stars or rosettes by various editions of France's powerful *Guide Michelin*. A three-star rating,

---

* Not long after my experience at Troisgros, I had another run-in with beef at a three-star restaurant. I was having lunch at Taillevent (see page 145) with my friend Claude, and we ordered côte de boeuf as our main course. It turned out to be quite flavorful, and not at all overdone, but it was nonetheless rather tough, which I mentioned offhandedly to our waiter. "Ah, well," he replied, "you know for really tender beef, you must go to America. French beef is always somewhat this way." A few days later, downstairs at the modest wine bistro Ma Bourgogne on the Boulevard Haussmann, Claude and I ordered their version of côte de boeuf, just as an experiment. It was flavorful, perfectly done, and gloriously tender.

according to the guide itself, means "Superb food, fine wines, faultless service, elegant surroundings." (The guide adds, "One will pay accordingly!")

The first *Guide Michelin* appeared in 1900. It had 399 pages (the modern-day guide averages 1200 or more) and was distributed free by Michelin tire dealers to their customers. It did not list restaurants as such, though it did recommend hotels where one could both stay and dine, as well as grocery shops, garages, gas stations, and other services that an automobilist of the time might need. Separate restaurant entries, and the star rating system itself, first appeared in the 1926 edition of the guide. The first three-stars were named in 1931—18 of them, all in provincial France. (Six Parisian restaurants were added to the three-star roster in 1933.)

As I write this, there are thirty-one three-star restaurants in Western Europe (the only part of the world for which the guides are published). There are nineteen in France, three each in Germany and Belgium, and two each in Great Britain, Italy, and Spain. (The numbers usually change a bit from year to year, but not dramatically.) I've eaten at slightly more than half of the current crop, and count some of them as favorites—Taillevent in Paris, L'Espérance in Saint-Père-sous-Vézelay, La Côte d'Or in Saulieu, Pic in Valence, Auberge de l'Ill in Illhaeusern, Comme Chez Soi in Brussels, Zalacaín and Arzak in Spain. There are several others at which I've eaten well enough.

The rest? I frankly think they're mostly self-satisfied, pretentious bores. These are restaurants that typically greet patrons with upturned noses; offer stuffed-shirt service, often neglecting the customer's basic needs while observing complicated empty protocol; serve fussy dishes made with deliberately pricey ingredients (their *dégustation* menus nearly always include caviar, truffles, foie gras, and lobster); and charge $200 or more per person—with only modest wines. Is it any wonder that I so often walk out of such establishments wondering why I've bothered—

and wishing I'd followed my instincts and gone to that pleasant-looking little bistro down the street instead?

But at least the food, however fussy, is usually very *good* at three-stars, isn't it? Hell no. I know from personal experience of one three-star restaurant that cooks all its lobsters for the evening's service by 10 A.M., then reheats them when necessary. Another—one of the most famous and influential of them all (not Troisgros)—regularly incorporates canned peaches and frozen chicken thighs (from England!) into its menus. In fact, virtually all the poultry and maybe half the fish used by this particular superstar restaurant is frozen. Then there's the three-star that (quite correctly) has no freezer to begin with, but that once found itself oversupplied with fresh (French) ducks just as business slumped. The waiters were instructed to "push" the duck. Duck was added in every form possible to all the *prix fixe* menus. As the birds' flesh putrified and grew striped with green, they were trimmed and roasted, and used for flavoring in salads and stocks, until finally they were used up. At no point, apparently, did anybody say, "These ducks are no longer good enough for a three-star restaurant to serve." Nobody had to. Why not serve them? Nobody would complain. Nobody would *dare* to complain.

How can three-star restaurants get away with offering less than the finest to their customers? They've got three stars, that's how. They've got it made. They don't have to cater to their clientele. They don't have to be polite or warm. They can charge what they jolly well feel like charging. And they can rest on their laurels: Once it has awarded three stars to a restaurant, Michelin will not take one away easily. (La Pyramide kept three stars for years after it had turned into more of a museum than an eating place. La Tour d'Argent in Paris is another establishment that held on to three stars long after it had ceased to be, by anybody's reckoning, one of the nineteen best restaurants in France.

A harsher critic of three-star restaurants than I is British food critic Richard Binns. Writing in 1986 in a publication called *The Three Course Newsletter,* he opined that three-stars have become "the culinary equivalents of fruit machine palaces [i.e., slot machine parlors] where, when three rosettes come up together, they greedily collect the jackpot. . . . [They] waste no opportunity to screw every franc, dollar, yen, mark and pound out of their three-star fame . . . [treating customers] as no more than jangling foreign coins to keep the cash registers tinkling away."

I don't think it's just a question of greed, though. I think three-stars have an attitude problem. It's not that the people who run them don't know how to be good restaurateurs. It's certainly not that their chefs (who are usually also their owners) have forgotten how to cook or to run an efficient kitchen. What's missing is the dedication, the care. All too many three-star chefs and restaurateurs have lost touch with their roots, with the love for cooking (and for humanity) that probably encouraged them to become chefs in the first place. They've ascended into the ozone of egoism. They've forgotten that a restaurant's first job, stars or not, is to feed people honestly and well—not to decorate and preen and wallow in publicity.

We, the customers, are partly to blame for this state of affairs. We ask to get treated badly by not complaining vociferously when it happens. We somehow suspect that if our experience is less than gratifying, it is our fault, not the restaurant's. We're blinded by starlight.

Maybe what's really wrong with three-star restaurants, in fact, is simply that we expect too much of them. The phrase "three-star" is a set-up. Like "twenty-four-carat" or "perfect ten," it implies the ultimate, the very best. The *Guide Michelin* itself, remember, promises us "superb," "fine," "faultless," "elegant." We've heard and read so very much in recent years about the glories of cuisine in general, about the wondrous character of handpicked ingredients, about the almost transcendental skills of three-star chefs, that we've come to demand much more of our most highly rated restaurants than just dinner. We've been told that food can be art, and so we expect each big-deal meal to be a Picasso. We approach three-star restaurants in a sort of acolyte's stew of awe and anticipation, as if a dinner served on Villeroy & Boch were somehow guaranteed to be a great spiritual experience, or at least great serious entertainment.

Is it any wonder that when we get a merely decent meal in a three-star, we're disappointed, and that when we get less than a decent meal we feel betrayed? If I had been served something flawed but nonetheless quite agreeable in a modest bistro, I wouldn't have minded a bit. At Troisgros, though, when I got an overdone steak, twice, it was as if a promise had been broken. Which in a way it had.

RECIPES

$\mathcal{P}$URÉE DE POMMES DE TERRE

SERVES 6

Why not try real three-star cooking at home? This is my translation (and slight adaptation) of Joël Robuchon's recipe for his famous mashed potatoes, as served at his almost religiously revered (and in my opinion highly overrated) three-star Jamin in Paris. The recipe comes from Robuchon's book Ma Cuisine pour vous, *and is not to be confused with the version offered in* Simply French: Patricia Wells Presents the Cuisine of Joël Robuchon. *The two are substantially different. Among other things, Robuchon specifies particularly waxy potatoes, while Wells counsels floury ones; Robuchon cooks the potatoes peeled, Wells*

unpeeled; and while Wells notes that the purée may be made up to an hour in advance and kept warm in a double boiler, Robuchon warns, "la purée n'attend pas et ne se réchauffe pas" *(the purée doesn't wait and doesn't reheat).*

2 pounds ladyfinger, yellow Finnish, or white rose potatoes*
of approximately the same size, peeled
Salt
10 ounces (2¹/₂ sticks) unsalted butter, cut into slices about ¹/₂"
thick†
7 ounces hot whole milk or half-and-half (do not allow to
boil)

Place potatoes in a kettle or large saucepan, then cover with cold water to a height of about 1" above the potatoes. Add about ²/₃ teaspoon salt per quart of water to pot, then bring to a gentle boil and cook uncovered until potatoes are easily pierced by a sharp knife.

Quickly drain potatoes and pass them through the fine sieve of a food mill, then return them to the pot.

Cook purée briefly over very low flame, stirring constantly, to evaporate moisture, then add the butter and beat it vigorously into the purée with a wooden spatula.‡

Stir in hot milk little by little, mixing very well as you do so. Add salt to taste.§ Serve immediately.

---

* *Robuchon specifies a waxy, yellow-fleshed French potato known as B.F. 15; to the best of my knowledge, these are unavailable in the United States. The closest equivalent, in texture if not in color, is the ladyfinger, which, like the B.F. 15, is a small, elongated potato. If these aren't available, white rose and yellow Finnish potatoes work reasonably well.*

† *Robuchon's recipe calls for 250 grams of butter (just over ¹/₂ pound), but he notes that quantity can be increased to as much as 500 grams, which is slightly more than 1 pound. When I've had this purée at Robuchon's restaurant, it seems so intensely buttery to me that I'd wager he uses more rather than less.*

‡ *"Il est très important de la travailler énergiquement pour la rendre élastique," notes Robuchon. In other words, give it hell.*

§ *Robuchon says that the reason he recommends adding so much salt to the cooking water is so that it won't be necessary to take the extra step of reseasoning the purée at the end.*

PART III

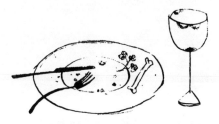

Satisfied Appetites

"He is well paid
that is well satisfied."

—WILLIAM SHAKESPEARE, *THE MERCHANT OF VENICE*

12

SEVEN RESTAURANTS

"[E]very like is not the same."
—WILLIAM SHAKESPEARE, *JULIUS CAESAR*

WHAT KIND OF FOOD DO I LIKE? IN COMMON with so many other food lovers, I find the cuisines of the Mediterranean irresistible, and I am especially fond of the "poor" cooking—based on simple, modest ingredients, but richly, grandly savory—of Catalonia, Liguria, and what's left of the Dalmatian coast. I like Moroccan food, and the straightforward cooking of Rome and Venice, too, and of course the wonderful fare of Spain's Basque region, which I consider sort of an honorary corner of the Mediterranean.

On the other hand, I think French cuisine, Mediterranean and otherwise, is in general the finest in the world, not least because it can accommodate and adapt ingredients and ideas from virtually any other culinary idiom (something that, for instance, Chinese cuisine finds much more difficult).

I haven't had much exposure to classical Turkish cooking, but I suspect that it might deserve a place in the pantheon often reserved for just Chinese and French. Speaking of Chinese food, I frequently enjoy it very much, and I marvel at its complexity and imagination. When I go out to eat, however, I'm more apt to favor Thai restaurants, maybe because Thai food seems more easily accessible, less intellectually demanding, more visceral than Chinese. Most accessible of all, it seems to me, is Mexican food—both the real thing, often surprisingly sophisticated, and the delicious clichés of Tex-Mex and Cal-Mex.

Japanese food sometimes tempts me with its maniacal concern for freshness and its appealing blends of sweet and salty flavors, but I find its rigidity a bore. I've eaten well in Vietnamese, Korean, and Filipino establishments, but these are cuisines that don't particularly entice me as a rule; I don't know why. Good Indian food, on the other hand, unfailingly dazzles me with its intense, mysterious, aromatic luxuriance. . . .

These are generalities, of course. When people find out what I do for a living, they tend to want specifics. They want names, addresses, suggested menus. And they want to know one thing above all: "What's your favorite restaurant?"

I can never answer that question. Or rather my answer is necessarily evasive, ambiguous, equivocal: I don't have a favorite restaurant—or else I have a lot of them. It depends on what you mean by "favorite." It depends on what you mean by "restaurant." It depends on how I'm feeling when you ask me—responsible, flippant, generous, foggy-minded.

When people ask me what restaurants I like most,

though, the names (and looks, and smells, and flavors) of certain places do tend to flash through my mind. They're not necessarily my "favorite" restaurants in any absolute sense, but they're places that I like very much for one reason or another. And I'd be very happy to be sitting in any one of them right now.

Here are notes on seven of them.

1. THE "THANK-GOD-I'LL-NEVER-HAVE-TO" RESTAURANT

There's an old joke about the young child from a wealthy family being driven off to nursery school in a chauffeured limousine. "Does she walk yet?" asks a friend of Mom's as the car goes past. "No," replies the woman, "and with her trust fund, thank God she'll never have to."

I sometimes think of Taillevent in Paris as the Thank-God-I'll-Never-Have-To restaurant. Never have to what? Never have to wait for a table I've reserved, for one thing, even for five minutes. Never have to sit at that table longer than three or four minutes without something to nibble on, something to drink, even if I'm the first one there, or am dining alone. Never have to unfold my own napkin, refill my own wineglass, ask for a fork, ask twice for a check. Never even have to find my own way to the men's room, for heaven's sake: A young *garçon* leads diners deferentially to the appropriate portal, then waits to lead them back to their table. At Taillevent, in short, I know that I'll never have to worry about anything that the restaurant's staff could possibly worry about for me.

"Taillevent" was the *nom de cuisine* of the legendary fourteenth-century French chef Guillaume Tirel. Tirel cooked for such illustrious masters as Philippe de Valois and King Charles V, and was ennobled and named as *maître queux* ("master cook") by King Charles VI. He also wrote, or at least compiled, a manuscript called *Le*

Viandier, which the *Larousse Gastronomique* describes as "the first professional cookery treatise written in France." (*Larousse* also suggests, incidentally, that Taillevent may have acquired his nickname, which means "wind cutter," on account of his prominent nose.) Tirel's coat of arms bore three *marmites* (cookpots) bordered by six roses.

Ironically, considering the culinary reputation of its namesake, what the restaurant called Taillevent is best known for is not its kitchen. The food prepared by longtime chef Claude Deligne is very good, even excellent—but it is hardly the most brilliant or innovative in France. Taillevent's distinction comes instead from its totality, from the way the diner's whole experience here is orchestrated.

Consider this example: I'm meeting my friend, another Claude, for lunch at Taillevent. I get there first. I'm greeted correctly, without a hint of the unctuous or the supercilious. I'm seated promptly in a comfortable boxed-in booth before a large, beautifully set table. After I've been there just long enough to settle in, a waiter appears to ask if I'd like an apéritif and perhaps (what a civilized idea!) a newspaper to glance at while I'm waiting for my companion. I decline the paper—I'd rather read the room—but order a glass of the house champagne. It appears almost at once, excellent Philipponnat nonvintage, served in an exquisite thin flute. With it comes a small plate of very light, delicious *gougères,* cheese-flavored puff pastries—just right to assuage the hunger without ruining the meal to come.

By the time Claude arrives, I'm thoroughly at ease. He sits down, orders a dry sherry, nibbles at a *gougère.* We talk for a few minutes. I just start to look up for our waiter when he magically appears, offering us menus. We peruse them, then order our meal: cold lobster soup *en gelée* (it is a hot day) and grilled turbotin in sea urchin cream for Claude, lobster sausage and fillets of baby sole in basil sauce for me. We choose a Raveneau Montée de Tonnerre from the superb and surprisingly reasonably priced wine list.

When the first courses arrive, Claude tastes his soup, nods approvingly, and says, "You must try this." He fills his deep-bowled silver spoon and passes it across the table to me. I sip the soup—it is delicious—and start to hand back the spoon. At that moment, something extraordinary occurs: Quietly, fluidly, almost without entering our field of vision, a waiter materializes, lifts the used spoon gently from my hand in midair, and, as if with the same motion, sets a clean one down alongside Claude's plate. Then he is gone. I think this is perhaps the most perfect single act of restaurant service I have ever encountered—thoughtful, unobtrusive, nearly clairvoyant, utterly without pomp, and above all *graceful*, both in the deftness with which it was accomplished and in its stylish elevation of what would otherwise have remained a quite ordinary restaurant moment. That act, in fact, defines Taillevent to me.

2. *CARROTS,* CROSNES, *AND PIG'S EAR FLAN*

One afternoon in 1983, in a small restaurant in Burgundy, I bit into a carrot. It was tiny and neatly turned and lightly glazed in butter, and I thought for a moment that it was perhaps the most perfect thing I'd ever tasted. Its sweetness and intensity of flavor were simply dazzling; its texture was astonishingly right. I believe that if a chunk of fresh black truffle had been offered to me just then, I would have turned it down in favor of this uncommon specimen of this most common vegetable.

The restaurant was Le Vieux Moulin, in the tiny village of Bouilland, a few miles from Savigny-lès-Beaune. Opened in the 1950s by one Raymond Hériot, it gained a following, and a star from the *Guide Michelin,* for its no-nonsense pre-*nouvelle* specialties—*pâté chaud de caneton, truite au bleu, coq au vin,* and the like. Hériot retired in 1981, selling the place to a young couple named Isabelle and Jean-Pierre Silva, the latter a Lyonnais-born chef who had lived on the Côte d'Azur for ten years, cooking at the well-regarded (now defunct) La Mourrachonne in Mouans-Sartoux, near Grasse.

I found Le Vieux Moulin in a roundabout way: In 1982, *Metropolitan Home* had published a long, beautifully photographed story about a famous restaurant in Busseto, in Italy's Emilia-Romagna region, called Cantarelli (it has since closed). The following year, the editors decided that they should give equal time to France, and charged me with finding a suitable equivalent place.

The criteria were simple: It had to be very good, young in spirit if not necessarily in proprietorship, and preferably not very well known. I asked my friend Claude if he had any ideas. He mentioned a little place he had heard about in a little village called Bouilland. A nice young couple, he had heard, had recently taken it over, and the food was reportedly very good. I asked a French-trained chef of my acquaintance in Los Angeles. He mentioned a little place he had heard about in a little village called Bouilland, where one of his ex–sous chefs had gone to do a *stage*. I asked a friend in the wine business. He mentioned a little place he had heard about in the same town where Rebecca Wasserman, the highly regarded American-born burgundy shipper, lived—a town called something like Bouilland. . . . Someone was obviously trying to tell me something.

Thus I went to Bouilland, and to Le Vieux Moulin. Besides that memorable carrot, I found a charming and enthusiastic young couple, an idyllic setting, an imaginative and intelligently chosen wine list, and in general some of the most personal and original contemporary French cooking I had ever encountered—a delicate *lapereau en gelée* with a salad of pickled *crosnes* or Chinese artichokes (a vegetable new to me), a dramatic fricassee of sea trout and foie gras with black cherry vinegar, a brilliant marinade of raw salmon and scallops with grapefruit juice and pink peppercorns, an exquisite breast of local baby pigeon (one restaurant guide later called it "as good as Kobe beef") with walnut oil and sherry vinegar dressing and an assortment of flawless little vegetables . . . I found, in other words, the perfect story.

Today, Le Vieux Moulin is a well-known restaurant, with two stars in the *Guide Michelin* and 17/20 from *Gault Millau*. Isabelle and Jean-Pierre Silva remain charming and enthusiastic, and the setting remains idyllic. The dining room—which used to be rustic-elegant, with tapestry-patterned chairs, subtle blue-and-gold carpeting, and a wooden carving of St. Vincent (patron saint of wine-growers) in one corner—has been remodeled in what I find a rather jarring eighties-modern style, complete with high-tech halogen spots glaring down on the antique oak trestle table in the middle of the room. (Interior design is not the strong point of restaurants in France.) But the food . . .

In my opinion, Silva has evolved, from already strong beginnings, into one of the best postmodern chefs in France. His mastery of technique is beyond criticism. His appreciation for (and skill at obtaining) the finest ingredients, from both local farms and far-off oceans, is positively inspirational. And his wit and imagination are nothing less than dazzling.

The dishes he made when I first visited Le Vieux Moulin are gone, but in their place are such astonishing creations as a *tartare* of scallops and black truffles, a *millefeuille* of hake and tuna belly in a sauce of nutmeg-spiked Banyuls, a roasted lobster served with little cannelloni filled with *boeuf bourgignonne* and moistened with sweet red pepper sauce (*le surf 'n' turf extraordinaire!*), sautéed fillet of gurnard (a delicious, firm-fleshed ocean fish) with a pig's ear flan, *suprêmes* of capon larded with bacon and poached in a broth flavored with *tête de veau*—and even such remarkable desserts (Silva is his own pastry chef) as a *feuilleté* of caramelized pears and grapefruit butter, and a crêpe-dough Napoleon filled with apricot preserves and served with chocolate sauce and pistachio ice cream.

In the hands of a lesser chef, food like this would be gimmicky, self-indulgent, maybe just plain silly. Silva is not a lesser chef.

3. GIRARDET'S ID

I like armagnac better than cognac, duck foie gras better than goose foie gras, the Stones better than the Beatles—and Stucki better than Girardet. Stucki and Girardet are almost certainly the two best restaurants (and the two best chefs) in Switzerland, which is no small achievement. Girardet, in fact, is often called the best restaurant (and chef) in the world. In 1990, *Gault Millau* dubbed Girardet himself, along with Joël Robuchon and Paul Bocuse, one of three *"cuisiniers du siècle"* (chefs of the century). And indeed, Fredy Girardet is a culinary genius and an artisan of sometimes breathtaking skill. His establishment in Crissier, near Lausanne, is one of the great wonders of the gastronomic world.

Given the choice, though, I'd take the Bruderholz Stucki, a comfortable old hilltop mansion in Basel. John Thorne, in a typically lapidary essay called "Fat Cook, Thin Cook" (collected in his book *Simple Cooking*), notes that "Cooks come in two classic sizes, just like clowns: fat and thin." The fat cook, Thorne proposes, cries out, "Eat, eat!" while the thin one asks only that we sample something. The fat cook is the one we turn to, he continues, when we are at peace with our hunger. "But we embrace the thin cook when we feel vulnerable, suddenly frightened of this act of eating.... The thin cook's hypercaution, his peckishness, his dizzy excitement over tiny tastes perk up even the most neurasthenic appetite."

Though neither exemplifies physical extremes, it is not at all inaccurate to say that Girardet is a thin cook, Hans Stucki a fat one. Girardet's food is delicate, dazzling, intellectual; Stucki's is hearty, joyful, visceral—not intellectual so much as intuitive. (*Gault Millau* have not named Hans Stucki as a chef of the century; instead, they simply call him *"la force tranquille de la grande cuisine suisse"*—the quiet power of great Swiss cooking.)

I don't mean to suggest for an instant that Stucki's style is somehow simple or naïve. Stucki thinks as much, and as smartly, as any chef alive. He is a great one for mixing and matching culinary references, in fact, discovering common (or complementary) qualities between them. A dish of crisp-fried *rougets-barbets* or baby red mullets, for instance, might be accompanied by thinly sliced artichoke bottoms and a light saffron-spiked aïoli—the trick being that not only do both artichokes and saffron contrast perfectly with the flavor of the fish, but that artichokes and saffron turn out to have strong notes of flavor in common, too. In another Stucki specialty, a bed of shredded endive and orange peel cuts the richness of wild duck breast superbly.

Foie gras puts up with accompaniments of many kinds—but Stucki's service of vaguely smoky-tasting grilled foie gras with a salad of *mâche, haricots verts,* and translucent slices of barely cooked turnip is positively brilliant. So is his "pojarsky" of rabbit—a patty of ground rabbit meat wrapped in caul fat, set on a bed of very lightly creamed spinach and surrounded with little sea scallop–sized pieces of rabbit loin. So is his *feuilleté* of strawberries and cream, made with pastry based on Laekerli, the traditional Basler honey cookie. I find this food unfailingly seductive, without ever seeming overwrought. "Sometimes," Stucki told me once when I asked him what had gone into a certain dish, "the most important ingredients are the ones you leave out."

4. ACROSS THE CANAL AND INTO
THE TAGLIATELLE

I first dined at Harry's Bar in Venice in the early 1970s, not exactly by mistake, but certainly without quite having intended to. I was rather threadbare financially at the time, not a student still but a working stiff, armed with a complimentary Eurail pass and a free (and quite exquisite) room at the posh Bauer-Grünewald Hotel—both of them secured through the good offices (and the office) of my Uncle Paul, who did travel-business public relations in New York. These unearned luxuries aside, I was counting pennies (or whatever the appropriate currency was at the time), staying in little hotels near railroad stations, and eating in lots of pizzerias, and on lots of park benches.

Well, there was one other luxury: Before I left, my parents had given me an introduction to an old friend of theirs in London, the American-born film producer Jules Buck, and Buck had generously entertained me, providing me with a treasure trove of complimentary theatre tickets. He had also, when he learned that Venice was on my itinerary, urged me to visit his old friend Gastone, who was then head barman at that city's famed and elegant Danieli Excelsior Hotel. This I duly did. Gastone was charming and full of information about Venice. But I think the fact that I came recommended by Buck and was staying at the Bauer-Grünewald gave him an exaggerated idea of my assets. Thus, in telling me firmly, and with the wisdom of a true Venetian, exactly which restaurants I must avoid and which restaurants I must sample at all costs, the latter tended to be places that cost a lot.

Chief among these was Harry's Bar, and for some reason—whether because I didn't realize quite how expensive it would be, or because I didn't want to disappoint him, or (most likely of all) because I had secretly longed to try the place anyway but hadn't quite had the courage—I let him make a reservation for me, and went off to see what Harry's was all about.

I fell in love with it. I remember precisely what I had: a not-at-all-Venetian but addictively delicious green *tagliatelle verde alla bolognese* (one of the restaurant's great specialties); a plateful of small scampi out of their shells, sautéed simply in olive oil; and a fresh fig tart. I drank the house soave, from a pretty little pitcher, and had an Amaro Averna with my espresso. It was perfect. Even more perfect, though, was the place itself: I felt bathed in a golden glow at Harry's. I felt important, stylish, *international*. And I felt superbly taken care of. I felt at home.

Then I got the check. In an era when one could still eat very well in Italy—even at such famous places as Piccolo Mondo in Rome, that great canteen of La Dolce Vita, which was for years another of my favorite restaurants—for around $6 or $8, wine included, my bill at Harry's came to something like $30. That should have covered my hotel for a night *and* dinner, and probably lunch the next day. I was appalled. But I was not sorry.

I've been back to Harry's probably twenty times since then, and I have always been superbly treated and superbly fed. My gastronomically sophisticated friends in Italy tend to dismiss Harry's these days as a tourist trap or a shadow of its former self. I don't buy that. Sure, tourists go there. (This is *Venice,* for heaven's sake, which would probably be a swamp full of ruins today were it not for the tourist trade.) And maybe it used to be better—or at least used to seem better when there were fewer other good restaurants around. But the food remains wonderful—the world-famous carpaccio (invented here), the creamy risottos with scampi or spring vegetables, the Venetian-style calf's liver, the whole roasted monkfish tail, the homemade ice creams—and the glow never fails to greet me when I walk through the door.

5. ONE LONG PLANNING TO RETURN

"... [A]ll my traveling," wrote Ford Madox Ford in *Provence*, "has always been one long planning to return. One should skim through a place and if one likes it establish little contacts, with a waiter, a marketwoman, an honest merchant, an eating place, or merely those contacts that are part of memory. Then, when one returns to stay a little, one has already made some sort of preparation for digging in."

I liked Casablanca the first time I visited it, and I quickly found an eating-place there that I wanted to establish a little contact with. The best-known of Casablanca's seafood restaurants, along the Boulevard de la Corniche near the lighthouse of El Hank—La Mer, Le Cabestan, Ma Bretagne, Au Petit Rocher, etc.—serve fish and shellfish in the French manner, to diners who are themselves either French or Francophone (and apparently Francophile) Moroccan. The food can be very good at these places— Le Cabestan is perhaps the best—but there is a certain sameness to them, and they tend to be a bit too reminiscent of the portside restaurants of the Côte d'Azur, which is presumably not what one comes to Morocco for.

The Restaurant du Port de Pêche is different. It occupies the top floor of a plain two-story building behind the gates of the city's hard-working fishing port. (Downstairs, there is a simple fisherman's café, with a blackboard menu written only in Arabic, which I hope someday to have the courage, and the Arabic, to try.) Both the dishes it serves and the people who eat them are considerably more diverse than you would find at Le Cabestan and its relatives. The clientele includes everyone from young German backpackers to elderly French merchants obviously long ensconced in "Casa" (as nearly every French speaker calls the city), from large Moroccan families in traditional dress to local swells in polo shirts and blue jeans—the good

154

boys drinking Coca-Cola with their meals, the reprobates some pleasant Moroccan rosé. The food is not so much French as all-purpose Mediterranean, with a few Moroccan seafood dishes not commonly found in the tourist haunts thrown in, and all of it is fresh, honest, delicious.

What attracted me to the place immediately, though, was something more elusive: It simply had a kind of buzz to it, a warm, rackety energy that told me right away that this was the place to be. Maybe it was the crowds: The restaurant seats about 150, and is always jam-packed, usually with a few dozen people waiting in line. (Reservations are not accepted.) Maybe it was the lived-in, or at least dined-in, self-confidence of the corny but comfortable interior, with its red tile floors, white stucco walls, red tablecloths overlaid with pink paper, fishnet curtains on ships'-stern windows, red-shaded table lamps, and fish prints and seascapes on the walls. Maybe it was the casual efficiency of the waiters, bustling this way and that, forever grinning, chattering, dispensing recommendations and cautions.

Of course, the pleasure that the food gave me doubtless enhanced my impressions of the place. On my first visit to the Port de Pêche, I ate a big bowl of sweet little carpetshell clams, steamed in butter and their own juices; a first-rate grilled langouste, so full of flavor that I had to suck and lick every bit of juice and roe and butter from its every crevice; and finally a *tajine* of sea bass, which included green peppers, green olives, tomatoes, carrots, and potatoes, and a blend of spices in which paprika and cumin seemed to predominate. It was exquisite.

On my second visit to the restaurant about six months later ("Why do you come so often to Morocco?" asked the customs official who examined my passport when I returned; "For the seafood," I replied, to his obvious astonishment), I started with one of the great secrets of Moroccan gastronomy: a platter of impeccable oysters from the village of Oualidia, fifty miles or so southwest of

Casa. People who have never visited this corner of Morocco are surprised to learn that there are oysters raised on this coast at all. In fact, the oysters of Oualidia are superb—medium-small, salty-sweet, wonderfully full of flavor. Next, I had a jumble of fried baby squid, whiting, and miniature sole. I finished with the redundantly named *boulettes de merlan kefta* (*"boulettes"* and *"kefta"* both mean "meatballs," in French and Arabic respectively), tiny dumplinglike spheres of ground, spiced whiting in a thick sauce flavored with cumin and coriander. My anticipation was not betrayed.

I don't know when I'll get back to Casablanca the next time—but I know there'll be a next time. And I feel confident that I have already made some sort of preparation there for, shall we say, digging in.

6. IS THIS THE BEST RESTAURANT IN THE WORLD?

One autumn evening at Eldorado Petit in Barcelona, as a group of us were sitting back after dinner, fairly drowning in ice-cold *cava,* my friend Betty looked up and exclaimed, with incontrovertible authority, "This is the best restaurant in the world!"

What had inspired Betty's effusion? I'm not sure, but I think it must have had something to do with the deep-fried miniature red mullets, the salad of raw ceps dressed with olive oil and lemon juice, the huge Mediterranean prawns lightly poached in seawater, the salad of paper-thin marinated salt cod with white beans, the sweet red peppers stuffed with *rascasse* mousse and cloaked in hollandaise, the rich Catalan seafood-and-potato stew called *suquet* (faintly flavored with grated chocolate and ground nuts), the whole gilt-head bream (the fish the French call *daurade,* and the Catalans *orada*) baked in a crust of salt and served with *allioli* (Catalan garlic mayonnaise), the John Dory roasted on a bed of potato slices, the *arròs*

negre or black rice (made with cuttlefish, which has sweeter flesh and richer ink than squid), the baby duckling braised with pears. . . .

But wait a minute. All this was undeniably quite wonderful—gloriously simple and unfailingly delicious. But "the best"? Surely not, I began to say. Surely there *is* no single best restaurant in the world—and if there were, surely it would be something more complex (and probably more French) than this.

But then I remembered an article I had read years before, called "Have I Found the Greatest Restaurant in the World?" written by Roy Andries De Groot—a writer whose articles in various magazines in the 1960s and 1970s had helped awaken me to both the romance of restaurants and the importance of the human ingredient in good food. This particular article proposed that the world's best eating place might in fact be the three-star Restaurant Troisgros in Roanne—and I thought it might be worth looking up De Groot's piece when I got back to America to see how his criteria for Troisgros might apply to Eldorado Petit.

The reception and the service at Troisgros had been flawless, wrote De Groot. (Check.) The dining room had been comfortable but not self-consciously "luxurious." (Check.) De Groot's dinner, which had been proposed by the proprietors themselves and was based on products from that morning's market, was wonderful, and "astonishingly light." (Check.) In sum, said De Groot, "there had not been the slightest pomposity about the food, the service nor the welcome." (Check and double-check.)

The meal De Groot describes at Troisgros and our own meal at Eldorado Petit, though, were dramatically different: Ours was loosely structured and composed of the simplest of dishes, sometimes almost ingenuous in their plainness, but always perfectly fresh and right. De Groot, in contrast, dined on terrine of foie gras, lobster in calvados sauce, roasted wild duck with peaches glazed in maple syrup, and a raspberry *millefeuille*.

Good though I'm sure this meal was, it sounds so foreign to our tastes today—so *old-fashioned,* frankly—that this notion occurred to me: If Troisgros was indeed the best restaurant in the world in 1972, insofar as such things may be judged, then maybe, in the same sense, Eldorado Petit has a fair claim to being the best one today—not necessarily the place where you'll find the most dazzling cuisine *qua* cuisine, but a kind of paradigm of restaurant virtues for the 1990's: fresh, seasonal ingredients; skilled but not overcomplicated cooking; a menu with a strong regional identity, but also a deft cosmopolitan finish; interior design that creates a warm, easygoing environment without calling undue attention to itself (the noted Barcelona designer Jaume Tressera is responsible); and just plain scrupulous professionalism on every level, from the prescient service to the bartender's art to the friendly imperturbability of the man who parks the cars out front.

Is Eldorado Petit, finally, then, the "best restaurant in the world"? De Groot answered the same question about Troisgros, twenty years ago, by saying that, of the "12,474" restaurants around the world in which he estimated he had dined since childhood, "As far as I can remember, not one of them was ever as good as Troisgros." I've probably dined at only a quarter or a third of that number myself, but one of them was Troisgros (see page 134)—and I can tell you this: I like Eldorado Petit miles better.

7. IS THIS THE MOST ORDINARY RESTAURANT IN THE WORLD?

And then there's the establishment I'll call Restaurant X. Restaurant X is a place I manage to visit about once a year. It is situated in a city that is a good many miles from either coast, in a building at the foot of an anonymous office tower. The interior is *faux* bar & grill, with floors that are alternately hardwood slats and white terrazzo. There are reproductions of appropriately bar-&-grillish paintings on walls, and the tables are comfortable but not particularly large, and furnished with white tablecloths and dark green napkins, neither of the finest linen. There is a long mahogany bar, and, just inside the door, a blackboard listing specials of the day and wines available by the glass.

The service is casual but attentive here. (One day I noticed a waiter actually *looking* at every one of his tables every time he passed them, which is something precious few waiters do even at most three-star restaurants in France.) And the food? It's okay. The Cobb salad, though not traditional, is about the best I've ever had—full of roast beef and chicken, with little bits of celery and green pepper lurking there and a light, creamy vinaigrette dressing with which the salad is thoroughly and deliciously coated. The gazpacho is excellent, the corn and crab chowder is very good, and the lobster quesadilla is unusual and very pleasant. The "steakburger" and the beer-battered shrimp I can take or leave. The fish—usually a good selection of it, simply prepared—is nothing special, but perfectly all right. The desserts are disappointing.

In a way, then, this is just an ordinary restaurant. It is also one of the restaurants I like best. Why? I don't know. Maybe it's a question of scale: It sets modest goals for itself and then achieves them easily, and with a certain off-handed flair. It is a restaurant thoroughly without pretension. It feels good.

And why don't I reveal its name? For purely selfish reasons. It's not that I'm worried that the ravenous foodies of America will suddenly descend on the place and eat up all the Cobb salad. (They probably wouldn't like it anyway.) It's me I'm worried about. I want to be able to continue going into this establishment whenever I'm in the neighborhood. I want to be able just to sit down and have a quiet and enjoyable meal without the chef watching what

I'm eating or the manager sending me free wine to thank me for the mention or, well, the waitress asking, "What's your favorite restaurant?"

RECIPES

HOMECOMING CHICKEN

SERVES 3 TO 4

When I set off on one of my eating trips, the meal I look forward to the most has nothing to do with my favorite restaurants in Basel, Barcelona, or wherever. The meal I look forward to the most is the dinner that my wife inevitably cooks for me the night I get home. It is always the same—chicken roasted with carrots, shallots, garlic, and potatoes—and it is always superb. It is also, incidentally, a dish that can rest in the oven for an hour or two after cooking (which comes in handy if my plane is late or the Customs hall at LAX is even more of a bordel than usual).

2 *sprigs fresh rosemary*
1 *3¹/₂- to 4-pound roasting chicken**
2 *garlic cloves, minced*
¹/₄ *cup extra-virgin olive oil*
1 *tablespoon* herbes de Provence
1 *tablespoon coarse salt*
2 *teaspoons freshly ground black pepper*
¹/₂ *lemon*
4 *medium-small White Rose potatoes, unpeeled, quartered*
2 *large carrots, peeled and cut into sticks about 3" long and*
    ¹/₂" thick

---

* "Use a perfect chicken," warns my wife. "A really, really good one. Otherwise it will get tough."

4 shallots, peeled and separated into cloves
1 cup dry, full-bodied white wine*

Preheat oven to 400°.

Place rosemary sprigs in cavity of chicken. With fingers, separate breast skin from breasts and push minced garlic under skin, spreading it around as evenly as possible. Rub surface of chicken with olive oil, then sprinkle with *herbes de Provence,* salt, and pepper. Squeeze lemon juice over top of chicken.

Lightly oil a lidded cast iron or other metal roasting pan just large enough to hold the chicken with an inch or so of space around the edges. Distribute potatoes, carrots, and shallots around the roasting pan, then place chicken, skin side up, on top of them.

Roast chicken, uncovered, for 1 hour, basting it with pan juices after 20 minutes. After another 20 minutes, pour wine over chicken. At the end of 1 hour, baste again with the combined wine and pan juices.

Turn off the oven, cover roasting pan tightly, and let chicken sit in the oven for at least ½ hour, but for as long as 2 hours if necessary.†

---

*"The one you're drinking while waiting for your husband to get home," my wife notes.

† "If you leave it in the oven for an hour or two," adds my wife, "the chicken is obviously going to be very well done. But it won't dry out, and will still taste very good."

13

WAKING UP IN ROME

"... [It was] a typically Roman repast of aromatic artichokes,
spring lamb and impressionistic salad...."
—HAROLD ACTON, *MEMOIRS OF AN AESTHETE, 1939 – 1969*

*I*T WOULD BE AN EXAGGERATION TO SAY that I discovered food in Rome in the 1970s—real food, of the kind that now composes so great a part of my daily diet—but it would not be too much of an exaggeration.

I went to Rome frequently in those days, if not always as a primary destination, then as a stop tacked on whenever I went anywhere else in Europe. What drew me there, besides the obvious attractions of the city itself, was a good friend from Los Angeles named Karen, who had moved there several years before. Karen was (and for that matter still is, even now in Pennsylvania) a terrific cook and a great lover of good food, and she and I and her Italian friends seemed to spend our days and nights in Rome doing little else but going from one *caffè, trattoria, ristorante,* market, and wineshop to another—or else sitting around the dining table at Karen's apartment (first in the center of the city, off the via del Corso, and then on the Monte Mario) eating wonderful dishes she had cooked up in a sort of California-Roman style.

I wish I could remember the particulars of my first meal in Rome precisely. The best I can do is to summon up disconnected images of it, a little blurred around the edges. I was certainly with Karen, and we were almost certainly in a casual trattoria. There was probably one of those huge buffets of antipasti I grew to love so much—filled with things like tepid shrimp and whole small squid crisscrossed with grill marks, parsley-dusted mussels on the half shell, lengths of zucchini stuffed with bread crumbs and fresh herbs, butter-soft baby artichokes submerged in olive oil, filleted anchovies as thick as cheap sardines—all (I came to learn) the usual things.

There was pasta, of course—fiery *penne all'arrabbiata,* or maybe (if it was a Tuesday or a Friday, fish-market days in Rome) *spaghetti alle vongole.* For a main course, I'm sure we must have had *abbacchio arrosto,* roast baby lamb scented with rosemary, crisp and juicy, surrounded with leathery but delicious roasted potatoes. Then probably Parmigiano Reggiano and maybe grapes. . . .

Whatever it was that I ate, I had certainly never encountered anything quite like it before. It was in vivid contrast, in fact, with everything I had known or thought I'd known about Italian food: Not counting Chef Boyardee and Franco-American (and it's been a long time since I've counted them), I probably first encountered Italian food of some sort when I was fourteen or fifteen, and I had become a certified lover of the stuff by the time I was twenty-one. But Italian food in America in those days was not what it is today. If, indeed, you are what you eat, then by the time I had achieved my majority I must have been at least 10 percent ravioli with meat sauce and another 10 percent veal parmigiana—both of them heavy, cloaked with tomato sauce, and choked with cheese.

It's hard to remember—or even to believe—today, but in the mid-1970s, outside perhaps of a few hard-core ethnic enclaves scattered around the country, no one in America had ever heard of sun-dried tomatoes, porcini mushrooms, radicchio, arugula (or *rucola*), balsamic vinegar, *pancetta, polenta,* or *bufala mozzarella* (not "buffalo," incidentally; you can't get milk from an animal with an "o" at the end of its name, at least not in Italy). Sweet red peppers were a rarity, sold fresh in supermarkets for perhaps a few weeks a year, and otherwise available mostly in cans or jars, cut into little strips and called "pimentos." Olive oil, if it was to be found at all amongst the Mazola and the Planter's, came in tiny flasks and was measured out in half-teaspoons, and folks still sniggered when you called it "extra-virgin." Parmigiano was parmesan, a sawdustlike substance you shook out of a green cardboard container. Carpaccio was an artist.

I recall vividly, just back in the States from my first trip to Rome, trying to describe to friends *bruschetta*, which, in its pure form, is simply grilled country bread rubbed with raw garlic cloves and drizzled with olive oil. They were incredulous. "You can't make garlic bread without cheese," one of them informed me. (By 1988, "*bruschetta*" had earned the designation "household word" in *Metropolitan Home*—not at my instigation, I hasten to add.)

Beyond the sheer sensory intensity and sybaritic joy of eating and drinking in Rome, then, the thrill of the city's restaurants and markets was primarily for me a thrill of discovery. I doubt that my life has ever again revolved so completely and satisfyingly around food as it did during those visits to Rome. At virtually every meal, I experienced little gastronomic enlightenments. My eyes got opened almost as often as my mouth. I woke up to food

in Rome—not just to Italian food, but to food in general—
and to the integrity of raw materials and the authenticity
of flavor.

I remember discovering, for example, and positively
luxuriating in, the grilled *scamorza* cheese at Er Cucurucù
on the via Caporati, overlooking the banks of the Tiber.
(Who knew you could actually *grill* cheese, other than
inside a sandwich?) I remember my first-ever white truffles, grated into the *insalata Verushka* at Taverna Flavia; as
I bit into a piece of one for the first time, I felt as if I had just
unlocked some great earthy secret, slightly naughty,
slightly mad. (It was a foregone conclusion that I would
order this particular salad: I clipped pictures of Verushka
herself out of magazines in those days, and was thrilled
beyond reason to see her striding across the piazza di
Spagna one afternoon in person.)

At Sabatini in Trastevere, I was introduced to grilled
porcini mushroom caps, as big and meaty as thin steak—
and sat there stunned, since I had always detested mushrooms of any kind in America (probably, I later figured
out, because the only ones we ever had at home were the
rubbery, bland little ones that came in cans). And I remember my first *puntarelle,* the roots of a kind of chicory,
dressed with olive oil and anchovies, at Piccolo Mondo;
my first rectangular *pizza rustica* topped with thinly sliced
potatoes at a stand on the campo del Fiore; my first
braised oxtail at Piperno; my first roast pork in sweet-and-
sour sauce at Al Moro, beneath a window painted by
Raphaël.

Most of all, though, I just remember sitting there in the
garden of one restaurant or another, breathing in the rich
perfume of fried garlic and roasting meat, watching while
a legion's worth of Romans attacked great quantities of
simple food with busy relish and white-shirted waiters
worked their way around and through a veritable logjam
of full tables, popping wine corks, dousing salad greens

with oil and vinegar like madmen, rattling off the irresistible bill of fare.

And there I was, fingers glazed from hands-on eating, face flushed from consuming positively un-American quantities of wine and salt, feeling, at least for the moment, almost indecently in love with Rome, with Italy in general—and with the whole idea of food.

RECIPES

$\int$PAGHETTI CACIO E PEPE

SERVES 4 TO 6

Of all the famous pasta dishes invented in or adopted heartily by Rome—spaghetti alla carbonara, all'amatriciana, or alla puttanesca, maccheroni alla ricotta, penne all'arrabbiata, fettuccine Alfredo *(see page 247), and the rest, this is my favorite. I don't recall exactly where I had it for the first time—maybe at Piccolo Mondo, or at the modest trattoria called La Buca di Ripetta—but I know that it surprised me with both its simplicity and its intensity of flavor, and that I subsequently ordered it often. I also know that I was never quite able to reproduce it in my own kitchen until I got this recipe from Roman-born restaurateur Mauro Vincenti, who today runs Rex Il Ristorante, Pazzia, and Fennel in Los Angeles, and who learned the secret of the dish from his chef at Pazzia, Umberto Bombana.*

Actually, I should probably say a secret of the dish. Sacramento-based wine-and-specialty-food purveyor Darrell Corti, who is extremely knowledgeable about Italian cooking (among many other things), says that using pancetta *is absolutely wrong. "This was originally a Lenten* dish," he says, "and so it couldn't have any meat products in it at all. You should coat the spaghetti with olive oil instead—and instead of draining it very well, you should leave a little moisture on the pasta. The cheese will melt and stick to the spaghetti better." If you're confused by the contradictions between Vincenti's and Corti's rules for making this dish, you should hear them on the subject of spaghetti alla carbonara! This, in any case, is Vincenti's recipe.

Salt

¹/₂ pound fatty pancetta (unsmoked Italian-style bacon), sliced ¹/₆" thick

1 pound spaghetti*

6 ounces well-aged Pecorino Romano†

Freshly ground black pepper

Bring 6 to 8 quarts of amply salted water to a boil in a large covered pot or pasta cooker.

Meanwhile, cook *pancetta* over medium-low heat in a large, deep skillet or Dutch oven until it gives up most of its fat. Remove skillet from heat and discard *pancetta* or save it for another use. Reserve ¹/₄ cup *pancetta* fat in the same skillet, draining off excess, if any, for another use.

When water comes to a full boil, add spaghetti and cook at a boil, uncovered, for about 6 minutes, or until slightly firmer than *al dente.*‡

While pasta is cooking, grate Pecorino Romano (using small grating holes, not larger shredding holes) into a small bowl, grind a generous amount of black pepper into bowl, and mix cheese and pepper together very well.

Just before spaghetti is cooked, return skillet with *pancetta* fat to a medium heat. Drain spaghetti well, then add to fat and toss to coat thoroughly.

---

* Vincenti prefers Martelli or Gerardo di Nola brand pasta. Under no circumstances use egg noodles or freshly made pasta.

† This particular kind of Pecorino may be difficult to find, but it is available in the United States, and it really does make a difference.

‡ Romans like their pasta firmer than al dente—what they call "filo di ferro," or "iron string."

Remove skillet from heat, and sprinkle a third of the cheese over pasta. Toss well to coat pasta with cheese. Repeat this process until all the cheese has been added and each strand of spaghetti is evenly coated with cheese and pepper.

Serve immediately.*

---

* *Italian etiquette dictates that you should start eating pasta and risotto the moment you are served, regardless of what anyone else is doing.*

14
CLAUDE'S CHALLENGE

"For Claude, the party was always just beginning."
—ROBERT HARDY ANDREWS, *A CORNER OF CHICAGO*

*C*LAUDE AND I HAD JUST FINISHED LUNCH
at L'Artois in Paris, in the days when it was still under the
ownership of the now-deceased Isidore Rouzeyrol and his
wife, and still one of the best old-fashioned Auvergnat-
style restaurants in the city. We had eaten the kind of meal
we had often in those days: foie gras followed by simply
roasted *bécasse,* or woodcock (commercial hunting of this
bird, the most intensely delicious of all feathered game,
had not yet been banned in France), on thick, wonderfully
soggy croutons made from country-style bread. We had
finished with big slabs of Cantal cheese the color of old

ivory, and slices of sweet blue plum tart. We had consumed the wines we usually drank here—a bottle of sancerre and a bottle of cahors—and were now sipping Rouzeyrol's highly palatable *vieille prune* and smoking our luncheon-sized Monte Cristos.

At this point, Claude looked once around the restaurant, leaned back a bit in his chair, squinted, and said, "You know, if I were still a young man, I would now challenge you to eat exactly the same meal with me again, but backwards this time, starting with the plum tart and ending with the foie gras." He paused. "Only this time," he continued, "perhaps we would have the wild boar instead of the *bécasse. . . .*"

Fortunately for my well-being, Claude was seventy-five at the time and didn't feel up to such a feat of gourmandise himself. It was a close call, though—because if he had issued his challenge instead of merely threatening it, I would have felt compelled to accept it. I wouldn't want to let the old man down.

Much of what I know about eating in Paris, and in France in general, I have learned from Claude. He has several advantages, from my point of view, over younger or more conventional commentators on the subject: His very age, to begin with, and the sheer depth of experience in eating and drinking that that implies. His long membership in a number of gastronomic societies of the old style—organizations with names like Les Poètes Chevelus (The Hairy Poets; members must be bald or nearly so to qualify), La Queue de Poêle (The Pan Handle), the Académie Rabelais, Les Mâchons de Paris (a group of dedicated trenchermen who meet for hearty Lyonnais-style meals—at nine in the morning!), as well as a now-defunct association of food-loving Anglo-American newspapermen in Paris known variously as the Royal Gastronomic Society, the Trough, the Bistro Anonymous, and the Bombay Duck—through which he keeps up with food-world gossip and continues to enrich his already considerable knowledge of French culinary tradition. And, probably most of all, his unbridled skepticism and disdain for the pretensions of chefs and restaurateurs.

Claude, who spent his life (before retirement) in the newspaper business, is my unofficial adoptive father. The bonds between us are both historical and sentimental: In the late 1920s, as a young man working for the Parisian daily *Le Quotidien*, Claude was sent to the United States for a year to work at the *Chicago Daily News* (he already spoke reasonably good English through family connections in Great Britain) so that he might acquaint himself with American standards and methods of news reporting. In Chicago, he met my father, who was a few years older than he and himself an editor and writer for the paper. They became fast friends and drinking companions—but after Claude returned to France in 1931, the two lost touch.

In the early 1960s, my father wrote a book about his newspaper days in Chicago. In it, he devoted some pages to "a young hurricane from Paris named Claude," who, he said, had arrived in Chicago "prepared to scalp red Indians on State Street and spit right in Al Capone's eye."

As he describes his friend, Claude was already outspoken, and had already developed prodigious appetites: "In Hy Green's speakeasy," my father writes at one point, "[Claude] drained a waterglass of gin in one great gulp, and gasped that he much preferred it to his father's best Courvoisier. Then he passed out cold. But ten minutes later, he was up and roaring for more."

Later in the book, though, my father describes loading Claude, weeping, onto the *Twentieth Century* for New York, from which he was to sail back to France. (In fact, Claude says, it was the *Sunset Limited* for San Francisco; he was to sail back to France the long way, through the Panama Canal.) "I never saw or heard of him again," concludes my father. He told me later that he had always believed Claude to have been killed in France during World War II.

Following publication of the book, though, my father heard from another *Daily News* veteran, author Mac-Kinlay Kantor, who informed him that Claude was still very much alive in Paris. The two men were reunited by mail—but since my father's travels of the period were mostly to the Far East, I met Claude before my father saw him again, on my first trip to Paris, in 1966. When Claude and his wife, Pepita, came to my hotel to pick me up for dinner in Paris, Claude later told me, he recognized me immediately from afar. "I could have been looking at your father as he was the last time I saw him," he said.

I got along with Claude and Pepita well enough on that first meeting, but on my next trip to Paris some four years later, Claude and I discovered that we genuinely liked each other and could talk to one another freely about almost anything. He and his wife had never had children, and I became a kind of part-time stand-in son for them. For my part, I was hungry for any and all connections with France—and, I suppose, for a kind of parental frankness that I couldn't count on from my own father. Our relationship soon became familial.

Since my second trip to France, I've probably been there at least twice a year on the average, and Claude and I have dined together endlessly on these visits, not just in Paris, but in Alsace, Burgundy, Provence, and the Charente. (Pepita joins us sometimes, but most of the time leaves us to our "boy talk" and serious consumption of food and drink.) Claude's age—he is eighty-six as I write this—has diminished neither his capacity nor his desire for the pleasures of the table. He has oftentimes proved more resilient than I, in fact.

One afternoon a couple of years ago, for instance, we were discussing our dinner date the next evening on the phone. He had just been in the hospital and had been advised to take it easy with his diet. Reading him some restaurant descriptions from *Gault Millau*, I came to the splendid establishment called Apicius, and mentioned that one of their specialties was an escalope of foie gras in a sweet-and-sour sauce—quickly adding, "But that's probably not the sort of thing you'll want to eat so soon after the hospital." He replied, "Well, you know, foie gras doesn't sound so bad. And after all, it is in a sense already half-digested, and so ought to go down pretty well." As it turned out, we went to another establishment. Claude didn't have foie gras. He had lamb kidneys instead.

On another occasion, I had an assignment to write about the newly refurbished La Coupole, and I met Claude there for lunch. I ordered oysters for us to share to start— a half-dozen Belons and a half-dozen freshwater Belon-dines. "Probably that's not enough," Claude said. I agreed, so we asked for six *plates* from Holland, too. "And maybe we should have some *bouquets roses,* too," he added, referring to a kind of delicious little rose-pink prawn. I agreed again. At that point, our waiter departed—but Claude held on to the shellfish menu, scanning it with a not-quite-satisfied grimace, perhaps considering the clams, the mussels, the cockles, and the winkles. At that moment, though, our waiter returned bearing a couple of complimentary appetizers—a small bowl of those winkles (or *bigorneaux*) and another of *crevettes grises,* baby brothers to the *bouquets.* Claude smiled as if to say, Well, now we'll have enough. We ate everything. Then we went on to our civet of wild boar.

"You know," Claude told me as we ate, "when this place opened back in 1927, I was one of the regulars at La Ro-tonde, across the street. We were very loyal to La Rotonde, and all the guys there swore that they'd never even set foot in this newcomer. But the bosses here gave such a great opening party, with everything for free, that most of us snuck over here anyway—and pretty soon, well . . ."

This was good fodder for my article on the place, of course. But the next night, away from Montparnasse, over dinner at the two-star Duquesnoy on the avenue Bous-quet, one of our regular haunts, Claude told me a much better tale of the *quartier*. One day when he was about forty, he began, he had lunch with some colleagues at a bistro in Montparnasse. Heroic quantities of wine and brandy were consumed, and afterward, carrying under his arm a carton of American cigarettes he had obtained at great difficulty for his wife (this was just after World War II), he headed home. Along the way, he stopped at a number of his favorite local bars and cafés. "This is what you did then," he explained, "seeing friends, having a drink with them."

Some hours later, he found himself at one little place near the Gare Montparnasse that he remembers vividly for two reasons: The milk trains—in the literal sense of the term—arrived from Brittany daily just outside this particular café, delivering big metal milk cans to be distributed (even then) by horse-drawn carts around the city. The clanging of those cans being loaded, he told me, still rang in his ears. "The other thing I remember about that place," he continued, "was that I met a man there, drinking at the bar, who had a cage on his back full of white mice which he was delivering to a scientific laboratory."

Finally hailing a cab to take him home to the apartment he and Pepita then shared on the rue Dareau, Claude invited the taxi driver to stop and have a glass of white wine with him when they passed another of his favorite cafés. The driver agreed. As they continued on their way, Claude spotted yet another place to stop. Again the driver agreed. The third time this happened, the driver—not up to the challenge, as it were—pleaded that he'd had enough. "We're almost to my house," said Claude. "Just one more glass." The man acceded yet again. Incredibly, Claude added, when he finally did get home, he discovered that he still had Pepita's cigarettes.

Pepita was mad anyway, though, and worried. She would have called the prefecture of police, she told him, but she had called his office first, and his coworkers had calmed her fears. Pepita was doubly angry because she and Claude had invited another couple over for dinner that night—Claude had forgotten—and they had already arrived. Furious, she put Claude into the bathtub, from which he proceeded to sing loudly for some minutes. Then he somehow arranged himself and went in to dinner, which he apparently survived without mishap—other than the fact, he now recalls with some embarrassment, that he got into a big argument with the rest of the table over their insistence that a true *civet de lapin* (the evening's main dish) was thickened with the rabbit's blood. (It is.)

"The couple that came to dinner," Claude went on, "were Louis-Émile Galey and his wife. He had been director of the cinema for the Vichy government, but he really wasn't a bad guy. He always made sure that the good directors had enough film stock, and so on. His son Matthieu became a famous critic and author, and wrote, among other things, some interesting volumes of memoirs, which are only just now being published, posthumously. He died rather recently, and there was quite a scandal because a woman who had been in love with him, even though he was a homosexual, claimed his body and took the coffin to the place in Provence where he had wanted to be buried. Well, it seems that along the way, she stopped for the night at a hotel in Carpentras, and brought the coffin into the room, and . . .

"*Merde!*" Claude exclaimed at this point, realizing that he had gotten somewhat off the track. "What the hell am I talking about?"

But, ah, I had been thinking in the meantime, so *that* was Montparnasse.

RECIPES

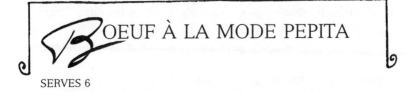

BOEUF À LA MODE PEPITA

SERVES 6

Some of the best meals I've ever had with Claude, our extensive restaurant-going aside, have been at his apartment on the avenue Gambetta, with Pepita doing the cooking. One of her best dishes—a French classic now difficult to find in Parisian restaurants, much less in the United States—is boeuf à la mode. This is her recipe, and it is very French, complete with larding for the beef (you'll need a larding needle), a calf's foot in the sauce for texture, and not one but two instances of flambéeing. There are plenty of good all-American recipes for pot roast, braised beef, and the like that don't demand larding, flaming, or the inclusion of animal paws, and readers who find these details too intimidating or distasteful are invited to consult such simpler formulae. But a recipe without these elements would not be Pepita's, and would not be half as good.

Anyway, the French attitude, to which I heartily subscribe, is that while there's nothing wrong with eating simply, when you do choose to cook a serious dish, you ought to cook it correctly—and worry about your calories and cholesterol another time. (Leftovers from this dish are excellent cold, incidentally, especially when encased in the delicious gelatin that the calf's foot will yield.)

¹/₄ *pound beef suet or strip lard cut into 5 long strips (or 10 shorter ones)*
3¹/₂-*pound rump roast*
3 *tablespoons unsalted butter*
1 *calf's foot, sawed crosswise into thirds*
Salt and freshly ground black pepper
1 *cup cognac*

1 tablespoon flour
1 bottle côtes-du-rhône or other good red wine
6 large carrots, cut in 1" rounds
1 large onion, peeled and stuck with 4 cloves
12 small white onions, peeled but trimmed only slightly at
      the root end (so they will hold together in pot)
1 bouquet garni (3 sprigs parsley, 1 sprig thyme, 1 bay leaf,
      and a few celery leaves, wrapped tightly in cheesecloth)
1 garlic clove, crushed
1 piece orange peel (about 2" × 3")
1 small dried red chili pepper

With a larding needle, lard roast lengthwise, inserting one long piece of suet or lard (or two shorter ones, one after the other in the same incision) in the middle of the roast and arranging the other four (or eight) pieces around it evenly. Melt butter in a deep roasting pan large enough to hold roast with 3 to 4 inches around it, then brown the roast slowly on all sides. (This should take 15 to 20 minutes.)

Meanwhile, place calf's foot in a large pot with cold water to cover, bring to a boil, and continue boiling for about 10 minutes.

When beef is well browned, add salt and pepper to taste, flambé half the cognac over it, then sprinkle flour on top. Add wine to the roasting pan to just over half the height of the beef, adding water if necessary to attain that level. Flambé remaining cognac over beef. Add calf's foot, carrots, large and small onions, bouquet garni, garlic, orange peel, and chili pepper to liquid, and bring to a boil. Reduce heat and simmer, lightly covered, for 2 hours. Baste beef frequently with pan liquid, and turn it over after 1 hour.

Remove beef and calf's foot and allow both to rest for about 5 minutes. Slice beef across the grain in 1" to 1½" slices and arrange on a serving dish that will hold liquid. Add calf's foot and surround beef with carrots and small onions. Strain all the liquid over the meat, discarding the solids. Serve with coarse salt and good mustard.

$\mathcal{H}$OMARD AU WHISKY

SERVES 6

Sometimes, though, Claude does the cooking. This is one of his specialties—inspired, he reports, by a dish he used to indulge in sometimes at Maxim's.

2 *onions, minced*
1 *garlic clove, minced*
2 *tomatoes, peeled, seeded, and chopped*
1 *bouquet garni (3 sprigs parsley, 1 sprig thyme, and 1 bay leaf, tied together firmly)*
Olive oil
Salt and freshly ground black pepper
6 *live lobsters, 1 to 1½ pounds each*
Good-quality Scotch whisky, warmed
2 *cups dry white wine*
6 to 8 *saffron threads, lightly toasted and crushed*
Tabasco sauce

In a large Dutch oven, cook onions, garlic, tomatoes, and bouquet garni in olive oil over low heat for at least 1 hour, or until very soft and thick. Season mixture to taste with salt and pepper.

Cut the lobsters into large pieces along the separations in their shells.* Detach and crack the claws. Cut the head in two lengthwise, reserving the light green tomalley

---

* *Claude maintains that this operation must be performed while the lobsters are still alive for optimum flavor. ("Their claws must be bound with rubber bands," he notes, "or they will fight back.") Clearly, this is not an operation for the squeamish. A workable alternative, recommended as humane by the Universities Federation for Animal Welfare in Great Britain, is to plunge the lobsters first into a large quantity of rapidly boiling water (about a gallon per lobster—do it in batches unless you have a very large stockpot), for about 30 seconds. Then remove them and proceed. Alternatively, you can ask your fishmonger to prepare the lobster as described.*

(liver) and, if present, pink coral in a bowl. Discard dark portions.

Sauté the lobster tails and claws in olive oil in a large pan until the shells just turn red. Immediately flambé them with about 1 cup of warm whisky. Mix lobster pieces in the whisky until well coated.

Add wine to the onion mixture, bring to a boil and reduce slightly, stirring constantly. Add the lobster pieces and whisky sauce to the pan. Add saffron to mixture, stir well, and place the split lobster bodies on top. Cover pan and let the lobsters cook over medium heat for about 15 minutes.

Remove lobster from the pan and let cool slightly. Meanwhile, continue cooking sauce, stirring occasionally, until it is thickened. Remove the lobster from the shells. Crush tomalley and coral (if any) with a fork, then add 1/4 to 1/2 cup of it to the sauce. Add a few drops of Tabasco sauce, to taste, and a splash of whisky, stir well, then return shelled lobster pieces to the sauce and heat through.

Serve with plain white rice.

15

HAMBURGERS AT CHEZ PANISSE

*"[A] man might limit his boasting to saying that he was a good
trencherman, and yet be vain since he may delight in wolfing down
what, in the realm of the haute cuisine, is mere garbage."*
—FORD MADOX FORD, *IT WAS THE NIGHTINGALE*

ONE EVENING IN THE MID-1980s, I STOPPED
in alone for dinner at a casual, comfortable, vaguely pub-
like restaurant in Santa Monica and ordered one of my
favorite (casual, comfortable) meals: a Caesar salad and a
cheeseburger, with a bottle of good red wine on the side.

The restaurant's host apparently recognized me, and (I
learned later) ducked into the kitchen to warn the chef that
an Important Food Critic was in the house. As the evening
had been a slow one and the hour was late, the chef had
been getting ready to go home. Under the circumstances,
of course, he couldn't think of leaving. He did a quick

inventory of raw materials and picked out what he thought was best. "Tell him about the red snapper," he told the waitress who was assigned to my table. "Tell him about the tuna. Tell him about the venison." She did so, dutifully. But I was not to be swayed. "A Caesar salad and a cheeseburger," I said.

A year or so later, that same chef, who had subsequently become a friend, asked me, "Do you remember that night you came in and ordered the Caesar and the burger?" Yes, I said, I did. "Do you know that when I got that order," he continued, "after I'd stayed late and all, I was so damned mad at you that I threw food clear across the kitchen?"

On another occasion, I dined with my friend Ciro at a well-known restaurant in a major East Coast city. Ciro had been out running before dinner and was ravenous. I was, as usual, ravenous myself, without having bothered to run. As we were being shown to our table, Ciro noticed bowls of tortilla chips and salsa on the bar. As an immediate sop to our hunger, he quickly sweet-talked our waitress into bringing us some of these while we considered what to order. The chips were fresh and crisp; the salsa was delicious. We ate enough of both to stave off our hunger pangs and leave a pleasant taste in our mouths.

At about this time, our waitress reappeared to tell us that the chef would like to choose our dinner for the evening. (Ciro is himself a chef of some repute, and this sort of thing happens to him as often as it happens to me. When we dine together, it is virtually inevitable.) The first dish the chef sent out was cornmeal pancakes with caviar and smoked salmon in dill sauce. It was fine. But it also seemed somehow fussy and silly. Not one of the dishes that followed, in fact, though some of them were quite imaginative and well cooked, gave either one of us anything approaching the pure sensual pleasure we had drawn from those simple chips with salsa. Ciro said as much. I agreed. "And you know," I added, "there aren't a whole lot of people walking around loose out there who would understand what the hell we were talking about if we told them that. . . ."

I have dined extensively in the great restaurants of Europe and America, and in the course of so doing, I have sometimes encountered food of almost transcendental refinement and subtlety. I appreciate precision, craft, art (in the loose sense of the word) in cooking. Food of great finesse is one of the priceless treasures of the race, and I devoutly hope that it survives fad and fashion and economic downturn. I certainly do my part to help support it, both with words and with credit cards. But I don't want to eat it every day. And I find such food palatable only when it is done genuinely well, with confidence, good sense, and skill.

Otherwise, frankly, I'd rather have chips and salsa. I mean that literally—and I don't even mean that the chips and salsa have to be fresh, homemade, and unusually good. I'd settle for Salsa Rio Doritos with Rosarita hot sauce if that was all I could get—and like it a damned sight better than most of the ersatz *"bruschetta"* and soggy-crust "designer pizza" and oversauced, gummy pasta I encounter regularly at the hands of Oh So Creative young American chefs.

What I mean is that I like fine food but I don't like mediocre food masquerading as fine food. And I like plain food, too—not just chips and salsa, of course, but meat loaf, steak, smothered pork chops, tuna salad sandwiches, cracked crab, old-fashioned onion soup, chocolate ice cream, biscuits and gravy—and, of course, hamburgers.

When, for reasons that still escape me, I was included in the late *Cook's* magazine's first "Who's Who of Cooking in America," I was asked to name my favorite food. Hamburger, I replied, without a moment's hesitation. I got kidded about that at the "Who's Who" banquet, and more than one of my colleagues asked me, "No, but what's the *real* answer?" That was the real one. The only answer I liked better than mine—and one I wish I had given, as it would have been an even more accurate expression of my tastes—was Craig Claiborne's. His favorite food, he said, was "Any ground-meat dish."

I like hamburgers because they taste good. They're succulent. They're satisfying. They're even reasonably well balanced nutritionally, including as they do (in their classic form, at least) not only meat and bread but also cheese and at least two different vegetables—lettuce and tomatoes. I think they're just about the perfect food, in fact, and I don't quite understand why chefs who put them on their menus in the first place then sometimes treat them as an embarrassment and feel insulted when a supposed food expert like me orders one.

I order them myself at all the best places. I've had them made by (or under the supervision of) Lydia Shire, Jeremiah Tower, Jonathan Waxman, Wolfgang Puck, and Bradley Ogden, among other famous American chefs. I even once had a hamburger at Harry's Bar in Venice, though I probably wouldn't do so again; the chicken sandwich is much better. Oh, and I'm also probably one of the few people in the world who has ever eaten a hamburger at Chez Panisse. It was on the lunch menu at the Café there one day in 1987, and I never even considered ordering anything else. It was compact, juicy, delicious. "I don't think we ever served it again," proprietor Alice Waters now says.

RECIPE

*T*HE ALICE WATERS HAMBURGER

When I asked Alice Waters for the particulars of the hamburger she had once served at the Café at Chez Panisse, she could not recall them. But, she said, she did "have some ideas about hamburgers." Here they are, but in a slightly edited version of the form in which she gave them to me:

"The bread is vital. I use a relatively soft roll, not too thick, with lots of taste. The roll is cut, toasted, drizzled with olive oil, and rubbed with a clove of garlic.

"The meat is vital. I buy hormone-free ground chuck with a medium amount of fat. I chop up a little garlic finely and mix it with the meat, then form the meat into hamburgers and salt and pepper them. I slice up an onion and fry it in the same pan with the meat, adding a touch of olive oil if necessary. Or, ideally, I cook the meat over charcoal and grill the onion slices. Either way, I always brown the meat, and it's always rare inside.

"The garnishes are vital, too. I use a slice of ripe tomato, lots of rocket (arugula), and a little mustard. (I also like the taste of lovage instead of rocket, but you can't use too much of it.) I serve my hamburgers with dill pickles and home-fried potatoes. C'est tout!"

16

IF YOU ARE DETAINED
AT CALAIS . . .

"Everything written before our time was written for our instruction. . . ."

—ROMANS 15:4

"*T*ORTONI'S HOTEL RESTAURANT [IN LE HAVRE]," begins a passage in my favorite restaurant guide, "must not be confounded with the Brasserie Tortoni quite close to it, which is a bachelor's resort; and which I, as a bachelor, have found very amusing sometimes after dinner." Another passage begins, "If you are detained at Calais (and every man at least once in his lifetime is detained at Calais) . . ."

Clearly this is not your Zagat or your *Guide Michelin* talking. This is an urbane, witty, highly evocative, information-packed little volume called *The Gourmet's*

Guide to Europe, by a man who signs himself simply Lieut.-Col. Newnham-Davis—a book devoted to the dining customs, menus, and after-dinner entertainments not just of Western Europe, but of Russia, the Balkan countries, even Turkey.

Sounds good, you say? Sounds like something you might like to pick up at Brentano's before your next trip across the Big Pond? Well, maybe. But you'd never find it, and it would be of limited practical use today if you did: It was published in 1903.

I collect old restaurant guides, particularly (though not exclusively) those dealing with Paris, London, New York, and Los Angeles. Not everyone appreciates the appeal of such volumes. Isn't collecting old restaurant guides, they ask, a bit like collecting old telephone books or old calendars? Aren't old restaurant guides like yesterday's papers?

The answer is, of course, that old restaurant guides are of little use today as *guides,* but that they can tell us a very great deal, culinary and otherwise, about earlier times and other places. For instance, I thought I knew what Chateaubriand was, until I read Newnham-Davis on the subject. The real Chateaubriand, he writes, "is a steak of great thickness, with two thin slices of rump-steak tied above and below it. These slices are burned in the cooking and are thrown away, the steak done-through being passed over a bright fire before being served, to brown it."

He adds that the dish was invented at Champeaux on the place de la Bourse in Paris,* where "the cuisine has

---

*There is in fact a lot more to Chateaubriand than that. According to popular tradition, this preparation of beef (sometimes rendered in French as châteaubriant) was named after the famous author/statesman Vicomte François Auguste-René de Châteaubriand (1768–1848). The Larousse Gastronomique quotes the noted chef Henri Paul Pellaprat (1869–1950), who had worked at Champeaux before its demise in the early 1920s, as suggesting ("probably wrongly," notes the dictionary) that the dish was created at the restaurant to honor Châteaubriand upon the publication in 1811 of his book L'Itinéraire de Paris à Jérusalem.

Another theory has it that it was invented not at Champeaux at all, but in Châteaubriand's own kitchen, by his personal chef, Montmirail (Jean Conil in his always been of the best," and tells what he calls "a pretty story" about that establishment: "Champeaux, its founder, as a poor boy came to Paris, starving and without a sou. A kindly restaurateur gave him at daybreak a dish of broken food. When he himself was prosperous and a restaurateur he ordered that all the food left over should each morning at daybreak be given to the hungry poor, and this is still done."

Who was Newnham-Davis? "If Colonel Davis knew as much about the arts of war as he did about the pleasures of peace," wrote Charles Browne in his own *The Gun Club Cook Book* (1939), "he would certainly have long ago been entitled to a Field Marshal's baton." Newnham-Davis was by all accounts an incredible character, educated at Harrow, a veteran of "The Buffs" or the East Kent Regiment (so called for the buff-colored facings of its uniforms). He saw active service in the so-called Zulu War of 1879 and later served in India, China, and the Straits Settlements. He subsequently became one of the great gastronomes and bon vivants of his era.

Known to his intimates in London as "The Dwarf," apparently on account of his sturdy size, he was said to have been the quintessential "clubman" after his retirement from the army in 1894—capable of telling colorful war stories at the Naval and Military, trading theatre lore at the

---

Haute Cuisine, *who identifies Châteaubriand only as "Ambassador in London, where dishes were named after him," says that the chef's name was Lefort), or even that it had nothing to do with him at all, and was in fact a reference to cattle bred near the town of Châteaubriant, southeast of Rennes.*

According to Joseph Favre in his Dictionnaire universel de cuisine practique, *the Chateaubriand of the early 1900s (the era in which Newnham-Davis wrote his guide) was a beef fillet as thick as two large steaks, grilled and served with maître d'hôtel butter and glace de viande—but he goes on to claim that Montmirail's original recipe called for a thick piece of fillet to be cut open horizontally to form a pocket, and then stuffed with sautéed shallots, beef marrow, glace de viande, minced scallions, cayenne, and salt, closed with a skewer, and grilled. Nowhere, in fact, have I been able to find corroboration of Newnham-Davis's description of the dish. But Pellaprat does add that, because the Chateaubriand (in its 1900s version) is so thick, it must be cooked very slowly, lest a hard shell form on the outside while the center remains uncooked. The sliced rump steak method would certainly address the problem.*

Garrick (he was himself the author of at least two West End plays, "A Day in Paris" and "Lady Madcap," and of several ballets), and expounding on food and drink at the Beefsteak. Whether by accident or design, he had also been put in charge of German internees in London during World War I—a group whose numbers happened to include many of the city's top chefs and maîtres d'hôtel. This presumably aided him greatly in his pursuit of the gastronomic pleasures after the war. Newnham-Davis was also an accomplished journalist, having for a time been editor of two magazines, *Town Topics* and *Man of the World,* and a contributor to the *Sketch, Punch,* the *Pink'Un,* and the *Pall Mall Gazette.*

Of his book *Dinners and Diners,* a collection of restaurant pieces originally published in the *Gazette,* one writer was later to note, "[A]ny novelist who wished to reconstruct the social scene of 1900 [in London] would save himself many blunders by consulting Newnham-Davis." One thing I could not discover about the good Lieut.-Col. for some time was his first name—which does not appear on any of his books. (The third, besides the aforementioned *Gourmet's Guide* and *Dinners and Diners,* is *The Gourmet's Guide to London.*) A brief appreciation of him by John Fuller in the Wine & Food Society quarterly *Wine and Food* in 1944 calls him "N. Newnham-Davis," but that was as far as I could get—until I found a citation from the *Gourmet's Guide* in a little book called *Spirit of Place/ Provence,* in which his name is given—I know not on what authority—as Nathaniel.

One interesting characteristic of Newnham-Davis's guides is that though they deal extensively and in great detail with restaurants, they don't waste a lot of time yakking about food. He does reproduce menus, recommend certain dishes, and offer opinions of the overall quality of the cooking at the places he includes; but he also acknowledges, at least implicitly, that restaurants are social arenas and repositories of tradition and not just feed-troughs. His books are thus full of personality, full of life—books in which chefs are human beings, not celebrities, and in which a meal is only as good as the spirit by which it is animated. Oh, and he doesn't give stars.

Neither does a slightly later guidebook author, Julian Street (a popular writer whose nongastronomical works included *My Enemy the Motor, Ship-Bored,* and the short story on which the classic 1926 W. C. Fields silent movie *So's Your Old Man* was based). Here is his review of a Parisian boîte called Adrienne, reproduced in its entirety from his *Where Paris Dines* (1929):

> Into this restaurant I chanced one night by accident. Entering alone, I was greeted by female yelps in the 'Here comes Charley!' manner, but having got that far, and being hungry, I sat down and dined while terrible old harridans cavorted and sang. The wine was good enough, and the dinner was so far from bad that it surprised me, yet I found the place entirely unpleasant.

What precisely did Street eat and drink? Who cares? What more could anybody possibly need to know about the place than what he tells us? And how, for heaven's sake, could anyone assign a rating to it?

Or consider *Le Guide du gourmand à Paris* (1922) by one Robert-Robert. Although basically a commonsense catalogue of Parisian eating places, with brief notes on some of the dishes served at each establishment, this volume is full of enlightening little asides that sometimes flirt with sheer poetry—as when the author writes of a restaurant called simply Marie, *"La mère Marie est belle à voir dans le rayonnement de ses fourneaux"* (Mother Marie is beautiful to see in the radiance of her ovens). He can also evoke a whole world in a simple phrase, as when he notes of Maxim's that its very name *"fait frémir les mères"* (makes mothers tremble)—a line that I think reveals as much about Parisian society between the two world wars as it does about Maxim's itself. (How sound Robert-Robert's gastronomic judgments are is apparently open to question: Next to his favorable notice on a place called Au Boeuf à la Mode, some earlier reader has scrawled in my copy of the guide, *"Estampage sole frite 12F vin exécrable"* (A rip-off. Fried sole for 12 francs. Abominable wine).

Journalist Sommerville Story, author of what is perhaps the most readable of my Paris guides, *Paris à la Carte* (undated, but c. 1922), states the food-isn't-everything philosophy plainly in his preface:

> The charm of Paris restaurants lies not only in the choice food they supply, but in the characteristics, habits, and peculiarities of the people who frequent them, the famous habitués of the past, and the little tags of history which help to give interest to one's meal.

Some of Story's richest and most colorful passages, in fact, aren't about restaurants at all. In mentioning the cafés of the Latin Quarter, for instance, he pauses to explain to us that the 1920s version of the traditional *grisette* or easygoing working girl, of the quarter

> is represented by a young lady, under whose high-waisted corsage a heart beats and blood flows as of old, only to-day she dresses in the latest *mode,* she is more independent and perhaps a bit more intelligent, and certainly she is rather more *désalée* than her predecessor. "Unsalted" is a delightful slang expression to signify that she knows her way about and probably knows "what's what."

(*Dessalée,* to give the word its modern French spelling, is usually translated as something like "cunning.")

And then there is the passage, attached to a reference to a Provençal establishment called Restaurant Blanc, in which Story tells his readers how "real" *aïoli* is made—in prose that shades palpably into the purple.

Take a mortar, or rather place one between the knees of a brown-faced, dark-haired youth of Provence and watch him while he crushes into it a few *gousses* of garlic and a little *piment* with a wooden pestle. He adds to this the yoke [*sic*] of a fresh egg. Then the girl he loves, standing over him as he sits with the mortar, pours delicious olive oil from a long-necked bottle over the mixture, as he goes on grinding with the pestle, slowly at first, but gradually getting quicker and quicker. The garlic, egg and oil form a delicious silky paste which gradually rises until it fills the mortar, and stiffens until, when the oil bottle is empty, the youth in triumph leaves the pestle standing upright in the mixture.

Aïoli, indeed! (Story adds, incidentally, as if in afterthought, ". . . [N]o one can guarantee that all *aioli* is made exactly in this way!")

In their *A Guide to the Restaurants of Paris* (1929), Thérèse and Louise Bonney (who, French names aside, obviously lived in America) offer a chatty overview of Parisian dining rather than a restaurant-by-restaurant list. They also include a rather flip glossary (*"SUPREME DE VOLAILLE:* Always a delicacy. The breasts of chickens with this and that added unto them in the clever French fashion"), a section on wines, a chapter called "Ordering a Meal in France," and—most fascinating to me—a series of menus for various occasions recommended by a number of notable Parisian restaurateurs and maîtres d'hôtel of the era. This section reveals not only how much French philosophies of both cooking and eating have changed in the past sixty years or so, but also how different they were from restaurant to restaurant even then.

M. Louis of Foyot, for example, proposes a *déjeuner intime,* such as a young man might offer to his true love, of caviar, *suprême de sole Foyot, caneton à l'orange, petits pois frais,* and *crêpes Suzette,* washed down with old sherry, Château d'Yquem 1899, Richebourg 1896, and Grande Fine Napoléon 1884.

J. Choulot of L'Ane Rouge gets even more elaborate, proposing an intimate luncheon of his own that begins similarly with caviar and *suprêmes de sole Choulot,* then goes on to Pauillac (i.e., lamb) *boulangère,* foie gras *truffé* with *le salade de saison, fromages variés, soufflé au Grand Marnier,* and "*tous les fruits,*" plus montrachet of an unspecified vintage, Baron 1919 (presumably Château Pichon-Baron-Longueville), musigny 1911, and Champagne Moët et Chandon 1906.

Compare these menus with the infinitely more sensible *déjeuner intime* counseled by Henri Sécheresse at Laurent: *omelette Laurent, foie de veau à l'anglaise,* corn on the cob (!), and a carafe of ordinary rosé—a menu a good deal more likely to engender intimacy, I should imagine, than those of Messrs Louis and Choulot.

On at least one occasion, a passage in one of my old restaurant guides has greatly enhanced my experience of a present-day establishment. Shortly before I first visited the resuscitated Rainbow Room at New York City's Rockefeller Center, after it reopened in 1988, I happened to obtain a copy of *Round the World with an Appetite* by Molly Castle, published in London in 1936. In it, the English-born Castle describes a lavish party she attended at the Rainbow Room a few days after its original opening in 1934—a bash so exclusive, she reports, "that Mr. Rockefeller himself was heard to say . . . that he had been lucky to have been able to secure an invitation." (I think Castle deserves extra points, incidentally, for that elegant display of auxiliary verbs.)

In the midst of this grand affair, Castle reports, she found herself helping a girl in the ladies room ("a very pretty girl . . . curved in all the right places") to repair a stocking. The girl, who had "always thought English dames were so frozen that they wouldn't put out a hand from a boat to save a drowning person if they hadn't been introduced first," warms to Castle, and tells a remarkable story:

It seems that the local Junior Leaguers had decided that modeling was a ball.

> They like to see themselves dressed up to the eyes: jewels by Cartier, furs by Revillon, and their pictures in all the illustrated weeklies, by heck. They didn't even get paid most of the time—as long as there were enough photographers lined up on the sidelines. . . . [T]hings began to get so bad that the shops we professional models had been working in even started turning off their regular girls, hoping that they'd always be able to get a customer to take their place . . . and the ones who depended on piecework didn't get but one job in two weeks, instead of two a day. . . . *And* curves were coming in, causing a need to eat regular. So . . . [w]e got a meeting together, and one of the girls had a boy friend that worked on a newspaper and he came along. And what a neat scoop that boy got! We gave out an ultimatum through his sheet that if the Junior Leaguers didn't lay off our jobs we were all going gunning for their sweethearts. And they photographed all of us in our underwear, and the sweethearts came right down and lined up in queues. So it all worked out quite well. Didn't I tell you that was young Vandeburg I had out there?

I guarantee you that no other visitor to the new Rainbow Room after its reopening saw the place through quite the same eyes that I did.

Even so purposefully dry and utilitarian a work as *Adventures in Good Eating,* the Duncan Hines guide, can offer unexpected insights into the popular culture of its time: When the book describes (in my 1947 edition) the restaurant called Stoddard's Atop Butler Hall, at Columbia University in New York—wherein the eponymous Mr. Stoddard (also the inventor, it is noted, of the Ampico Reproducing Piano and the U.S. Pneumatic Mail Tube) had installed an automated kitchen in which cooking times for all the dishes were preset and controlled by clockwork—it seems to encapsulate in a few pithy phrases all the technological hopes and dreams of early postwar modern America.

And sometimes old restaurant guides can knock the wind right out of you. Browsing one afternoon through John Drury's *Dining in Chicago,* published in 1931, wondering what the Alaska mountain goat at Wiechmann & Gellert might have tasted like, or maybe just the chicken shortcake at the College Inn, I suddenly and quite unexpectedly met my late father. He was there, listed as "Bob Andrews, the novelist," among the celebrity habitués ("Thomas Ross, the actor; Aline Stanley, the actress; Jess Krueger, the newspaperman and American Legion official . . .") of a restaurant on East Delaware Place called Casa de Alex. The food at Casa de Alex was American, reported Drury, "prepared in an appetizing style," and Spanish dishes were available on special order. There was, he added, "Dancing in the evening, [but] no rowdy stuff allowed. Afternoon teas attract many women, but there are no gigolos." It sounds like an okay place. I like to think that the old man, as a bachelor, might have found it very amusing sometimes after dinner.

17

SOMETIMES A CIGAR

"Good cigars don't stay lit."
—GEORGE BURNS, IN A NEWSPAPER INTERVIEW, 1989

*C*IGARS ARE LIKE MOTORCYCLES. BOTH CAN be objects of great sophistication, carefully crafted and capable of giving real pleasure to those who know how to handle them. And both can, in the hands of the parvenu, the showoff, the schmuck, become loud agents of contempt for one's surroundings and the people who inhabit them. The unmuffled Harley roaring down a quiet street at midnight and the cheap smoldering panatella waved arrogantly about in a crowded room both deliver the same message: I do what I want. I don't care what anyone thinks. Fuck you.

I am not a smoker. I don't call myself one, anyway, because I don't smoke very often. But when I do smoke—whether it's a fine cigar after a good meal or just a nice strong French or Spanish cigarette in a bar or in my living room—I enjoy it mightily. I enjoy it for a simple reason: Good tobacco, especially in cigar form, smells and tastes wonderful. If a cigar is like a motorcycle, it is also, sometimes, like a well-made sauce, an exquisite perfume, a wine of noble character—something to be savored, to be appreciated sensually and sometimes more than merely sensually.

Frankly, I'm always a bit surprised when people who appreciate other gustatory pleasures dismiss tobacco as some noxious, foul-smelling weed. How can any true wine lover or gourmet, I wonder, fail to recognize the subtlety and complexity of flavor and aroma that a good cigar can offer? I realize, of course, that habitual tobacco use can affect one's sensitivity to the gastronomic niceties. But I've also met enough Gauloise-chewing winemakers and Monte Cristo–puffing chefs who are nonetheless at the tops of their respective trades to realize that the human sensory apparatus must be capable of remarkable adaptability—and that though a smoker might not taste wine and food quite as "purely" as does a nonsmoker, he can nonetheless apparently still taste them well enough.*

Cigars and cigarettes, of course, are very different creatures—as different as, let's say, brandy and wine, which (like them) also share a common botanical origin but also are substantially different in strength and charac-

---

* It is said that when the aging dean of California winemakers, André Tchelistcheff, was ordered by his doctor to quit smoking, he at first obeyed—until he found that, without cigarettes, he had lost his ability to blend wine. Whenever folks start nattering on about how delicate nuances of flavor are lost on smokers, I like to invoke Tchelistcheff's name, pointing out that his smoke-defiled palate created, among other wines, Beaulieu Vineyard's legendary Georges de la Tour Private Reserve cabernet, for decades the standard against which all other California cabernets were judged.

ter. It is practically an article of faith in this country today that cigarettes are a deadly indulgence, virtually guaranteed to induce lung cancer, heart disease, and other illnesses not only in the smoker himself but in anyone unfortunate enough to inhale his "secondhand" fumes. Because this tenet is now held so unshakably, even militantly, by so many people in America, I have pretty much given up trying to explain, much less justify, my own occasional appetite for cigarettes. Smoking one is just something I do when I feel like it, and when I am in the company of other smokers, or alone—when, that is, I think that I can get away with it.

Though my father was a habitual smoker in the two-to-three-pack-a-day range, I never touched a cigarette myself, not even to take a single, forbidden puff behind the barn, until I was eighteen. And when I did try one, it was sheer exotica—a sweet, aromatic Egyptian oval some friends had brought back in a tin box from Cairo. They looked so chic and Levantine and racy that I couldn't possibly resist them. Since that time, I've smoked off and on, but never regularly. I'm one of those cigarette smokers other cigarette smokers hate, entirely capable of going through a pack of Ducados or corn-paper Gitanes or Camels (when I do smoke, I want a cigarette that *tastes* like something) in a day's worth of café-sitting or bar-hopping, and then not even thinking about cigarettes for another six months. In fact, it has just now occurred to me that I haven't had a cigarette in two or three years. No big deal. I'll have one (or a pack of them) again some day, I'm sure—and like it just fine.

Cigars are another story. Health hazards have certainly been imputed to them, but these aren't as serious to the smoker as those assigned to cigarettes, both because cigars are seldom inhaled and because their use tends to be occasional, even ceremonial, and not quotidian. Secondhand smoke from cigars is rarely a problem for nonsmokers, either, for a simple reason: They usually object so violently to the merest whiff of it that cigar-smokers immediately retreat.

Why do nonsmokers find cigars so loathsome? "Because they stink" is a common answer. That, of course, is a matter of opinion. Anyway, garlic and cheap perfume "stink," too, but nobody gets hysterical when they get a snootful of those. No, I think there's something rather more to it than that: Cigars push buttons. Even when they're not being brandished by some nicotinic Hell's Angel as a weapon of aggression, they intrude, encroach, pervade. The sense of smell is our most immediate sense, the one connected most directly to our brain. Cigar smoke, then, isn't just a symbol, but a symbol that invades the cerebrum.

Whether you welcome this invasion (as I do) or not depends, of course, on what it is the cigar symbolizes to you. Journalist David Shaw, a dedicated cigar smoker who calls his nightly after-dinner cigar "just about the only activity that I find truly, utterly relaxing," has pointed out that women often behave more indignantly in the presence of a cigar than men, and suggests that this is perhaps because there is something "so resolutely masculine about cigars that the very sight of one—the very idea of one—enrages certain women." The cigar, Shaw continues, might well be taken by some women as "emblematic of the abhorrent sexist discrimination, exploitation and exclusivity that many men have long practiced and that women have rightly struggled to overcome."

I don't know about that, but I do know that when I've asked women I've dined with over the years if they'd object to me smoking a cigar after a meal, their responses tend to fall into one of two categories: "Oh, please don't. I *hate* cigars. My father smoked them." Or, "No, I don't mind a bit. I like cigars. My father smoked them." I will leave it to practitioners of other disciplines to interpret these responses.

I've pretty much given up trying to smoke cigars in America. My wife claims she can smell them even when I smoke them outside on our balcony, with the sliding glass doors into the living room shut tightly. (Cigars are not, in any case, best smoked on the veranda; air currents make them burn too fast and hot. Automobile air conditioning is a great enemy of cigars for the same reason.) Most of the restaurants I frequent, at least in southern California, ban cigar smoking at the table, some of them permitting it (grudgingly) in the bar and others forbidding it altogether. Even in restaurants where cigars are theoretically welcome, I find that I am often requested to extinguish mine— or am at least subjected to the sort of nose-holding, "phew-phew"ing, and exaggerated coughing with which the anticigar faction so frequently seeks to demonstrate its disapproval of delicious smoke.

I am sometimes tempted to defy my adversaries—to ask them, for instance, how they can accuse me of polluting their lungs, and then drive off home in an internal combustion–powered automobile, belching hydrocarbons into the common, already plenty murky air. I rarely if ever stand up for my stogie, though. Because, as David Shaw suggests, smoking a cigar is above all a *relaxing* pursuit, I take no joy in continuing to puff away under strained circumstances. I give up, ostensibly gracefully— though nearly always, I must confess, with some measure of smoldering contempt for what I consider my sophomoric, candy-ass opponents.

There is one circumstance under which I will not automatically give in, incidentally: If I'm asked by people who are themselves smoking cigarettes to extinguish my cigar—which happens more often than you might think— I will usually offer to put out mine if they'll put out theirs. I have yet to be taken up on the deal.

Fortunately for my affection for cigars, I travel frequently to Europe, where cigar-smoking is by and large still seen as a civilized pleasure and an adjunct to a good meal.* And in Europe I am occasionally able to extract an admittedly childish but highly satisfying revenge on the kinds of nonsmokers who bedevil me in my native land.

Here is an example: One afternoon at one of my favorite Paris restaurants, Arpège, Claude and I found ourselves seated next to a particularly prissy-looking young American couple, very expensively turned out. The man seemed cold and colorless. His wife appeared to be (to put it politely) more than a little high strung, and complained throughout their meal about this thing and that—the weather, the desk clerk at their hotel, the prices of the food. She scarcely opened her mouth except to complain, in fact. ("My God!" Claude exclaimed at one point in French, "to think that a couple would be married and have only things like *that* to say to one another! *Merde!*")

As it happened, these two finished their lunch about the same time we did, and had ordered coffee, when I—maliciously, knowing full well that the act would strike terror into their hearts—asked our waiter to show us the cigar selection. Lingering over our choice, discussing the characteristics of this cigar and that with the restaurant's cigar-savvy maître d'hôtel—no doubt prolonging the adjoining couple's agony—I heard to my pleasure precisely the kind of whispered, terrified chatter I had hoped for. "Oh my God, he's going to smoke a cigar." "I can't believe they let them do that." "You get the check. I'm going to the bar." (This last from the woman.) Ha! I thought. You're on *my* turf now! We lit up. Our neighbors disappeared. My cigar was especially delicious.

---

* *How much longer this will remain the case is uncertain: Shortly after I wrote these words, the French government unveiled details of a new antitobacco campaign, which includes a ban on tobacco advertising, the institution of warning labels on cigarette packs, an annual "tobacco-free day" nationwide on May 31, and serious plans to outlaw or severely limit smoking in the workplace—and even in restaurants.*

PART IV

Wine as Money,
Wine as Life

"Wine is a mocker . . . and whosoever is
deceived thereby is not wise."

—PROVERBS 20:1

18
THE EMPEROR'S NEW WINE

"Vins fins means, simply enough, 'finished wines,' that is, wines that did not turn out as well as might have been expected."
—JAMES THURBER, "HOW TO TELL A FINE OLD WINE"

*M*OST SO-CALLED "GREAT" WINES ARE junk. No, that's probably too strong. Let's say instead that most wines to which "greatness" is commonly ascribed—the big names, the famous labels—don't begin to live up to their reputations. They certainly don't live up to their prices, which are preposterous almost without exception. Half the time they don't even taste very good. Half the time they don't possess even a modicum of the qualities most of us (I presume) look for in wine: an agreeable bouquet, some measure of complexity, good balance of constituent elements (for instance, tannin, acid, fruit), and, of course, good old-fashioned pleasant *flavor*.

I generalize, of course. But I've tasted a very large number of "great" wines, old and new, over the past twenty-five years or so—and I'd estimate that, once I've filtered out their historical or romantic value, I've found maybe 15 or 20 percent of them at the most to be genuinely enjoyable. And I honestly don't think it's just me. I'd wager that if such wines didn't have famous labels and/or impressive price tags on them, most of us wouldn't accord them a second sip if there was something else to drink in the vicinity.

And yet they do have those labels and/or those price tags, and we do drink them—and pretend that we enjoy them in spite of ourselves. Why? Because, in a word, I think that we've been snowed. I think that as we've learned the lore of wine, we've simultaneously accepted as gospel a lot of secondhand and questionable judgments about it and indefensible assessments of its quality. I think we've swallowed the snake oil, bought the bunkum. What's more, I think we know it. I think we realize, way deep down, that a lot of the famous wines we encounter aren't what they pretend to be, and that unglamorous "everyday" wines often provide more real pleasure. But what can we do? We can't very well come right out and say that we actually enjoy that $10 zinfandel more than that $100 burgundy. One, after all, is just table wine; the other is art, or maybe poetry.

Once a wine's qualities have been apotheosized by several dozen noted wine authorities (and validated by high apparent monetary worth), who are we to criticize it? What business do we have finding fault with some enological masterpiece that has earned a perfect 100 score from America's leading consumer wine publication, or from the most influential wine writer in the world—or even merely fervent kudos from the guy down at the wineshop, who obviously knows what he's talking about? Who are we to buck the experts? And anyway, what if it's all our fault? What if we're just not good enough at this wine game yet to appreciate the subtleties of grand-cru burgundy or first-growth bordeaux? What if we don't *deserve* great wine?

And there's another problem: Once we've paid $250 (or even $50) for a bottle of wine, or been given a pricey bottle as a gift, we *have* to like it. There's too much at stake, both in terms of money and honor. Thus we react to the wine itself not as our senses (and our good sense) might tell us to react, but as we know full well we're supposed to react. Everybody else loves the stuff, so we love it, too.

There's a term for this phenomenon, and it has to do with a certain lofty potentate and what he is or isn't wearing. The only difference is that, in the case of wine, the external trappings are there. It's what's inside that's wanting.

I would go so far as to say that there's really no such thing as great wine—or at least that we should be very sure that we understand the sense in which we use the word "great" when we apply it to wine. Wine is lush fodder for the senses, and can stimulate and gratify the spirit. I love wine. I revel in it. It enriches my life.

But I don't believe that wine is art. Winemaking might very well be an "art," in the sense of a craft requiring great skill and intuition, but the finished product is not an object demanding aesthetic response on the level of the Brahms Requiem or "Les Demoiselles d'Avignon." Likewise, a certain wine might quite reasonably be said to be "great" in the sense that you just heard a great new Psychedelic Furs CD or the tomatoes from your garden were great last summer. But I think it's very important to remember that that's not greatness in the ennobling, universal, eternal sense. To start thinking that maybe in some way it *is* that kind of greatness—that maybe a 1961 Château Latour or a 1971 Erbacher Marcobrunn Trockenbeerenauslese or some such is a timeless, irreproducible museum piece—is to confuse the metaphorical with the literal, or at least the mountain with the molehill. I mean, come *on*. We're talking about fermented grape juice here, for heaven's sake. We're talking about a pleasant alcoholic beverage, meant to be drunk and enjoyed and maybe talked about affectionately later or anticipated in return acquaintance— assuming that it was any good to begin with.

When apologists for "great" wines—and they are legion—hear somebody say that they don't much like some supposed *chef d'oeuvre* of the vintner's trade or other, they tend to start looking around for something other than the wine itself to blame. If they're too polite (or insecure in their own abilities) to question the acuteness of your palate or the sophistication of your experience, then they'll probably suggest that you sampled the wine in question when it was still too young, or already too old. Or maybe it wasn't stored properly. Or was too warm (or too cold) when you consumed it. Or should (or shouldn't) have been decanted. And maybe they're right. Maybe there is something to one or more of these explanations. But what we're left with, in any case, is a, say, $250 bottle of wine that we have to make excuses for.

Why should any bottle of wine cost as much as $250 (or more—sometimes very much more) in the first place, no matter how good it is? In some cases because it's rare, an old vintage of which there are probably only a few bottles left in the world. In some cases because the people who produce the wine, or who sell it, have decided that it ought to cost a lot, and have been able to convince other people that they're right. High prices of this sort are usually justified by their assessors in one of five ways:

1. "We're as good as they are." This is the comparative theory of wine pricing. If somebody else is getting $100 a bottle for their plonk, and I think mine's as good or better, why shouldn't I charge $100, too? I suspect that this reasoning was behind Angelo Gaja's decision, in the late 1970s, to start releasing single-vineyard barbarescos

priced at $30 or $35 a bottle (in an era when most barbarescos went for $10 or $12; his new releases are now priced in the $100 range, and his older wines from good vintages can cost $150 or more). At the time, he was the Italian distributor for the spectacularly overrated, overpriced burgundies of the Domaine de la Romanée-Conti—and I would almost bet you that at some point he said to himself, "Hey, my wines are *much* better than this stuff." (He was right, of course.)

A more recent if less focused example of this philosophy comes from Al Brounstein, proprietor of Diamond Creek Vineyards in the Napa Valley, who promises to price his 1990 Lake Cabernet Sauvignon at $150 a bottle—on the grounds that "American wines are world class, but until now have not achieved price recognition."

2. "Do you know how much it costs to make this stuff?" My favorite example of this approach dates from the mid-1980s, when I visited the then-new Château Woltner winery in the Napa Valley. Though the facility is located in an area (near the top of Howell Mountain) best-known for cabernet sauvignon and zinfandel grapes, and is owned by the family that had earlier owned Château La-Mission-Haut-Brion in Bordeaux, a region to which Burgundian grape varieties are pretty much a stranger, Château Woltner had decided to dedicate itself to chardonnay—and to ask $35.95 a bottle for the initial release of its top-of-the-line Titus Vineyard offering (now, incidentally, up to $58). How could the winery justify this price? I asked proprietor Francis Dewavrin-Woltner himself that question. "We charge so much for our wines because they are great," he replied without a trace of shame, "and thus they are expensive to produce. And we are lucky that our wines are great and not merely good, or we would have to go out of business because we would not be able to charge enough for them to make up for what they cost." This dazzling little piece of circular reasoning revolves around the "greatness" of the wine, but who conferred this great-

ness? Woltner himself—though of course anyone who buys his wine at the prices he asks in effect confirms that opinion.

3. "Do you know how little of this stuff there is?" There's some of this one in the Château Woltner pricing philosophy, too (only about 200 cases of the Titus Chardonnay are made)—but the Italians are the real masters of this approach. In Italy, it seems, it doesn't matter any more if the wine is good; if it's scarce, it's expensive. The famous picolit dessert wines of the Friuli region, for instance, can command as much as $125 a bottle when new—for what is to me mostly pretty flabby, shallow wine. "Why does picolit cost so much?" I once asked a Friuli winemaker. "Well," he answered, "you have to understand that the picolit vine has a genetic flaw in it, and it sets very little usable fruit. Thus the yield per hectare is extremely low, and the process of selecting the good grapes takes a great deal of time." I nodded politely at his explanation—but what I was thinking was along the lines of, "Hey, did you guys ever stop to think that maybe Mother Nature was trying to tell you guys something about picolit with that genetic flaw stuff?"

4. "It got 100 from Parker." Even 95 or so would probably do it. Parker is of course the highly knowledgeable and hard-working Robert Parker, without question the most powerful wine critic in the world today. With the scores he assigns to wines in his various books and in his newsletter *The Wine Advocate,* he can literally make or break a wine. Not only gullible customers but (I can only assume) cynical wine merchants buy on the basis of Parker points. A high Parker score given to a wine that is already in short supply will have the effect of turning that wine into an instant collector's item—for which those who happen to own a few bottles can charge virtually anything they like. For example, in late 1990, Parker gave California's Groth Winery 1985 Reserve Cabernet Sauvignon a perfect 100 score. The winery, which made only 525 cases of this wine,

had already priced it at a heady $30 a bottle (see "Do you know how little of this stuff there is?"). Within a week of the appearance of the Parker score, every bottle had been bought up from the winery; within a month, private collectors were offering it for sale for as much as $400 a bottle.

5. "It sold for $2,500 a bottle at auction." Wine auction bids shouldn't have anything to do with retail wine prices. Real commercial wine auctions—like those held regularly by such firms as Sotheby's and Christie's in England and Butterfield's in the United States—usually deal with odd lots of older wine, and the prices these bottles bring can vary greatly from one auction to another (and are often surprisingly reasonable, especially in England).

The wine auctions that get all the publicity, though, are what I think might fairly be called publicity-stunt auctions—almost always tied to some charitable cause or other. These auctions, the most famous of which is the annual Napa Valley Wine Auction (which benefits three local health-care facilities), have three purposes as far as I can tell: to raise money for a worthy cause; to gain public (and media) attention for participating wineries and high-bidding retailers; and to satisfy the whoever-has-the-most-toys-wins mentality of certain private buyers.

The prices commanded at such events are sometimes astounding. At the 1990 Napa Valley auction, for instance, a six-liter bottle of 1987 Grace Family Vineyard (*who?*) Cabernet sold for $20,000—about $2,500 a bottle. And though the winery obviously isn't going to try to charge that kind of money for its regular retail product, it might very well refer to the price paid in its promotional materials, the implication being that any wine that brings that much at auction must be worth a lot in ordinary circumstances, too.

But what relation, other than an accidental one, does an amount like that have to the quality of the wines sold, and to the prices the same or similar wines ought to command on the regular retail market? About this much: In 1991, during the early months of the Iraqi occupation of Kuwait, a celebrity cook-off and food auction was held in Abu Dhabi, in the United Arab Emirates, to raise money for displaced Kuwaiti families. Bidding on one culinary specialty offered for sale at the event, Shaika Fatima, wife of UAE president Sheik Zayed ibn Sultan al-Buhayan, paid $2.7 million for a foil container of *baid al-qata*—a Kuwaiti delicacy described in a Reuters dispatch as consisting of "mashed eggs and sand grouse." It was an exceedingly generous charitable gesture. I trust my point is clear.

Ultimately, of course, expensive wines cost what they do because somebody is willing to pay the price. I think that's fine as far as it goes. Anybody has a right to ask whatever he wants, and anybody has a right to *pay* whatever he wants, for a bottle of wine—or for that matter for a steak dinner, a new car, a house in Malibu, or any other luxury you'd care to mention. But if the steak dinner costs $1,000, and the new car $1 million, and the house in Malibu $1 billion, then I think the purchaser ought to realize that he's getting cheated if all he really needed was a meal, a means of transportation, or a place to sleep. There's got to be some reason beyond the simple identity of the thing itself for such excessive prices. And what I'm arguing is that wine should probably *always* be bought for what it is—not for what it's supposed to be, or for what it represents, but for the sheer sensory enjoyment it gives the person who consumes it.

The corollary to this is that if a certain wine doesn't give much enjoyment, then no matter what it's called, it isn't worth a dime.

RECIPE

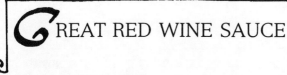

REAT RED WINE SAUCE

MAKES ABOUT 1½ CUPS

*Using truly "great" and expensive red wine won't neces-
sarily make this sauce taste any better, but it's a good way to
get rid of stuff you don't really want to drink—and to horrify
your wine-snob friends. I recommend this sauce with steak,
roast beef, hamburgers, lamb, or venison dishes.*

2 cups "great" and very expensive red wine*
3 or 4 shallots, peeled and finely chopped
1 sprig parsley
½ carrot, diced
1 bay leaf
1 tablespoon freshly squeezed lemon juice
1 tablespoon meat glaze (glace de viande)
4 tablespoons (½ stick) unsalted butter, at room temperature
Salt and freshly ground black pepper

Place all ingredients except butter, salt, and pepper in a
heavy saucepan, bring to a boil, then reduce heat to medium and simmer uncovered for 15 to 20 minutes, or until
liquid is reduced by about half.

Strain liquid and return to saucepan over low heat. Whisk
in butter and mix well, then add salt and pepper to taste.

**Though it goes without saying that the wine you use for this sauce shouldn't be
something you consider good enough to drink with pleasure, on the other hand you
should not use an unsound wine (one that is corked or oxidized or otherwise dam-
aged).*

19

LIQUID GOLD AND
EMPTY BOTTLES

*"[A wine] cellar is an interesting place to fill, to contemplate when
filled, and to empty in the proper way."*
—GEORGE SAINTSBURY, *NOTES ON A CELLAR-BOOK*

AM NOT A WINE COLLECTOR. I DISLIKE THE
very idea of collecting wine. I think collecting wine is
stupid, and quite possibly immoral.

Simply *amassing* wine, of course, is an age-old pursuit,
dating back at least to the ancient Greeks. Buying wines
you like in some quantity and then drinking them over a
period of time—maybe keeping a few bottles back for a
special occasion, or just to see what will become of them—
makes perfect sense, and probably even qualifies as a kind
of conservation, or at least wise husbanding of resources,
to be admired and encouraged. But accumulating wine as

217

a commodity, with no intention or desire ever to consume it, seems to me both wrongheaded and potentially quite harmful to the everyday appreciation of wine in general.

Some people collect wine for the usual eccentric collector's reason: simply to be able to say they have it. I find this curious, because wine collected but not uncorked is wine left unappreciated. At least if you collect rare books, you can thumb through them (carefully) on occasion; if you collect glass paperweights or model ships, you can *look* at the darned things. You can look at wine, too, of course—but, with occasional exception, one wine bottle tends to look pretty much like another. More to the point, what it looks like is not what gives wine its value in the first place.

The more insidious kind of wine collecting, which also leaves the wine itself untouched, is the acquiring of it as an investment. There is no question that certain wines increase considerably in value over the years. Noted New York wine merchant William Sokolin once proposed that some wines could appreciate, "[c]onservatively . . . at the rate of 15 percent per annum."

Why do certain wines increase so much and so predictably in value? The answer curls into a kind of vinous vicious circle: Because they're rare. And why are they rare? Because there aren't very many of them in circulation. And why aren't there very many of them in circulation? Because collectors buy them. And why do collectors buy them? Because they increase so much, so predictably, in value. . . .

Wines also appreciate because they carry within themselves the promise not only to endure—to last long enough, that is, to make holding on to them a safe bet—but actually to improve in the bottle, thus justifying their appreciation in price, at least theoretically, with a corresponding appreciation in quality. I am highly suspicious of this promise. Sure, wine can improve with age. Sure, it often needs time to settle down in the bottle, to soften up, to knit together. But for most wines, a little age goes a long way.

In his definitive disquisition on the subject, the privately published *Old Wine, Fine Wine?*, Roy Brady notes:

> There is a considerable literature of old wine by André L. Simon (1877–1970) and the school of English wine writers of which he was the most eminent member. They wrote mostly in the 1930s, 1940s, and 1950s. That is not far away in years, but it is eons away in attitudes toward wine, in technology, and in economics. Their views have been transmitted across the gap in increasingly exaggerated and distorted form and applied in ways that would have astonished Simon.

Brady demonstrates, in fact, that Simon and his colleagues repeatedly recognized the weaknesses of many of the old wines they tasted. In 1944, Simon spoke thus of the once-praised bordeaux of the 1923 vintage: "It was a great disappointment to watch some of the best of them fade away to sugar-and-water at much too early a stage of their career."

Brady further suggests that the English developed their well-known preference for old wines in the first place as an expression of social exclusivity: It was seldom possible to buy old wines in the nineteenth century. Since vintage-dated wine in bottles probably wasn't laid down in wine cellars until the 1770s, there simply wasn't yet much of it around. Thus, says Brady,

> The only way to have old wine in [quantity] . . . was to inherit it from one's father, grandfather, great-grandfather, and so on. . . . As long as old wines in quantity could only be had through the provision of one's ancestors, one was securely beyond emulation by any parvenu, however rich. . . .

Imputing great value to old wine, in other words, was a way of showing off, of impressing lesser mortals with one's own superiority. It continues to fulfill this function to this day. The difference now, though, is that the would-be show-off doesn't have to inherit old wine. He can merely buy young wine that will become old wine—expensive young wine, that is, that is expensive *because* it will (supposedly) grow magnificent as it ages. I think treating wine this way debases it.

The Wine Spectator introduced its new wine auction column in 1990 with a piece about the one-of-a-kind sauternes called Château d'Yquem. In the column, headlined "Auction World's Liquid Gold," correspondent Thomas Matthews quotes Simon Lambert of International Wine Auctions of London as saying, "Over the past 10 to 15 years, Yquem has ceased being a drinking wine, even an expensive one, and become a true collector's item—a gilt-edged security." In other words, buy d'Yquem, but don't drink it.

The same year, in a letter to *The New York Times Magazine*, the aforementioned William Sokolin cites the story of a young stockbroker of his acquaintance, who had lost his job and gone through a divorce, and was left with little but his wine cellar. This fortunate young man, says Sokolin, was able to sell his wines—which he had bought for about $100,000 in the 1970s—at auction for a net of $455,000. The lesson to be drawn from this anecdote? "Drink $7 bottles of Chilean wines. . . . Save your Pétrus and Lafite for appreciation."

Yes, but if nobody ever drinks d'Yquem, Pétrus, or Lafite, why do they have value? Or, rather, on what basis can their value possibly be determined? What earthly *good* is wine that is not meant to be consumed? Its change in status, however unwilling, from the ephemeral to the immortal, robs it of its franchise. It turns into something false, something empty. If certain wines are never to be consumed, then why even bother bottling and shipping them? Why not treat them like pork bellies or municipal bonds, and obviate the need "wine collectors" have to take physical possession of them? Why not just collect by phone or by computer, reducing wine to a line of figures on a spread sheet?

Better yet, why not just leave wine alone? Why not go play with some other commodity and put wine back where it belongs—in the hands (and cellars) of people who like to drink it? In the hands (and cellars) of people who collect experiences and memories of wine instead of blind, dumb, useless, closed-up bottles?

Postscript: Shortly before this book went to press, wine merchant Sokolin started taking out ads in *The New York Times* that sang a different song: They were headed, "WINE PRICES ARE DOWN." Among the bargains listed in one of them were (in the ad's own curious typography), "1986 Ducru Beaucaillou—was $45. Bottle now $30. THE ABSOLUTELY INCREDIBLE CHATEAU MARGAUX 1987 case was $650. NOW CASE $390. . . . 1987 LAFITE ROTHSCHILD—TERRIFIC was $600 case now—$440." So much for 15 percent appreciation per annum.

20

SNIFF THIS

*T*HERE'S NO SUCH THING AS A PROFESSIONAL wine-taster. Nobody gets paid for tasting wine. At least nobody, to the best of my knowledge, gets paid for doing nothing *but* tasting wine. There are, on the other hand, a great many people to whom wine-tasting is an integral part of their professional routine. I'm one of those people. Although I don't get paid for tasting wine, I do get paid for writing and sometimes talking about it, and obviously I've got to taste the stuff (and remember and/or make notes on what I taste) in order to know what the heck to write and sometimes talk about.

By "tasting wine," I don't necessarily mean a lot of complicated swirling, sniffing, sipping, and slurping—the kind of thing people usually seem to have in mind when they say, with what always sounds to me like a mixture of awe and disapproval, "Oh, so you're a *wine-taster.*" I really just mean paying attention to wine in some deliberate but unelaborate way, noticing things about the way it looks, smells, feels in the mouth, *tastes.* I just mean trying to figure out what makes it tick.

Tasting wine is not always fun. It is not, in general, something done in paneled studies, in dinner jackets, with crystal goblets sparkling in the candlelight. It's more likely to involve standing off in the corner at a noisy party, sticking your nose down into a glass while everybody else is having fun, trying to scribble notes on the back of a soggy cocktail napkin. Or maybe sloshing around in a damp, chilly cellar with some tyro *vigneron,* trying not to gag on barrel samples of his undrinkable $20 chardonnay. Or even sitting for long hours in a brightly lit, antiseptic room with a dozen or so colleagues, in total silence but for the soft arrhythmic sputtering sound of spent wine being spit into sawdust-filled buckets.

Sometimes I even taste wine alone at the dining room table, trying not to feel too stupid as I squint and sip and spit all by myself—while the neighbors, I suspect, pass by outside and whisper, "Poor fellow! No wonder he can't keep a steady job!"

Nonetheless, I like tasting wine. I like exercising (and testing) my sensory acuity and sense memory—fine-tuning a portion of my human machinery, almost in the way (I like to tell myself) an athlete does. Okay, so maybe I can't run a marathon; but can the average marathon runner tell the difference between a barrel-fermented chardonnay and one fermented in stainless steel? (Incidentally, I'm not sure which activity, the running or the differentiation, I consider the more pointless in the larger scheme of things.) I also like the fact that tasting wine nearly always

224

teaches me something about wine, both specifically and in general—surprising me or confirming a prejudice or posing a whole new set of questions—extending the game a little. Oh, and I like the fact that it provides a good excuse to drink a fair amount. Not everything gets spit out.

Anyone can taste wine. Anyone who ever touches the stuff in the first place *does* taste wine. Every time you tug at a plastic tumbler of chenin blanc at a gallery opening or casually wash down a burger with a bit of beaujolais, certain physical receptors in and around your nose and mouth register certain sensory impressions and transmit them to the brain. Unless your physical receptors are somehow impaired (or your brain is), you can't stop the process. It's automatic—autonomic, even.

Even if you don't know or care a fig about wine, the impressions transmitted to your brain tell you something: that what you're drinking is wine, for instance, and not carrot juice or buttermilk. You might even notice idly that the wine is dry or sweet, that it does or doesn't make your mouth pucker, that it smells like perfume or like fresh fruit. You will almost certainly be able to tell whether you like it or not. Whether you realize it or not, when that happens, you're a wine-taster.

But how is it that some people are able to tell so much more about a wine than just whether it's dry or sweet, or whether they like it or not? How can some people distinguish cabernet from pinot noir, pauillac from st-émilion, Ruffino from Ricasoli? Experience, mostly. How can you tell the difference between chocolate and vanilla—or between Haägen-Dazs chocolate, say, and some supermarket brand? How can you tell the difference between Frank Sinatra and Tony Bennett, or between Nirvana and the Jesus and Mary Chain? Simple: Repeated exposure to the same or similar stimuli. Habitude.

People who taste wine professionally get more or less the same information about it everybody else does. They just process the information a bit differently. The professional, or the interested amateur, looks for elements in the wine that the casual taster probably wouldn't recognize, and probably doesn't need to notice. I think serious wine-tasting can be a kind of code-breaking: The taster isolates and then organizes and interprets the impressions his brain receives so that they yield up intimate details about the wine—the wine's secrets. But do we have to know these secrets in order to enjoy the wine? No, of course not. Wine is enjoyable at face value.

Why delve deeper, then? Why try to crack the code? Sometimes there's a good reason. When people taste a single bottle of wine professionally, they are often in effect tasting a whole batch of it. The single bottle they open is a sample—a metaphor for perhaps 10,000 bottles—and on the basis of that one sample (sometimes, in fact, not even in a bottle yet) they must make educated predictions about what the sample represents.

I'm not talking about people like myself, who taste wine as an adjunct to another job. If I make a mistake about a wine, I can always shrug it off as a matter of personal preference; if I make a lot of mistakes, I can always go back to reviewing restaurants for a living. But there are people whose very livelihoods depend on wine, and on the accuracy and consistency with which they taste it and react to it—winemakers, vineyard owners, wine scientists, wine shippers and importers, wine retailers, and so on. If these people make the wrong decisions, missing obvious faults (or obvious good qualities) in wine, they risk losing not just money but their professional reputations.

These are the people who originally started all that swirling, sniffing, sipping, and slurping. These are also the people who coined all the wine-tasting jargon that everybody always finds so funny—all that talk about "legs" and "nose" and "raspberries" and "vanilla"—but that, when used properly and with agreed-upon definitions, is an invaluable tool of communication between tasters. And these are the people for whom the University of California at Davis, America's premier school of viticulture and enology, designed the widely used (and misused) twenty-point "Davis Scale" for the evaluation of wine—a scale meant for the laboratory and the classroom, incidentally, and not at all appropriate to the amateur wine-tasting parties at which it is so often invoked today.

In professional wine-tasting, there are good reasons for all this ritual and vocabulary, and for some semblance of an objective scoring system: Swirling wine around in the glass, for instance, stimulates its volatility, giving tasters more to smell; sucking air into the mouth along with the wine, producing that awful and oft-parodied slurping sound, animates the wine still further; some wines smell or taste of vanilla because they draw a phenol called vanillin from the oak barrels they're aged in; a uniform scoring system allows the qualities of wines of very different types to be quantified for statistical and other formal purposes; and so on. Professionals need these tools.

What I don't understand, though, is why anybody would want to go through all this nonsense if they don't have to. Wine is just such an elegantly simple beverage at heart. Its basic virtues are available to almost everyone. It can be enjoyed on the most elementary level. You can go much further with it if you want to, of course. You can learn to recognize and interpret the sensory signals the brain receives. You can compare one wine with another, or try to put a wine into historical, geographical, or cultural perspective. You can learn all the wine-pro tricks for ferreting out the subtleties of flavor and aroma wine frequently possesses. But you don't *have* to do any of this stuff. And all this extra work won't necessarily increase your enjoyment of wine. It'll just give you enjoyment of a different kind.

RECIPE

𝒫ETITS CROQUES-MONSIEURS

MAKES 16 SMALL *CROQUES*

"Buy on bread, sell on cheese," goes the old wine merchant's saw—bread because it is a reasonably neutral "palate-cleanser," useful as a sensory interlude between wine samples; cheese because it makes most types of wine taste better. (And vice versa: Pierre Androuët wrote in his book The Complete Encyclopedia of French Cheese, *"Man has yet to find a better companion to cheese than wine.") One of my favorite preparations of cheese is a variation on that ubiquitous Parisian snack food, the croque-monsieur—a variation, I must confess, inspired by an elaboration of the basic sandwich called the* croque campagnard, *or "rustic croque," as served (in two slightly different versions) at two of my regular Parisian cafés, Le Départ and Le St-Séverin, both on the place St-Michel.*

Unsalted butter, at room temperature
8 large slices sourdough bread (no more than ½" thick),
*   crusts trimmed*
4 slices prosciutto di Parma, trimmed of excess fat
4 to 5 ounces aged Gouda, Cantal, or farmhouse cheddar
*   cheese, thinly sliced or shaved into small, thin pieces*
Salt and freshly ground black pepper

Butter bread generously on both sides, then make 4 sandwiches, dividing the prosciutto and cheese evenly between them. Cut each sandwich into 4 equal squares. Grill sandwiches in a bit more butter in a nonstick frying pan, pressing down on them with a spatula and turning them once, until golden brown on both sides. Lightly season the tops.
    Serve as hors d'oeuvres or as a light lunch accompanied by a small salad.

21
I THINK WE'RE ALL BOZOS
IN THIS WINE SHOP

*"An old wine-bibber having been smashed in a railway
collision, some wine was poured upon his lips to revive him.
'Pauillac, 1873,' he murmured and died."*
—AMBROSE BIERCE, THE DEVIL'S DICTIONARY

*"Occasionally Americans know altogether too much about
wine for their own good."*
—BARON ELIE DE ROTHSCHILD (ATTRIB.)

A FEW YEARS BACK, I CONDUCTED A PINOT NOIR
seminar at the Food & Wine Experience in Aspen, which is
a casual, highly enjoyable three-day event mounted every
summer by *Food & Wine* magazine, and attended mostly
by the (food-and-wine-loving) general public. I had as
panelists at my seminar several top winemakers who were
specialists in the pinot noir grape, and our discussion was
a lively one.

Following our presentation, there was a question period, and at one point, a serious-looking young woman in the front row, who had been taking notes assiduously throughout the seminar, raised her hand and asked, "Now, exactly what grapes is pinot noir made from, again?" We grimaced. (Had she understood nothing of what was said?) The crowd groaned. The woman was sadly misinformed, and probably should have done at least minimal homework before coming to the seminar.

But hers was not the stupidest question of the morning. That had come a few minutes earlier, when a man near the back of the room had asked the assembled winemakers, "So what do you guys do about the benzaldehyde problem?" One of the vintners quickly replied, "What benzaldehyde problem?" The audience laughed, and we moved on to the next question.

Benzaldehyde is an aromatic nonflavonoid phenol (C_6H_5CHO) derived from (among other places) oak wood. It shows up frequently in wines that have been aged in new oak barrels, especially those made from American oak, which is more porous than the French or Yugoslavian varieties also commonly used for wine aging, and thus lends its derivatives more generously to the liquid it contains. Like many other elements extracted from barrel oak, it can add pleasant qualities to wine in moderation, but too much of it can overwhelm other characteristics of flavor and aroma. It is entirely possible, then, that pinot noir—or any other oak-aged wine—could indeed have a "benzaldehyde problem," and that winemakers might have to find a way to solve it.

But this was a casual seminar at a sun-and-fun consumer event, remember, and not a technical symposium. This was an environment in which "What foods go well with pinot noir?" or "How long will pinot noir improve in the bottle?" might have been legitimate questions, but "So what do you guys do about the benzaldehyde problem?" was not.

If the man who asked it had been a fellow winemaker, or

for some other reason had been genuinely interested in how these particular panelists would deal with this particular technical winemaking problem, I suspect that he would have quietly asked them about it off-stage. And if he knew enough to pose the question in the first place, he must have known that very few, if any, of the nonwinemakers in the room would have the slightest idea what he was talking about; and that his question was not one that could be answered in a few words anyway. So why *did* he ask about benzaldehyde? Simple. He was showing off. He was a wine bozo.

The wine bozo is a well-known personality in the world of wine. He loves wineshops, haunting them like a teenager hanging out in a mall. (I speak of the wine bozo as "he" because, in my experience, there are very few females of the species. For whatever reasons, wine jargon and enological one-upmanship seem to be mostly a guy thing.) The wine bozo joins wine societies and attends wine festivals—but only the best or most prestigious of both—and often fancies himself as more of a guru than an acolyte. He visits wineries at home and abroad (probably still trying to get to the bottom of that pesky benzaldehyde problem), and then brags about all the great wines he has tasted "in wood" (i.e., in aging or storage barrels, not yet bottled—this implies preferential treatment from the winemaker).

The wine bozo knows more about wine than you do. He knows more about wine than I do. He calls important wine producers by their first names, and will often tell you about the time he had dinner with Angelo or lunch with Zelma (not always remembering to mention that there were fourteen other people at the table at the time, and that he had paid $75 for the privilege). He calls wine types not even by their first names but by jaunty abbreviations— "cab" for cabernet sauvignon, "zin" for zinfandel, "j. r." for johannisberg riesling. He applies similar nicknames to the chemical elements he delights in identifying (occasionally correctly) in wines, and asking questions about at seminars—perhaps not "benz" for benzaldehyde (at least I haven't heard that one yet), but certainly "v.a." for volatile acidity, and "bret" for brettanomyces—another favorite wine bozo word, referring to wild yeasts that give some wines what is usually described as a "horsey" or "wet-cardboard" character.

Winemakers and winesellers usually suffer wine bozos politely, answering their questions as best they can and even encouraging them—intentionally or not—in their pursuit of enological minutiae. Sometimes, though, as at that pinot noir seminar, a wine authority refuses to play the game. That happened, too, at a tasting of wines from Château Yquem I attended in San Francisco some years ago, when a wine bozo asked the estate's proprietor, the Marquis de Lur-Saluces, "What's the residual sugar in the '67?" The marquis—God bless him—replied, "I'm sorry, but I really have no idea. You'd have to ask my winemaker. But, anyway, why would you want to know that?" The wine bozo muttered something like, "Just curious," and sat down—no doubt thinking to himself (or saying to his companions) "Jeez, this guy doesn't know *anything*."

Wine bozos are always "just curious." They always have questions they'd like to have answered: "What's the residual sugar?" "What's the pH?" "What clone are you using?" And of course, "What do you guys do about the benzaldehyde problem?" Just what wine bozos do with this information if and when they finally obtain it, I'm not sure. Do they write it down in a little notebook for future reference so they don't have to ask the question again? Probably not.

When wine bozos aren't trading technical terminology, they talk a lot about numbers. Instead of discussing flavor or aroma, or maybe venturing an unguarded personal opinion about a wine, they tend to ask, "How many golds does it have?"; "What did it get in *The Spectator*?"; "What did Parker give it?;" and so on. "Golds" are the gold medals awarded—often with astonishing indiscrimination, I think—to wines at various state and county fairs and other wine competitions. *The Wine Spectator* is an attractive and informative monthly, and more or less the Bible (or at least the *Variety*) of the wine bozo, full of ratings and inside dope.

Robert Parker is the wine bozo's god (see page 212). Mention almost any prestigious wine—'66 Château Ducru-Beaucaillou, say, or '78 Phelps Insignia, or '90 Rosemount Show Reserve Chardonnay—and he will know its "Parker score." This is the number of points out of a possible 100 assigned to the wine by Parker in his newsletter or in one of his books. Parker takes the guesswork out of wine, and protects wine bozos from making embarrassing mistakes, like buying or even expressing favorable opinions of the "wrong" wines. Some wine bozos actually refuse to buy any wine that has less than an 85 or 90 score from Parker. ("Life is too short to drink bad wine," such bozos chirrup cheerfully. This is an example of wine bozo humor; another example is the bumper sticker that reads, "Life is a Cabernet.")

Now, wine bozos are not evil people. They are enthusiastic about wine, and often genuinely knowledgeable. Some of my best friends are wine bozos. What bothers me about them is that they cloud the waters and scare people off, making wine an insider's game, an arcane pleasure. Wine bozos don't know when to stop. They aren't content just to enjoy wine. They want to become part of wine. If wine could talk, it might well ask of the wine bozo (as Buddy the black jazz musician does of Murray, the white American hanger-on, in the classic Terry Southern short story called "You're Too Hip, Baby"), "What do you want from us?"

"Nothing," the wine bozo would probably reply. "Just curious."

PART V

Side Orders

"Contrive me a dish—
I am quick to surround it. . . ."
—PHYLLIS MCGINLEY, "TIRADE ON TEA"

22
CHICKEN À LA KING AND
BIDIMENSIONAL PIRANHA

"On no account should new terms or names
[for dishes] be created."
—L. SAULNIER, *LE RÉPERTOIRE DE LA CUISINE*

*J*N A LEO CULLUM CARTOON IN *THE NEW Yorker* in 1984, one Eskimo offers another a platter bearing a single, unadorned whole fish. "It's called fettuccine Alfredo," the first Eskimo announces.

Well, now, a plate of fish is obviously not fettuccine Alfredo—but then neither is most of what's served under that name in the restaurants of America today. Food nomenclature in this country in general, in fact, has degenerated in recent years into a hash of misnomer, a stew of garbled terminology.

Back in the Dark Ages of American gastronomy, say

fifteen or twenty years ago, the food we ate in restaurants may well have been frozen (or canned), overcooked, and underseasoned. But at least we knew what to call it—or, rather, when we saw what the restaurant called it, we knew more or less what it was going to be. Certain names implied certain ingredients and/or cooking methods, and any reasonably experienced diner knew which names meant what. Chicken à la king, for instance, was always chicken in a cream sauce with pimentos, served on toast or in a puff-pastry shell; veal parmigiana was cloaked in tomato sauce, with gooey cheese melted on top; sole Véronique involved green grapes. The particulars might have varied from one restaurant or chef to another, but standard definitions did exist.

Such definitions were given almost statutory weight by the French, in such books as the *Larousse Gastronomique, Le Répertoire de la Cuisine,* and Escoffier's *Le Guide Culinaire.* Culinary nouns, verbs, and adjectives had meanings that could no more be tampered with than weights and measures could be arbitrarily changed. Thus, *hongroise* implied paprika; Parmentier, potatoes; Vichy or Créchy, carrots. Even if he couldn't quote the textbook definitions of several hundred garnishes or sauces, anyone who went out to dinner regularly probably knew, for instance, that a dish described as *provençale* wasn't likely to be made with sour cream and dill.

Practical value aside, old-style food names in general— French and otherwise—are colorful, poetical, evocative. Some dishes are named after professions: *maître d'hôtel* butter, *poulet chasseur,* diplomat pudding; others are named for famous personalities—musicians (tournedos Rossini, steak Sinatra), writers (*poulet* George Sand, the Chateaubriand [see page 190]), statesmen (*jambon* Metternich), and both monarchs and their lady friends (the Napoléon; crêpes Suzette).

English food names, for instance, are often more interesting than the food they describe: angels on horseback (grilled oysters wrapped in bacon on toast), bubble and squeak (reheated mashed potatoes with cabbage or other greens), toad in the hole (sausage baked in pastry), tipsy parson (a relative of trifle).

The Italians like naughty food names. The best known of these is the famous Roman pasta dish, spaghetti *alla putanesca*—"whore style." In several parts of Italy, gnocchi, or potato dumplings, are known as *strangolopreti* or *strozzapreti,* meaning "priest stranglers," the implication being that even holy men consume them gluttonously. Then there are the notorious Sicilian convent pastries dubbed *fedde del cancelliere* (chancellor's buttocks) and *minni di virgini* (virgins' breasts), and the tiny Roman pasta called *cazzetti d'angeli,* which it is possible to translate no more delicately than as "little angels' penises."

The Chinese like metaphorical food names—Dragon and Phoenix (made with seafood or reptiles and chicken), Ants Climbing a Tree (minced pork with glass noodles, in which bits of meat are supposed to resemble ants), Lion's Head (pork with curly cabbage—the cabbage thought to resemble a lion's mane). Sometimes, metaphor becomes euphemism: In *Food in History,* Reay Tannahill notes that poor Chinese workers in medieval times ate such things as "brushwood shrimps" and "household deer"—grasshoppers and rats, respectively.

Another whole category of food names is intentionally ironical—names that make a joke out of the poverty of their ingredients. The most famous of these is "Welsh rabbit," made from melted cheese, ale, and mustard, implying that this blend of ordinary ingredients is what the Welsh eat when they haven't been able to shoot or trap any four-footed bunnies. (On the rabbit/rarebit question, I refer the reader to Ambrose Bierce, in *The Devil's Dictionary:* "RAREBIT, n. A Welsh rabbit, in the speech of the humorless, who point out that it is not a rabbit. To whom it may be solemnly explained that the comestible known as toad-in-a-hole is really not a toad, and that *ris-de-veau à la*

financière is not the smile of a calf prepared after the recipe of a she banker.")

There are countless other examples of this genre: Britain's Scotch woodcock (toast with anchovy paste and scrambled eggs); the Italian *uccelli scappati,* or "escaped birds," and the Niçoise *alouettes sans têtes,* or "larks without heads," both of which are little bundles of flattened beef or veal rolled around herbs and bread crumbs; the Sicilian *fegato ai Sette Cannoli,* a dish of sliced yellow squash in a garlicky sweet vinegar sauce, said to be the closest thing to liver *fegato* that the poor Palermo neighborhood of Sette Cannoli can afford. I wonder, too, if there isn't similar irony implied by the Catalan and Provençal words for omelette—*truita* and *troucho,* respectively— identical to the words in those languages for trout. The fisherman who comes home with an empty creel, that is, might have to settle for eggs for dinner.

About the most imaginative dish names I've seen in recent years are the surrealistic Spanish ones coined by Jimmy Schmidt and Ricardo Jurado-Solares at the original Rattlesnake Club in Denver in the mid-1980s.* These included *calamares atacados por piranas bidimensionales* (squid attacked by bidimensional piranhas), *aquarium vacio encostalado y frito con lava* (empty aquarium encrusted and fried with lava), and *explosion nuclear en el campo de calabezas* (nuclear explosion in the pumpkin patch). These were, respectively, fried squid with tomatillo sauce, spicy seafood wontons, and chicken and mushroom empanadas with pumpkin–blue cheese sauce. These names might have had no logic to them, and they certainly weren't traditional—but they were sure fun.

In contrast, the typical "New American" menu today is

---

* *The Rattlesnake Club in Denver was subsequently renamed Adirondacks, and Schmidt was bought out by his partner, Michael McCarty. At this writing, the restaurant is closed. Schmidt today owns the Rattlesnake Club in Detroit, along with several other restaurants in that city.*

apt to offer (to pick from several real ones at random) such things as "lobster with Scotch whisky and white bean ravioli in leaves of green chard," "chicken salad with baby lettuces, roasted peppers, sun-dried tomatoes, pine nuts and goat cheese," "braised veal ribs in white wine, roma tomatoes, apricots and fresh herbs, served with great northern white beans," and "charcoal grilled Szechuan beef, thinly sliced, with hot chili oil and cilantro shallot sauce." Those aren't dish names, those are recipes—or at least shopping lists.

At least with names like that, though, you know pretty much what you're going to get. Maybe old-style food terminology has lost its appeal simply because it has been so often and egregiously misapplied over the years in America, either through ignorance, laziness, or some misapprehension about the nature of "creativity" in the kitchen. As many times as you may have eaten "eggs Benedict," for instance, I'll wager that you've never eaten *eggs Benedict,* the real thing, served on Holland rusk with a slice of tongue instead of ham, and garnished with thick slices of black truffle. Tournedos Rossini, beef Wellington, and dishes as simple as the Cobb salad or the *salade niçoise* are similarly misinterpreted as a matter of course.

And then there's fettuccine Alfredo: Supposedly invented in 1920 in Rome by Alfredo di Lellio at his Alfredo restaurant on the via della Scrofa ("street of the Sow"), and supposedly named in his honor by Mary Pickford and Douglas Fairbanks, Jr., who ate the dish while in Rome on their honeymoon, fettuccine Alfredo has become one of the most popular of all pastas in America. But fettuccine Alfredo isn't what you think it is.

Let's not even mention the peas or mushrooms or prosciutto that often get stirred into something masquerading under Alfredo's name; the fact is that real fettuccine Alfredo contains *no cream.* Here is a contemporary description (from 1931) of the way Alfredo himself used to make the dish, from *Conducted Tour* by Gil Meynier:

When steaming platters of *fettucini* [*sic*] were brought in, Alfredo himself came and stood at the head of the table.... A spoon in one hand, a fork in the other, he made a few graceful passes over the dishes on which butter, cheese and *fettucini* were waiting to be mixed by the master. The spoon delved into the heap of flat, golden, ribbon-like spaghetti [*sic*] and lifted it toward the caress of the fork which in its rapid movements carried a piece of fast melting butter. The grated cheese penetrated into the lower layers of the deftly malaxated mass. Alfredo was no longer smiling. A minute longer and it would be ready to serve. An almost imperceptible gesture of the head warned his attentive aide to have the plates ready. One more stroke ... he dug into the dish and with an upward gesture drew from it a first portion which he piously deposited on the first plate. In three movements he emptied the dish in three miraculously equal shares. And started on the next lot.

There was originally nothing in the dish, in other words, but noodles, cheese, and butter. Of course, the cheese was the finest Parmigiano Reggiano, and the butter was extraordinarily rich. Most accounts of the dish maintain that cream was first added because American butter wasn't rich enough. Nonetheless, what was probably the first recipe ever given for the dish in this country, in restaurateur George Rector's *The Rector Cook Book* (1928), was a pure one, calling for cheese and butter only. (Rector calls the dish simply "noodles Alfredo," without specifying the kind of pasta to be used, and appends the recipe to something called marinated beef, Alfredo.) The fact is that it is entirely possible to make a credible, authentic fettuccine Alfredo in this country (see page 247)—and it's worth the trouble.

As food changes and develops, of course, so do dish names and their interpretations. But I think there have to be some commonly agreed-upon definitions—perhaps not as stringent or all-encompassing as those of Escoffier or Larousse, but at least ballpark meanings. I think we ought to have at least some menu shorthand, colorful or not, and that we ought to agree on what that shorthand stands for. And I think that while chefs certainly have the right to improvise, they don't have a right to call any old thing by a famous name. It's not just a matter of cream in the fettuccine Alfredo. It's the whole idea of reestablishing some kitchen basics around here. Otherwise the day will soon and surely come when we'll order steak tartare and get beef stroganoff—or order fettuccine Alfredo and get a plate of fish.

RECIPES

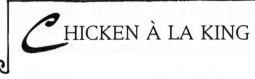

CHICKEN À LA KING

SERVES 6

You can call this dish "diced chicken in egg-thickened white-pepper sherry-cream sauce with pimentos and mushrooms on toast," if it makes you feel more contemporary.

4 *skinless, boneless chicken breast halves*
1 *celery rib, halved*
1 *carrot, halved*
1 *small onion, peeled and halved*
1 *bay leaf*
4 *tablespoons (¹/₂ stick) unsalted butter*
1 *tablespoon olive oil*
¹/₂ *pound small fresh mushrooms, quartered*
Salt and white pepper
2 *cups heavy cream*
2 *egg yolks, lightly beaten*
1 *4-ounce jar red pimento strips, drained and diced*
¹/₂ *cup good-quality dry sherry (e.g., La Ina or Tío Pepe)*
6 *puff-pastry patty shells or 6 thick slices of crustless white toast*
2 *parsley sprigs, minced*

Place chicken breasts, celery, carrot, onion, and bay leaf in a medium pot and cover with cold water. Bring to a boil, then reduce heat and simmer, covered, for 10 to 12 minutes. Set chicken breasts aside to cool, discarding liquid and vegetables (or save to use as the basis for stock). When chicken is cool enough to handle, dice into ³/₄" cubes.

Heat butter and oil in a large skillet and sauté mushrooms for about 5 minutes, stirring occasionally. Add chicken, mix well, and add salt and white pepper to taste. Add cream, raise heat to high, and stir well as mixture comes to a boil. Boil for 2 to 3 minutes, stirring constantly, then remove from heat. Adjust seasoning if necessary.

Stir in egg yolks, pimento strips, and sherry. Allow mixture to rest for about 5 minutes, then return to heat and reheat without bringing to a boil. Serve immediately over patty shells or toast, garnished with chopped parsley.

C ALAMARES ATACADOS POR PIRANAS BIDIMENSIONALES (FRIED SQUID WITH TOMATILLO SALSA)

SERVES 6

This was one of my favorite of Jimmy Schmidt's fancifully named dishes at the original Denver Rattlesnake Club.

6 ripe tomatillos, husked, rinsed, peeled, and diced
3 or 4 scallions, trimmed and minced
2 or 3 parsley sprigs, minced
Juice of 2 limes
1½ teaspoons salt
6 tablespoons extra-virgin olive oil
Tabasco sauce
Corn or canola oil
1½ cups flour
½ cup dried red pepper flakes
3 large eggs, lightly beaten
1½ cups whole milk
6 whole squid with bodies 4 to 6 inches in length, cleaned
  and with tentacles discarded
Freshly ground black pepper
1 large bunch watercress or mizuna greens, washed and
  dried
Salsa

Combine tomatillos, half the scallions, parsley, lime juice, and half the salt in a small bowl. Stir in olive oil and add Tabasco sauce to taste. Set aside.

Fill a deep skillet or Dutch oven with corn or canola oil to a depth of about 3 inches and warm over medium-high heat until temperature reaches about 350° or oil begins to crackle.

Meanwhile, mix flour, red pepper flakes, and remaining salt together in a medium-sized bowl.

In another medium-sized bowl, lightly whisk eggs and milk together.

Pass each squid body through the egg mixture, shake off excess, then dredge in seasoned flour, coating evenly.

Shake excess flour off squid, then deep-fry in oil (in two batches if necessary, to avoid them touching) until golden brown on both sides, about 3 minutes altogether. Drain on paper towels, and sprinkle with pepper to taste.

To serve, arrange watercress or mizuna evenly on six plates. Place one squid on each plate. Spoon a bit of salsa over each squid, then evenly sprinkle remaining scallions over them. Serve additional salsa on the side.

And, of course . . .

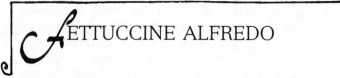

ℱETTUCCINE ALFREDO

SERVES 4 TO 6

There are two slightly tricky parts about making this dish properly: One is finding butter with a high fat and low water content (or "making" it yourself—see p. 248). The other is learning how to mix the cheese and butter into the pasta with the right, swift movements. Practice once before you make this dish for company. And, please, use only the finest Parmigiano Reggiano you can obtain.

6 ounces (1½ sticks) unsalted butter, well chilled (in coldest
   part of refrigerator, not butter compartment)
1 pound fresh or dried fettuccine
Salt
½ pound finely grated (not shredded) best-quality
   Parmigiano Reggiano, at room temperature
Freshly ground black pepper

Wrap butter securely in a very clean kitchen towel (make
sure it doesn't smell of soap or bleach), then knead butter
gently but firmly for 5 to 10 minutes or until a considerable
amount of moisture has been extruded from it. Unwrap
cloth and scrape butter up with a dinner knife or wooden
spatula, forming it into nut-shaped pieces and putting it
on a plate. Allow to soften to room temperature before
cooking pasta.*

Cook pasta in generously salted water until *al dente* or
done to your taste. (Fresh pasta cooks much faster than
dried.)

Place half the butter in a large, shallow-rimmed bowl.
Drain pasta well and add to the bowl. Place the remaining
butter atop the pasta, and scatter about half the cheese
over the top, then very quickly lift pasta up from platter
with a fork and large spoon and let drop back down, doing
this frequently until butter and cheese coat pasta thoroughly. (Work as quickly as possible so that pasta doesn't
cool.) Repeat the process with half of the remaining
cheese.

Serve immediately with remaining cheese and freshly
ground black pepper on the side.

---

* If you have access to home-churned butter or other fresh butter with very high fat
and low water content (the Plugra brand is widely distributed), disregard this step
and begin with the butter at room temperature.

23

THE NOTEBOOKS OF
CAPTAIN CAMILLE

"Performing seals have to be fed. So do the film stars in the
Hollywood Zoo."
—MOLLY CASTLE, *ROUND THE WORLD WITH AN APPETITE*

NE OF THE OCCUPATIONAL HAZARDS OF
being a writer is that people with "incredible stories to
tell" are forever foisting half-written manuscripts upon
you or begging you to listen to their extraordinary tales, in
the hope that you might be able to "do something" with
them. Thus it was that my father, who was at the time a
busy screenwriter and novelist in Hollywood, came into
possession—probably in the late 1940s or early 1950s—of
a notebook kept by a restaurant captain named Camille.
Camille had served a veritable Who's Who of celebrities
during his long career, and recorded his observations—

by no means always flattering—of their social behavior, romantic inclinations, and habits of eating, drinking, and tipping. He thought that my father might be able to use his notes as the basis for a book or even a screenplay of some kind.

In fact, the notes turned out to be sketchy, repetitious, and often scandalous, and my father apparently saw no way to adapt them. Whether or not my father kept the original notebook, I don't know, but if he did, it has long since disappeared—as has Camille. At some point, though, my father did transcribe excerpts from the document, copying Camille's spelling, punctuation, and grammar verbatim. I found it among his papers after his death.

Who was Camille? At which establishments did he ply his trade? And what years does his notebook cover? The time frame may be deduced approximately from internal evidence: In his entry for Al Capone, Camille refers to Chicago mayor Anton Cermak in the present tense; Cermak was shot (not by Capone) in mid-February, 1933, and died the next month. In writing about Rudy Vallee, Camille notes that the entertainer has just married for the second time—which he did in 1931. I would guess that Camille first started setting down his observations, then, around 1932 (though he obviously includes earlier recollections). The latest date specified in the notebook is 1945, the year Camille says he got *"ma vengence"* on actor Wallace Beery.

As to where he worked, there are specific references to his employment at two celebrated Chicago establishments, the College Inn in the Sherman House Hotel and the Pump Room in the Ambassador East Hotel, and to the fact that he worked somewhere (unspecified) in Galveston, Texas. And in his entry on Maurice Chevalier, he notes that he had served the entertainer in Paris, Buenos Aires, and Hollywood, in addition to Chicago. At which restaurant or restaurants he might have worked in Hollywood, I have no idea.

As to Camille's identity, his entry on Lucius Beebe, a reporter and columnist for the *New York Herald Tribune*, and a famous bon vivant and railway buff, gave me my clue. In it, Camille thanks Beebe for "in your last book ever ... the cute story you tell between Mrs. E. Byfield the Second and I." Chicago-based Ernie Byfield was one of the great American hoteliers of his era, and among his properties were the aforementioned Sherman House and Ambassador East. (When once Byfield was asked how he got into the hotel business, he replied, with a straight face, "I was standing in the lobby of the Sherman Hotel one afternoon when my father, the owner of the hotel, strolled in and spotted me. He took an instant liking to me.")

I had no idea which Beebe book Camille was referring to, unfortunately, and the only Beebe titles in most libraries today are railway-themed—*The Age of Steam, High Iron, Mansions on Rails,* and so on. Then I got lucky. Browsing in a used bookstore in Santa Barbara one day, I happened to spot a book by Beebe called *Snoot If You Must.* It sounded promising. I checked the index and found one entry under Byfield, Kitty. I looked it up, and found the following passage: "Camille Duplieux, the maître d'hôtel and 'Frenchy' to the intimate great, used to be a room-service waiter [at the Ambassador East] until one day Kitty Byfield said to Ernie: 'We have the duckiest floor waiter named Camille. He always tucks me in mornings after he brings my breakfast,' and next day Frenchy had charge of the Pump Room." That, then, is what I know about Camille.

Here is a slightly abridged version of my father's partial transcription of the notebook of Camille Duplieux. It isn't exactly about food, but it most certainly is about restaurants, and the things folks get up to in them. It might also, incidentally, serve as an object lesson to some of today's celebrities: That waiter or captain you abuse or show off to or shortchange might just possibly be keeping a notebook of his own, and might one day tell the plain truth about your background or your behavior or the size of your tips. In fact, I hope somebody *is* keeping such a record, though they're probably not. Today's waiters and captains are probably all too busy working on their screenplays.

ANNABELLA. Very good dancer. But hoola-hoola!!! Poor Tyrone Power. That night he look so embarrassed on the dance floor. She looked like a snack snake. Love champagne. Chicken king. When at the table very shie. This will be a short marriage.*

EDWARD ARNOLD. Love cocktail at cocktail time highball at highball time goulash and stew is favorite I think. Of course never refuse salade. Very sweet personne. I fell shame of taking tips from him.

FRED ASTAIR. Lovely man to talk to. Dont drink. Here betwen trains. His wife very charming. Like tomato juice very much. Solf shell crabs and asparagas.

PHILL BAKER. Double or nothing 64 dolars question a good comedian. Proibition or not always as good liquor and love to use it but I think his wife will exchange few things about him.†

LUCILLE BALL. What a tall drink of water. Love to jump from one booth to a other. Beautifull white fur coat. Love to put it on dance-floor and dance on top of it. Just out of the humburger line will learn very fast to eat caviar??

TALLULAH BANKHEAD. She is like a good bottle wine good wintage older she getting better. What a memory I get from her. One morning at 4 A.M. she want to her balcony of the hotel and call few peoples by name. She land in police waggon. Oh! boy what a fun the lady of the south was kicking up.

JOHN BARRYMORE. The poor man he was realy per-

---

* *Annabella and Power were married on April 23, 1939, and divorced on January 26, 1948.*
† *Phil Baker (1899–1959) was a famous radio comedian and musician of his era—and was, among other things, the original host of the hit radio quiz program* Take It or Leave It, *which evolved into* The $64 Question *(and later, without Baker, into the*

secuted by womens olds and youngs to. His test was gone. Many time in night I use to give him some cold tea in a shot glass. He mix with watter thinking it is Scotch didn' know the differents. Nevers eat in 3 months. I was mostly is bodyguard. He puts me many times in very bad spots mostly in the colors dixtric in Chicago. Oh oh boy the Avalon hotel I will nevers forget also the young 16 years old girl from Philadelphia. Mrs. Potter bleu book lady of Chicago will remember him always. She had her nose put back in place. I saw his play more than 20 times and every time his lines were not the same. What a great actor drunk or sober.

LUCIUS BEEBE. What can you writt about such a perfect gentleman in every sence of the word. Love Don Perrignon 1921 a fin gourmet no gourmand. His great hobby is rail road. Lucius thank many many times for all the bigs breaks you give me in your paper and in your last book ever for the cute story you tell between Mrs. E. Byfield the Second and I.

ROBERT BENCHLEY. You nevers know if is drink or sober. He talk to you but his mind is 1000 miles away. He don' have to act just be himself in his shorts pictures. Food he know little about it but drinking as long as is liquide and as kick like a mule that go down. As storys teller he is marvellous. But please slow down or you are going to meet your Maker soon.*

WALLACE BERRY. Very big on structure very bully. One night for no reason at all he K.O. me because when he came to the College-Inn I ask for his name. Oh oh boy that was the end of a beautiful day. But in 1945 at the Town-House I get him. He wanded a very good steak not a

---

scandal-ridden $64,000 Question *TV* series). *The wife in question was either dancer Irmgard Eric, whom he married in 1945, or, more likely, one-time actress Peggy Cartwright, who divorced him in 1940. In any case, by all reports Baker proved resistant to "exchange" until his death. I know because Cartwright is my wife's grandmother.*
* *Benchley died in 1945.*

ordinary steak but a good steak. Ah there was ma vengence! No no steak. He was hot after me. He is what I call a very poor Americain. Food—zero. Drink—plenty of it. Actor—very very good. But you are a sucker for women. Mostly drug-store blondes.

JOAN BLONDELL. Blind like a bath but always carrie her eyeglasses on top of her hairs. One she complaint the steak was tough. I said to her please the knife is turned upside down. Always ready to eat (nice and plum). Oh boy love to drink. But she is nice.

HUMPHREY BOGART. Like to be tought but in side of him he is solft. Oh poor Escoffier this guy can murder your good food. But it is the best friend of the whiskey and more whiskey. Eat at my place very much.

CLAIRE BOOTHE. Tipicale New England lady. Know what she wants. But to me she still cheap polititian. Know good food. Love her Scotch. Ware beautiful cloths.

CONNIE BOSWELL. What a great trio very swell girls what a voice togethers. But Connie will nevers forget Galveston July 1934 when everybody left the club even her future husband.* She was cryint very hard and calling for help. I run in the club. There was over a foot of water. I run to the piano and carry her to safety. She don' know me no more when she see me.

CHARLES BOYER. Ah ah poors Americaines women you are so easy to decieve. To me he is the Jack Benny of France (you know what I mean). He is so cheap he smell. When his mother come to this country I was the ambassador for good will to her. I am still waiting for a thank from him. He is very fussy regarding his burgundy wine.

---

*This is a very curious story: Connie (or Connee, as she later spelled her name) Boswell had been partially paralyzed with polio at the age of four, and habitually sang from a wheelchair. She had been discovered originally by artists' manager Harry Leedy, whom she married in 1936. It seems inconceivable that he would have intentionally deserted the handicapped Boswell at the height of a flood, having both a personal and a professional interest in her.

Oh you should see him without his toupet. His head look like a gristal ball gaiser. Poors waiters or capitaines don' break your neck you will get just the same one big dollars and boy you sure earn it. You are on top now but boy watch when you go down! Please make a reservation at the Casbah.*

JOE E. BROWN. Don' worry you will find the road of comeback some day!!! What a swell guy. His hart is bigger than his mouth. Thank for the Cesar Salade you gave me in 1936. Don't drink but love good food.

AL CAPONE. Did plenty good during winter 1930–31–32. He had some big bread lines in Chicago for all the poor peoples. Always did they own justice. He is a goumet and well dress man. Very genereux always pay in gold. I bet you Mayor Cermack will win against Al. But poor Cermack if you do you are sure on your way to see Saint Peter.†

MAURICE CHEVALIER. My father remember his mother when she had a little store at Marche aux Puces. Tall very charming his shirt and tie always the same material. Drink little. First waited on him in Paris, after in Buenos Aires in Hollywood and in Chicago. He ask me if by any chance I am follow him all over the world.

GARRY COOPER. Very nice gentleman. Always think twice before he talks. Drinking very little. Food—likes Americains dishs the best.

JACK DEMPSEY. A plain good sport. Do not drink. Love double orange juice. Nevers refuse a autograph to the youngsters.

MARLENE DIETRICH. Not a spring chicken but she is

---

* *In his 1938 film* Algiers *(a remake of the vastly superior 1936 French film* Pépé le Moko, *which starred Jean Gabin in the title role), Boyer plays a fugitive from French justice, who cannot leave the safety of the Algiers Casbah, or native quarter.*

† *Anton Joseph Cermak was mayor of Chicago from 1931 until his death in March of 1933. He was killed not by Capone but by a stray bullet fired by anarchist Giuseppi Zangara, who was attempting to assassinate Franklin D. Roosevelt.*

a lovely lady and a good sport. Love and know food. Her drinking is moderate and at the proper time. If a piano there she is always willing to play you a tune or two. Used to come often with Jean Gabin and look like she is looking for real friendship and real love.

IRENNE DUNNE. Lovely lady of the cinema. She could be a queen. Love good food. No drinking except good wines.

DOUGLAS FAIRBANK JR. Very English type gentleman. As a very solft spot in his hart for Gertrude Lawrence. Love roast beef and very dry martini. Don't expect too much service. Off the stage a perfect guest.

ERROL FLYNN. Don't beleive always the news papers critics. To me he is a perfect gentleman. A very fine connaisseur of good food and very good wines. P.S. Do you know his license auto number—R You 18.

KAY FRANCIS. The cloths don' make her she make the cloths. She carry her tall structure very well. Not very chesty but what a look. What a perfect and lovely lady. Love good food good champagne.

GREER GARSON. Just came from England. Cute red hair. The face full of frikles. Hollywood will take care of that. Watch moviegoers she is going far way in your hart. Ernest Byfield call me to be at the station to meet her. Love good food and know good food.

BETTY GRABLE. 1942. So round. So ferm. So slapy. So vulgare. You think she is from Main Street. The first time I saw her I thought she was a refugee from a burlesque. She loves to exebite her legs.

ALAN HALE. What a lovely gentleman. A fine caractere actor. Very nice personnality. Very actif out of the studio on different other bussiness. Love his little bourbon and my crepes suzettes and eat most anything. Very good to the helps.

HELEN HAYES. Eat very good. The drinking in the family is done by her husband. They have a lovely little girl.* Very good actress for Shakespeare. Appreciate very good service. But poor waiter, he sure cannot do the same about her generosity.

WALTER HUSTON. Tipical caractere actor. Great sence of humor. One minute he could be a perfect pastor the next a good roughneck of the Wyoming prairies. Love good food and take his time to enjoie it.

GEORGE JESSEL. Sommetime with toupet sometime with out. Very nervous. Love beef any forme or shape. With his wife act like a lamb. With others a big show off. Love to be reconnaise. And those cigars!

GUY KIBBEE. A real connaisseur of better thing. Love good old wine and young girl. Very fine old man. Ware a very funny hair cut. A good gastronumm.

GERTRUDE LAWRENCE. She is too good to be English!!! The gret lady of the stage. I am creahated a dessert and named after her. Loves stuffed celery with raw meat and very dry Martini. Of course we must use English gin. I will never forget her white Xmas tree. So good to the help. She maded the Pump Room famouse.

VIVIAN LEIGHT. What a sad sac out of the screen. Always refused autographs to the kids. She calls me many times to chase those dirty kids like she says. But I told her some days "those dirty kids" will make her or brake her. It is too bad *Gone With the Wind* the wind was stronger and blod her to England for good. A perfect pair with her English husband. [See Laurence Olivier, next page.] Food and drink very hard to please.

OSCAR LEVANT. Lovely personne. Like very thin minute steak cottage fried potatoes coffe coffe and more coffe.

* *Hayes was married to hard-drinking newspaperman-turned-playwright/ screenwriter Charles MacArthur (coauthor with Ben Hecht of* The Front Page *and* Twentieth Century), *and speaks openly of his drinking in her numerous autobiographies. Lucius Beebe notes that MacArthur, presumably while intoxicated, once attempted to steal one of the elevators from the Ambassador Hotel, "but was unable to work it out of its shaft after several hours of experimenting." Hayes and MacArthur's daughter Mary died of polio in 1949.*

MARY MARTIN. What a swell girl. She is going places in the stage. Very good looking but dont take any advantage of her look or great talent. Food don't know much but she will. Drinking no.

ELSIE MAXWELL. Very slopy woman. Loves apple juice waffles or pancakes. What a epicurian ah ah! Who told her she could arrange a party? Really if you get planty bull you go a long way.

JEANNETTE MCDONALD. What a lovely lady. What charmes what smile. She got everything to please the most difficult personne in this world. I am sure her husband way in England must miss her beautiful red hair.* Don' drink. Love international humburger and real pineapple sherbet. Also ask for many of my recipes. I wish I could be her butler.

ADOLPH MENJOU. Very distingtif. He looks like he is made to weare good cloths. He is a real actor not a funny from Hollywood. Good food fins dishes and vintage wines are he hobby. Lanson Champagne his favorite.

GRACE MOORE. A great artist a great singer but a paine in the neck in private life. I made a fish dish named after her. Loves rare wines. Once we had some very old wine fly from N.Y. for a special party. I had to make the same salade seven times once. Her husband is like a puppet.† She likes Size 14 in dress but Size 20 fill better. Very jealouse of others opera artiste.

LAURENCE OLIVIER. Great actor. Only live for the stage and England. Very selfish nasty and ignorant personne. Likes to make you believe he know food but that too stinke. Better get out of this country.

LUELLA O. PARSONS. She will nevers forget the Polo Room at the Ambassador Hotel where we had a special breakfast party for her. We bring in the dining room 20

---

* *MacDonald was married to actor Gene Raymond.*
† *Moore was a famous Metropolitan Opera soprano and sometime movie star. Her husband was singer Valentín Parera, the so-called "Valentino of Spain," whom she met on the Île-de-France in 1931 and married shortly thereafter.*

beds. We put man and woman in each bed. Her partner was the good Ernest Byfield. They et the food in bed.

LILLY PONS. Tres coquette. Very simple to talk to. Every time she go to a new city there is some Americaine Beauty roses from her husband.* She loves cold white-fish. Sherry-wine is her drink. Before she goes on the stage she always eat some lumps of sugar. She own a beautiful chinchilla coat. Every Xmas she sends me a card.

CLAUDE RAINES. Very quiet fellow well manners. Love hors d'oeuvres et more hors d'oeuvres with few very dry Martini. Here at the Pump Room 1940 betwen trains. But it is very hard to know what his next move is going to be.

SALLY RAND. Thank to her she saves the 1933 World Fair in Chicago. It is too bad Barnum is dead. Off the stage a perfect lady. Don' know good food but sure she loves to eat good food.

EDWARD G. ROBINSON. What a sweet fellow. He as two lovely girls. His wife is a good artist paint.† His carac-tere is tought in picture but his hart is very soft. Like Lanson Champagne roast beef.

WILL ROGERS. He was a great humanitarian nevers like anybody to fuss over him. Do not like ringside table. Always went to the kitchen see what the helps eat and him eat the same. His favorite dish were pot roast and bake beans. I will say good Americains food. What a party we had a nite at College-Inn. He just flew from N.Y. and came at the door of College-Inn. When the guests saw him they went nuts and Maurice Chevalier Ben Bernie Amos et Andy graded him and dance in the midle of floor. The week before he craked in Alaska I give the tel. call from Willy Post the pilot. That was a great lost for America.

MICKEY ROONEY. Please Mickey stay out of public

---

* Lily Pons, the famous coloratura soprano, was married to conductor André Kostelanetz.

† Robinson was married to actress Gladys Lloyd, a sometime artist, who was herself the daughter of painter/sculptor C. C. Cassell.

eyes off stage you are so different. You act so shie with
your mgr. and you are really a perfect brat. Eat mostly
salades and sandwichs. I bet you will be married soon but
poor girl!!*

FRANK SINATRA. Do he loves to make sure everybody know he is here! About food and drinks he knows
NOTHING NOTHING.

SHIRLEY TEMPLE. Very cut little young lady lovely
dimples and smile so young yet and drink coffe. She likes
to be herself but don dare to.

SOPHIE TUCKER. "Open House Sophe" the only one
you are happy to pay good money to get insulted and love
it. Dont drink. Love scrambled eggs very hard. What a
woman. Love to do charity work.

RUDOLPH VALENTINO. After breaking so many
dishs as a poor dishwasher he came to Hollywood do
some more breaking but this time was women hearts. I
will never forgets my first meetting with him in August
1926 when he try a Hollywood on board of S/S "Paris" in
N Y C. The poor woman. What a fight. He try to put
overboard a little hunchback. That dit it. He got the best
bitting of his life.† Then few weeks later we learned his
dead. We were not so very sad.

RUDY VALLEE. You just took your second wife. You
will not stop there.‡ Quit your band and go alone. You will
do better. By the way how old you are you old goat? Like
good food. Very stingy.

ERICK VON STRONHEIM. What a prince is what a
gentleman. The woman who get him she is very lucky. Love

---

*Rooney indeed became notorious for the frequency with which he entered into
matrimony. His eight wives (to date) include actresses Ava Gardner and Martha
Vickers.

†I have found no reference to this tantalizing story, nor even any mention of a boat
called the Paris in any of the several biographies of Valentino I have consulted—
though the movie idol did spend the first weeks of August traveling back and forth
between New York, Chicago, and Atlantic City. He was stricken August 15 and died
August 23, of what was diagnosed posthumously as peritonitis.

‡Vallee was married four times before his death in 1986.

caviar, filet, crepes suzettes, and Cordon-Rouge Champagne. What a fameux actor in Grand Illusion and 5 Graves to Cairo.* Look very hard in picture but is hart is very soflt.

ORSONS WELLS. What a fine fellow with or without whiskers. Give up drinking. While in the Pump Room use to served him some Coca-Cola in the champagne bucket. Very smart on the stage or off it. Love good food good cigar. Great director! Great actor!! Always thinking of the under dogs.

MAY WEST. Why dont you come up and see me some time. Of course off the stage I am a good lady!!! Yes she is. A great personne. Always with her mother. Don't smoked don't drinked and a speak well English.

LORETTA YOUNG. Face of an angel. Face who belong to a convent Catholic. So sweet so simple to talk to. Love and know good food. Give her some of my own little food secrets. Her husband Major T. Lewis a real guy. I hope to work for him some day.

RECIPES

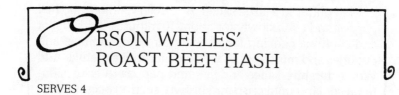

ORSON WELLES' ROAST BEEF HASH

SERVES 4

Orson Welles was one of the most famous of Hollywood gastronomes, as legendary for the breadth of his waistcoat as for that of his talent. As long ago as 1941, in fact, columnist Sidney Skolsky wrote that Welles was the only actor ever to have had a dish named after him at Chasen's, the ultimate Hollywood restaurant. Skolsky didn't identify the dish, but

---

* *Two of Eric von Stroheim's most famous film roles were in Jean Renoir's* La Grande Illusion *(1937) and Billy Wilder's* Five Graves to Cairo *(1943).*

noted that it involved *"a three- or four-pound piece of roast beef."* Welles later told an interviewer that the dish referred to must have been *"a roast beef hash that Dave Chasen had always made in the old days of vaudeville. I didn't invent it. It was something he used to make late at night at Chasen's, you know, when we'd stay up—and I liked it and finally he named it for me."* When I asked the restaurant's long-time manager, Ronald Clint, about the dish not long ago, he told me that he doubted that the dish had ever borne Welles' name. *"We've never named dishes after celebrities on our menu,"* he said. Nonetheless, he admitted, this simple, savory hash might well have been a Welles favorite.

2   cups cooked lean roast beef, diced
2   cups diced cooked potatoes
4   tablespoons (½ stick) unsalted butter
½   cup diced celery
½   cup diced onion
½   cup diced green bell pepper
1   small shallot, peeled and finely chopped
1   tablespoon Worcestershire sauce
Salt and freshly ground pepper

Combine beef and potatoes in a bowl and set aside.

Melt butter in a large skillet. Add celery, onion, and bell pepper and cook slowly for about 10 minutes. Add shallot and continue cooking for about 5 minutes. Add beef and potatoes and mix together well with a rubber spatula. Add Worcestershire sauce and salt and pepper to taste. Continue cooking until crisp and brown, stirring occasionally.

Serve with mustard sauce.*

* To make mustard sauce, add 1 teaspoon good-quality mustard to 1 cup white sauce or sauce béchamel.

CᖫRENCH APPLE PIE

MAKES ONE 9-INCH PIE

Of my own early food memories, perhaps the one linked most vividly with Hollywood is of French apple pie. My father loved this dessert, and when he was working under contract at 20th Century-Fox, a waitress in the commissary (once known rather grandly as the Café de Paris) always used to save a piece for him. I called the Fox commissary not long ago to inquire if by any chance they might still have the recipe from the 1950s. "Oh, no, we wouldn't have that," replied the manager's assistant. "Gee, the chef that made that is probably dead by now. Now all of our stuff comes in already made." And people wonder why Hollywood isn't what it used to be! In any case, in the absence of the old Fox recipe for this dessert—which of course is no more French than English muffins are English—I made one up, trying to capture as closely as possible (and as closely as I could remember) the character of the original.

28 *graham crackers*
¼ *pound (1 stick) unsalted butter, softened to room temperature*
2 *pounds apples (preferably Rome Beauty), peeled, cored, and coarsely chopped*
¼ *cup yellow raisins*
¾ *cup granulated sugar*
½ *teaspoon ground cinnamon*
¼ *teaspoon ground cloves*
1 *tablespoon flour*
⅓ *cup brown sugar*
¼ *cup plain dry bread crumbs*

Grind or crush 23 graham crackers into fine crumbs. Place about ⅔ of the butter in a mixing bowl and cream it with a whisk, then slowly add graham cracker crumbs until thoroughly blended. Lightly butter a 9-inch pie pan with a bit more of the butter, then press crumbs evenly against the sides and bottom of the pan. Cover lightly with plastic wrap and refrigerate.

While crust is chilling, preheat oven to 350°. Mix apples, raisins, granulated sugar, cinnamon, cloves, and flour together in a baking dish. Bake, uncovered, for about 45 minutes, or until apples are soft but not mushy.

Remove apple mixture from oven and cool to room temperature, then fill pie crust with it, tamping it down evenly.

Crush the remaining graham crackers more coarsely than for the crust and mix them with the remaining butter, the brown sugar, and the bread crumbs. Spread this mixture carefully over the top of the apple mixture, and chill for at least 1 hour before serving.

24
MEANWHILE, BACK AT
THE RANCH

"Nothing is invented and perfected at the same time."
—ENGLISH PROVERB

FIRST REALIZED THAT THE CREAMY, PLEAS-
antly sour buttermilk-based condiment called ranch dressing was no longer simply something you put on your
salad when I heard comedian/television personality Jay
Leno on the radio one morning exhorting me to try "Cool
Ranch-Flavored Doritos." Since ranches themselves are
generally composed of things like fenceposts and manure,
pickup trucks and barbed wire, I figured out pretty quickly
that the "ranch" with which these then-new corn chips
were flavored probably wasn't a *ranch* ranch. But that the
ranch in question was in fact ranch (salad) dressing was
not an easy notion for me to digest.

The American mass-food industry has a knack for turning individual dishes, or even whole genres of dishes, into flavors. Thus, ranch dressing *flavor* may be found today in such products as Keebler Wheatables Ranch Flavored Whole Wheat Snacks, Ranch Ruffles (potato chips), Light Ranch Flavor Pringles (reconstituted potato chips), and Fritos Wild 'n' Mild Ranch Corn Chips, in addition to the aforementioned Doritos. There are also corn chips said to be "taco-flavored." Similarly, "pizza" has become a flavor for crackers, pretzels, and other snack foods, and "fajita" for precooked French fries.

Never mind that "taco," "pizza," and "fajita" are all generic terms like "sandwich" or "pie"—and describe foods that draw any distinctive flavor they might possess from what goes inside them or on top of them. (Can you imagine "Sandwich-Flavored Doritos" or maybe "Pie-Flavored Cookies"?) The fact is that everybody understands that "taco-flavored" refers to a particular variety of taco, the standard one in this country, with ground meat, "cheddar" cheese, and lettuce enclosed in a crispy tortilla shell and seasoned with slightly spicy tomato-based sauce. And everybody knows that "pizza-flavored" refers to oregano-spiked tomato sauce and mozzarella cheese, and that "fajita-flavored" means ... well, whatever it means. But "ranch-flavored"? Had this comparative newcomer of a dressing really become so popular nationwide, and so widely tasted, that the very noun "ranch"—without even "dressing" attached—would summon up strong imagery of its flavor in the minds (and on the palates) of the general public? Apparently so.

When I was growing up, salad dressings in this country came in four basic flavors: vinaigrette (or simply oil and vinegar); blue cheese (which used to be called Roquefort until some sorehead pointed out that it usually wasn't made with genuine Roquefort cheese, and the truth-in-packaging boys got in on the act); French (a gooey, rather sweet tomato-spiked concoction totally unknown in

France); and Thousand Island (basically Russian dressing with a few minced pickles and pimentos thrown in). To these four occasionally were added Italian, which is more or less oil and vinegar with herbs and garlic.

Green Goddess dressing—which is basically mayonnaise flavored with anchovies and assorted green herbs, and was invented at the historic Palace (now the Sheraton-Palace) Hotel in San Francisco in the mid-1920s, in honor of William Archer's hit play *The Green Goddess*—enjoyed something of a vogue in California for several decades. Today it is pretty much limited to a few old-fashioned prime-rib restaurants and the Palace itself. Other dressings—honey-mustard, for instance—were mostly curiosities, often claimed by one restaurant or another as a house specialty, but never very widely popular.

Ranch dressing, which was often described, especially at first, as Hidden Valley Ranch Dressing, came out of nowhere (or so it seemed) in the mid-1970s. By the mid-1980s, it had conquered practically every salad bar and salad-dressing grocery shelf in America. It rode Thousand Island right off the menu. It ended up on corn chips. . . .

What was this stuff, anyway—and where did it come from? In early 1987, in an attempt to find out, I wrote a query to the letters page of *Nation's Restaurant News*. Almost immediately, I heard from a representative of the Clorox Company of Oakland, California. "Ranch-style salad dressing," he wrote, "was originated by the Henson family, owners of Hidden Valley Ranch, a guest ranch in the hills behind Santa Barbara. . . . Guests at the ranch raved about the 'house' dressing, and often requested samples to take home with them. This led to the Henson family starting up a small manufacturing operation, distributing packages of dry mix mostly to the western states in the period between the end of World War II and the early 1970s. In October 1972, the Clorox Company purchased the rights to trademarks, formula and product from the Henson family. The HVR Company, a subsidiary of Clorox, today markets the leading brand of Ranch-style salad dressing, Hidden Valley Ranch Original Ranch salad dressing, both bottled and in a dry mix, nationally."

After I published the preceding information in my "Restaurant Notebook" column in the *Los Angeles Times,* I received several more letters on the subject. One was from Linda B. Ebert, manager of the test kitchen at Pennsylvania State University's Housing and Food Services Department, who offered to send me a "from-scratch" recipe for ranch dressing that she had developed. (I took her up on the offer; see page 271.) Another was from L.A. filmmaker/photographer Alan Barker—and this one told the ranch dressing tale in far more vivid terms:

I lived and worked at Hidden Valley Guest Ranch from about 1959 until 1963. Your information from . . . Clorox was largely correct. The dressing was invented in the mid-fifties. . . . It was concocted by Steve Henson, who opened Hidden Valley as a sort of country club, night club, dude ranch in the mountains. The ranch had been his longtime dream. He and his wife Gayle built it from a much smaller existing ranch with money they had made in Alaska in the plumbing business. The ranch was not received well and promptly went broke. During my stay, we lived on peanut butter sandwiches and leftovers from parties thrown there by UCSB fraternities and sororities.

The dressing, which was originally mixed with buttermilk and mayonnaise, had no name at first. We ate it on everything from steaks to, in a comical moment, ice cream. The guests at the ranch first began asking for jars of it to take home for themselves, then wanted larger quantities for their friends. They took it in liquid form in mayonnaise jars. The impracticality of this led to packaging the [dressing] as a powder.

The ranch had no resemblance to the cutesy farm pictured in the commercials [for the Clorox version of the dressing]. The only animal left was a dog. There was an animator from Hanna-Barbera, whose name I have forgotten, who used to pay for his stays at the ranch by painting Western murals around the place ... [and] I believe he and Steve came up with the name Ranch Dressing, ... and he designed the original logo which was a cowboy figure.

The Hensons had a saga of a life. Steve was a muscular, hard-drinking, tale-telling cowboy sort. He charmed most who came to the ranch. There were twenty different stories of how he had captured the bear whose skin hung in the foyer. The stories were so entertaining no one cared if they heard several conflicting versions. ... If I recall correctly, he found the bear-skin in the local dump where he got most of the "old west" decor that littered the ranch. Gayle cleaned, cooked as many as 300 steak dinners a night when the ranch was leased out for a party, and played an organ to entertain guests at night. They were the two hardest-working, most unwilling-to-give-up people I have known. Gayle once said that she married Steve "because I couldn't get rid of him ... and he beat up all my other boyfriends."

The Hensons made a minor bundle in Alaska, lost it all on the ranch, then made one ten times as big on the dressing. They lived hard. ...

Barker went on to say that he had lost touch with the Hensons after he moved to Los Angeles in 1963, but did see their son Nolan—who had been his best friend at the ranch—one more time in about 1968. Nolan was a photographer in the Army at the time, on leave from Vietnam.

Whatever may have happened to them, the Hensons are, in any case, long gone from Hidden Valley Ranch. The ranch is now the Hidden Valley Retreat Center—not open to the public, I found out when I called there one day, and not particularly interested in answering questions about ranch dressing.

That, I would have thought, was about the end of the Hidden Valley Ranch Dressing story. But about six months after I published excerpts from Barker's letter in my *Los Angeles Times* column, I received one more letter—not about the dressing exactly, but, in a round-about way, about the ranch itself. This one came from Bruce and Matt Coe at another Hidden Valley Guest Ranch, this one in Cle Elum, Washington.

The Coes were writing to tell me that they had always wondered about Hidden Valley Ranch Dressing, since visitors to their own ranch often asked them if it had been invented there, and were thus interested to read about Steve Henson in my column. "[K]nowing something of the gentleman who started our Ranch in 1947," they added, they thought they might "try to add a little to the story." This is some of what they told me:

> Tom Whited (pronounced White-head locally) bought an old homestead in the upper Kittitas County in eastern Washington State in 1947, renaming it Hidden Valley Guest Ranch. Tom and his wife Nita redecorated the ranch, added some log cabins which they skidded in from other ranches around the area and began the foundation of what has become the oldest continuously run guest ranch in . . . Washington. . . .
>
> Tom was at one time an old "Hollywood cowboy," meaning that he was at various times a stuntman, stable hand, wrangler, Indian, etc., and when he moved to Washington, he brought a little bit of Hollywood with him. He used to entertain the guests by balancing on the rear legs of a chair with his guitar and singing "The Strawberry Roan." . . . Tom, like Steve Henson, was a hard-bitten cowboy kind of guy, wiry and lanky, a hard drinker and a tale teller. They probably would have enjoyed each other if they had actually met. Either that or they would have fought a lot. But wait!!!!
>
> Maybe they did know each other. . . . HVR Santa Barbara would have been the kind of place that Tom would have been attracted to. Maybe they were war buddies. Maybe Tom worked for Steve at the ranch. Maybe they met up here when Steve worked in Alaska. Who knows. . . .

The letter concludes, "So, if Steve Henson is still alive, it might be some comfort to him to know that Hidden Valley Ranch is still alive and that yes, the pipes freeze, the horses get loose, someone else's cattle are always in our fields, the fences are always down, and the hired help is always in the local slammer for some sort of perceived indecency."

Talk about your cool ranch flavor.

RECIPE

*H*OMEMADE RANCH DRESSING

MAKES 1 PINT

This is an adaptation of a recipe developed by Linda B. Ebert, manager of the housing and food services test kitchen at Pennsylvania State University. She believes that it closely resembles the original secret recipe, and it tastes pretty ranchy to me. (Besides dressing salads with it, I sometimes use it in place of mayonnaise on sandwiches.)

1 cup mayonnaise
$1/4$ teaspoon salt
$1/4$ teaspoon garlic powder
1 teaspoon onion salt
$1/8$ teaspoon ground oregano
$1/4$ teaspoon white pepper
$1/4$ teaspoon dried chives
$1/4$ teaspoon dried parsley
1 cup buttermilk

Combine mayonnaise, herbs, and spices in a mixing bowl, then mix with an electric beater, first at low speed for about 5 seconds, then at medium speed until smooth. Scrape dressing down sides of bowl and pour in buttermilk slowly, mixing at high speed, until mixture is very smooth. Refrigerate for at least 12 hours. Stir well before serving.

25

THE BLUE BAR BLUES

"[That] 'The Algonquin' [is] something in and by and for itself . . . can never be quite explained to those who are outside the magic circle."
—HENDRIK WILLEM VAN LOON, QUOTED IN
TALES OF A WAYWARD INN BY FRANK CASE

*T*HE TROUBLE WITH NEWCOMERS WHO TAKE over venerable old hotels and restaurants and vow not to alter their essential character is not that they forsake their vows intentionally but that they mostly wouldn't recognize essential character if they dropped it on their foot. They invariably offer the same assurances: Nothing to worry about, folks. We're not going to change a thing. Just smooth out a few wrinkles and brighten the place up a bit. It never for an instant occurs to them that it was probably the wrinkles and the lack of modern brightness that made the joint worth bothering about in the first place.

Consider, for instance, what has happened at New York's legendary Algonquin Hotel. Founded in 1902 as the Puritan Hotel and renamed with its present moniker the same year (apparently at the suggestion of an employee named Frank Case, who became the hotel's proprietor in 1907), the Algonquin was well known, first under Case and then under his successors, Mr. and Mrs. Ben Bodne (who purchased the hotel from Case's estate in 1946), as Manhattan's premier literary/theatrical/artistic caravanserai. It was a bit worn, but comfortable—not-quite-shabby genteel. People loved it or hated it the moment they walked in the door, and, if they loved it, wouldn't trade a room there for a suite at the Pierre.

In 1988, the Algonquin was purchased by the Cesar Park Hotels International chain, a Brazil-based subsidiary of the Aoki Corporation of Tokyo. Cesar Park spokesmen were quick to reassure the Algonquin's many loyal customers and friends that the company fully understood the hotel's unique appeal, and would do nothing to jeopardize the special feeling of the place. Then they almost immediately replaced the plain, thick, coarsely fragrant Ivory Soap bars that had long been the only "amenity" in the bathrooms with a bunch of cute little Caswell-Massey toiletries flavored with assorted fruits and nuts. They set scowling security men in sensible suits to prowl the corridors with walkie-talkies, where formerly there had been only amiable maids with oversized carts, occasionally colliding with the ghosts of Alec Wilder and James Thurber. They moved the hotel's eminently civilized 3 P.M. checkout time up to 1 P.M. (Hell, you can check out of any hotel at 1 P.M. You don't need the Algonquin for that.)

Subsequently, they refurbished the hotel from top to bottom, put vaguely militaristic-looking new uniforms on the staff, closed the Oak Room restaurant off from the lobby, and turned the adjacent Chinese Room into what the first manager installed by Cesar Park once described to me as "a very English-looking, very *clubby* but not *pubby* bar." Oh, and they closed the Blue Bar.

The Blue Bar was the best bar in New York City. Why? Who knows? It was ridiculously small—an odd-shaped little room crowded with six or seven tiny tables, half a dozen mud-brown barstools, half a dozen mismatched chairs, a single J-shaped banquette, and a scattering of little tables topped in blue Formica. There was a big square-cut wood (or wood-faced) column in everybody's way on the customers' side of the bar itself. An ornate brass-and-pewter chandelier with fake-flame bulbs descended from an incongruous round recess in the ceiling. The only blue about the place, for heaven's sake, besides the Formica tabletops and some dark blue velvet half-curtains on a small room divider and on the brown-shuttered etched-glass windows, was the little backlit sign over the entrance.

Yet the Blue Bar was a wonderful place—unexpected, eccentric, as comfortable as home. In some uncanny way, it grabbed you, and held you. If you were the right sort of person for the Blue Bar (and many sorts of persons were), you knew it instinctively. It became yours. It was a place where you could duck in for a quick Martini, or sit and talk and think and muse all night. If you came from out of town, a few drinks at the Blue Bar could leave you feeling as if you had connected with Manhattan (or could insulate you from it cozily, if you preferred); if you lived in New York, the same few drinks would lend you new perspective on the goings-on outside the door—and maybe even help remind you why you lived in the city in the first place.

Part of the Blue Bar's appeal was certainly in the way it seemed intimately connected with the interesting past, as if the party there had never really stopped. The appropriately literary bartenders helped, too—one was a published novelist; another was a specialist in Russian poetry—as did the sheer demographic breadth of the regular clientele, which included everything from *New Yorker* writers and piano players and stage-door Johnnies to computer wizards and big-game hunters and vapid but amusing foreign fops. (It was always an actors' hangout, too. Olivier and his wife Joan Plowright were regulars at one point.) And the modest size of the Blue Bar was almost certainly part of its attraction: It felt boiled down, concentrated, as if it weren't just a bar but rather *the* bar, the essence of bar.

Its feeling of connection with the past notwithstanding, though, the surprising truth about the Blue Bar is that it wasn't really all that old, at least not in the form in which I knew it. Nobody seems to remember exactly when it opened. One former Algonquin employee dates it from 1933, but Frank Case's memoir of the hotel, *Tales of a Wayward Inn,* published in 1938, makes no mention of it. One thing is certain, though: It looked very different in its early days than it did when it closed. The ceiling of the original version was high and flat, reportedly giving the room a vaguely eerie, cavelike feeling. The bar itself was in the shape of a truncated horseshoe, curving out from the north wall. That square wood pillar was behind the bar, not in front of it. There was a blue mirror on one wall, and murals done by some now-forgotten artist of the Ashcan School.

The man who turned the room into the Blue Bar I so delighted in was Andrew Anspach, who became manager of the Algonquin in 1956 or '57 (he doesn't recall which). "Changing the Blue Bar was the first thing I did when I got to the hotel," he told me recently. "I did it with great temerity, because tampering with something like that was going straight in the face of tradition. But the old Blue Bar had changed over the years anyway. It must have been quite handsome once, but by the time I got there, the murals had been painted over and all kinds of little alterations had been made. Whatever charm it had had in the first place had been ruined by people fiddling with it. It was just ugly." His philosophy of renovation, he adds, was (and remains) "not that you don't change something, but that you don't change it in a way that *changes* it."

Anspach dropped the ceiling and installed a cove in the center of it. The chandelier, he notes, was something special—an unusual turn-of-the-century pewter piece made by the Caldwell Chandelier Company, "the Tiffany of Philadelphia." "Because pewter is so soft," says Anspach, "you almost never see it used for anything this large. That's why the designer strengthened it with copper." Two such chandeliers were produced; the other was installed in the smoking room at showman Billy Rose's uptown mansion. Both were decorated with a nautical theme. "I would have preferred to find a chandelier that had to do with the arts, or theatre, or music," notes Anspach.

Anspach also added fine mahogany paneling ("The room was actually constructed somewhere in Queens by the best people in the business"), and, at the suggestion of noted Broadway set designer Oliver Smith—who also redid the hotel's Rose Room restaurant and created summer slipcovers for the lobby—he had the windows facing Forty-fourth Street beautifully etched.

"The new Blue Bar worked from the first day," remembers Anspach. "It looked from the first day as if it had always been there. It was absolutely consistent with the feeling of the rest of the hotel. I remember that one day, shortly after it opened, I was standing there looking at it and I overheard a smart-looking young man in his twenties, with his arm draped around a young lady, saying 'This bar has been here forever. I've been coming here for years.' It was a moment of great satisfaction to me."

Nobody knows how the Blue Bar got its name. Anspach once asked Margaret Case Harriman, Frank Case's daughter (and herself the author of a book about the hotel) if she knew where the name came from, and even she had never heard an explanation. "Like a lot of things about the

Algonquin," Anspach concludes, "it's just something that nobody knows."

The Blue Bar closed for the last time early Sunday morning, March 11, 1990. I had meant to stop by for one last drink that night, but was having dinner with a friend, lost track of the time, and arrived at the Algonquin just as the bar was closing. I stepped inside for a moment anyway, just to pay my respects, and so can claim to have been the last non-employee out of the place—but I can't quite say the last *customer*.

Later in March, I wrote to the hotel inquiring about the fate of the room. The "executive assistant manager" replied, assuring me that the Blue Bar would reopen in substantially its old form on May 1, 1990—after it was cleaned up and given "a fresh coat of paint." (This was a bit unsettling in itself, incidentally, since the only painted surface in the place was the ceiling.) As it happens, it did not reopen, and the room has since been turned into an office—dun-colored file cabinets, fluorescent lights, and mustard-yellow office chairs behind that beautiful etched glass.

Today, the Algonquin's once warm and welcoming lobby has turned uncomely and inhospitable: A folding screen just inside the door blocks ingress, both physical and psychological, into the heart of the room; a service bar crammed into the corner behind the door and an unattractive coat-check counter now occupy most of its southern flank. And past the coat-check counter, above the threshold of Cesar Park's "very English-looking, very *clubby* but not *pubby* bar"—which is coldly lit, pointlessly roomy, and utterly without charm—there is now a little back-lit sign. It reads: The Blue Bar. Don't you believe it.

RECIPE

*T*HE WORLD'S BEST MARTINI

MAKES 1 COCKTAIL

The two most famous bartenders in the modern-day Blue Bar were Jimmy Fox, who worked days, and George Sroka, who had the night shift. Both of them had started there in 1946, before its renovation. When Fox retired in 1982, Sroka moved to days—and an ex-journalist from Brooklyn (by way of Los Angeles and Chicago) named David Grinstead took over in the evenings. Though Grinstead remained a writer at heart (he is the author of two novels, The Earth Movers *and* Promises of Freedom*), he was also a first-class creator of cocktails, among them a stylish Sazerac, a textbook-perfect Sidecar, a dangerous but engaging "New York Margarita," and, above all, what may well have been the world's best Martini. This is his recipe.*

As you will notice, Grinstead is quite specific about his choice of brands. "A number of other good gins don't suit a Martini in my opinion," he says. "Tanqueray's too per-fumey, Beefeater's a bit bland." It is also very important, he believes, to use a proper Martini glass—"clear, stemmed, straight-sided, V-shaped, chilled." The Pernod, which will certainly be seen as heresy by most dedicated Martini drinkers, is imperceptible if added in the properly meager proportions. It merely "brings out" the flavors of the other ingredients, Grinstead believes.

2 to 3 ounces Bombay, Bombay Sapphire, or Boodles gin
¹/₂ to 1 teaspoon Boissière or Noilly Prat dry vermouth
Pernod
1 good-quality Spanish olive

Fill a cocktail shaker or mixing glass with ice, then pour in gin and add vermouth. Dip a bar sip (narrow plastic straw) into Pernod to the depth of about $1/8$ inch, then swirl the moistened end into the gin. Stir 2 revolutions (no more!) and strain into glass. Add olive and serve.

26
RUMINATIONS

"So some strange thoughts transcend our wonted themes. . . ."
—HENRY VAUGHAN, "THEY ARE ALL GONE INTO
THE WORLD OF LIGHT"

1. WHAT IS A BISTRO?

A BISTRO IS NOT A BRASSERIE. THE TERMS ARE not interchangeable. Brasseries are Alsatian in origin. The word itself is French for "brewery" (if singer Pierre Brasseur were English, he'd be Pete Brewer), and the brasserie is so called because it was originally attached to a beermaking facility—or at least specialized in beer. Brasseries are by definition large, open, noisy places; their menus are usually long, and, whatever else they may offer, there are nearly always oysters, soup, and *choucroute* (and beer).

Bistros are by definition small, intimate, low-key. Though they exist all over France and may serve dishes from any region, they are above all a Parisian phenomenon, and there they tend to specialize in the cooking of Lyon, the Auvergne, and the Gascon Southwest. They are often family-owned and are (at least theoretically) moderately priced. Organ meats (calf's liver, pig's feet, sweetbreads, etc.) are basic to the bistro menu, as are small steaks and roasted chicken, and such homestyle "cooked" dishes as *boeuf bourgignonne, coq au vin, pot au feu,* and *hachis Parmentier* (the French version of shepherd's pie). There isn't usually much fresh fish on bistro menus (other than in the occasional "fish bistro"), though herring, sardines, and salt cod show up frequently. There are nearly always pâtés and terrines, potatoes in numerous simple forms, and plenty of white beans, lentils, flageolets, and such. Minor wines flow freely.

Bistros are the roots of French cuisine: They nourish it, giving it direction and support. They safeguard culinary standards and traditions. They even have an influence on sophisticated contemporary French cooking, providing chefs with a basic repertoire to challenge or improve upon and, increasingly, lending actual culinary vocabulary to far grander restaurants.

Nobody disputes that. What nearly everybody who has ever stepped inside a bistro seems to have a conflicting opinion on, though, is what the word "bistro"—or, as it is sometimes written, "bistrot"—actually means.

According to the *Larousse Gastronomique,* the word first appeared in 1884. (It does not say where.) There is a popular theory that the word derives from the Russian word *bystro,* meaning "quickly." The story is that Russian soldiers in Paris in the early nineteenth century used to sneak into local restaurants for a bite to eat against their officers' orders, and were always shouting *"Bystro!"* to the waiters so that they could get served before they got caught. That's an amusing conjecture, but it doesn't explain why the xenophobic French would so readily turn a Russian adverb into a noun describing a quintessentially French institution—or where the word languished between the early 1800s and its debut in (according to Larousse) 1884.

A simpler and perhaps more plausible explanation is that the word comes from *"bistouille,"* sometimes pronounced as *"bistrouille,"* a northern French slang term for coffee spiked with brandy—itself a contraction of *bis* (twice) and *touiller* (to mix). Still other theories suggest that it comes from *bistreau,* a western French term for cowherd, and by extension a jolly fellow of the sort who might frequent a pleasant little restaurant; from *bastringue,* an archaic term for dance hall; or from *bistre,* which is a yellowish-brown pigment whose color is not unlike that of smoke-darkened bistro walls.

Robert Giraud, in his lexicon of bistro slang, *L'Argot du bistro,* offers still another etymology for the word that is so stunningly tortuous, so rich in associations, that one wants to believe in it no matter how unlikely it might seem: It begins with *setier,* a now-obsolete liquid measure (corresponding to eight French pints). This, says Giraud, was first abbreviated to *stroc,* by adding the jocular suffix *"oc"* to the three consonants, *"s," "t,"* and *"r."* Next came the term *mi-stroc,* or half-*setier,* which was applied both to a liquid measure and by extension to a person who sold (potable) liquids.

Mi-stroc evolved into *mastroquet,* meaning an innkeeper, and *mastroquet* in turn, through mispronunciation and trips through several varieties of Parisian argot, became *bistroquet.* An obvious French abbreviation of this word would be *bistrot*—at first still referring to a person, but then eventually coming to mean the place where such a person presided.

This derivation also explains, adds Giraud, why early twentieth-century texts use both masculine and feminine forms of the word—so that a bistro owned by a man might be properly described as a *bistrot,* but one owned by a woman would more correctly be called a *bistrote.*

On the other hand, I guess, the word might have been coined by the ancient astronauts, or maybe by inhabitants of the Lost Continent of Mu.

2. *SPOON FOOD*

The spoon begins and ends it all. It is the first eating utensil most of us, at least in Western countries, are allowed to wield as babies. It is frequently the last utensil we are trusted with as well, when we are elderly and toothless. In-between times, we might stab and jab and pierce our food with forks, and slash and saw and slice our food with knives; we might even fumble inefficiently (or operate with unexpected grace) with chopsticks. But our life is bracketed by spoons—cradled, in a sense, in those con-cave bowls defined by blunt round edges.

Between the brackets, in conventional adult life, the spoon doesn't count for much. It is not a sexy article or, certainly, a dangerous one. (I'm sure that Scotland Yard has in its archives record of at least one or two cases of murder by spoon, but a spoon is obviously no knife in that regard.) The spoon is passive—in an earlier time it might have been safely called "feminine." (It doesn't penetrate; it accepts.) On the contemporary table, it is pretty much relegated to ancillary functions—stirring the tea or coffee, scooping out the marmalade or chutney, transferring such peripheral (unsexy) foods as oatmeal, ice cream, or boiled eggs from vessel to maw.

Oh, there's soup, of course. Soup pretty much demands the service of a spoon, and soup can be an interesting enough dish. But, frankly, soup is rarely *important* food; it's luncheon fare, or a minor part of a major dinner, or even sometimes just an improvised last-minute something to stave off a sudden hunger ("soup" and "sop" have a common etymology, remember), and thus can't be said to bestow any particular gastronomic distinction on the spoon.

But the spoon—soft-edged, capacious, linked to what might well be our earliest sensory memories—is the most reassuring of utensils, the most comforting. Spoons feel good to hold, and good to eat from. They sometimes seem almost part of the food—not tined weaponry to hold it wriggling, but intimate apparel, giving it shape. They're also the only implement that delivers food dependably to the mouth in context, complete with sauce, seasonings, precious juices, the accoutrements, the gestalt. The plain truth is that a great lot of food tastes *better* with a spoon. And, maybe at least partially because someone has noticed these qualities in the spoon at last (or admitted them), there are isolated signs abroad that the spoon might find new credibility on the table of the '90s.

There is, for instance, a popular Tuscan dish called *pappa al pomodoro* (literally "pap with tomatoes") that started out as fare for infants (and probably the very poor), and that has recently found its way onto the menus at many of the best Italian restaurants both in Italy itself and in America. Efforts to identify this concoction as a soup, which some restaurants have made, are ludicrous. *Pappa al pomodoro* is a thick gruel of country bread torn into pieces, soaked in olive oil, and mixed with fresh chopped tomatoes. It is mush, and (if made correctly) it is delicious. And it is eaten with a spoon.

Then there's the recipe for "duck you can eat with a spoon" offered by Paula Wolfert in her recent book, *Paula Wolfert's World of Food*. Based on a traditional southwestern French recipe called *canard à la cuillère,* this is a densely flavorful, almost (but not quite) disintegrated whole duck that has been pot-roasted for five hours with red wine, duck fat, and herbs. The preferred method of consuming this dish is hardly in doubt.

In another part of France, three-star chef Roger Vergé

(of the Moulin de Mougins in Mougins) places a fork *and* a large spoon alongside his famous *gigot d'agneau au côte-rôtie braisé pendant sept heures*—leg of lamb braised with pigs' feet for seven hours in good red wine—and while the fork might work perfectly well for the lamb, you'll need the spoon to taste the *cooking*. In London, Alastair Little serves his fricassée of lamb and lamb sweetbreads with peas and mint in a wide, low-shouldered bowl with a big spoon at the ready. In Los Angeles, Michel Richard recommends a spoon with his chicken and mushroom risotto.

The use of spoons can go too far, of course. At La Mamounia in Marrakesh, a spoon is proffered as the proper implement with couscous. This is one spoon too many. Spoons with couscous are for the gringos. The correct utensil here is formed with the thumb and first two fingers of the right hand. Come to think of it, that might work pretty well with *pappa al pomodoro,* too.

3. YELLOW PAGES

One December evening in Des Moines, about ten years ago, sitting around my hotel room waiting for the fun to start, I sort of accidentally started leafing through the local Yellow Pages just to kill some time. Not surprisingly, given my proclivities, I soon found myself deep in the restaurant ads. I wasn't looking for a place to eat. I guess I must just have thought that a quick glance at this catalogue of local eateries might tell me something I didn't already know about the town. And indeed it did.

I learned, for example, that "When in Rome it's Alfredo's . . . When in Des Moines it's Anjo's." I learned that there were sixty-two pizza places in the area—roughly one for every 3,000 inhabitants. I learned that there was a Chinese restaurant in town called The Conference Room of the Nine Dragons, which made me wonder just for a moment if maybe Des Moines wasn't in the forefront of

Sino-American economic relations. Oh, and I learned that ethnic sensitivity wasn't the community's strong suit—not with all those sandwich parlors advertising "guinea grinders" (and "geuinea grinders," and "guini grinders"), and with the Hilltop Restaurant and Lounge billing itself as "Home of the Da-Go Burger."

I was hooked. Since that evening in Des Moines, I've made it a point to turn to the Yellow Pages restaurant listings wherever I go, and I think I've learned a fair amount about this country, gastronomic and otherwise, by doing so.

The most obvious thing such listings reveal, of course, is what people like to eat in one place or another. And sometimes this is a surprise. That there are a lot of German restaurants in Milwaukee and quite a few Portuguese places in New Bedford, Massachusetts, will probably not come as a surprise to anyone who has an elementary grasp of ethnic distribution in the United States. But who would have imagined all those Mexican restaurants in Anchorage (though I suppose the fact that residents of a cold northern capital would favor colorful and spicy cooking makes perfect sense), or all those Greek places in Montgomery, Alabama?

Who, for that matter, would have guessed that fully a third of the restaurant display ads in the Gary, Indiana, Yellow Pages would name frogs' legs as a specialty, or that nearly a quarter of those in the Harrisburg, Pennsylvania, book would mention veal? And who would have guessed that J.J.'s Boiler Room in Waipouli, on the island of Kauai, would billboard a "Famous Slavonic Steak"?

Yellow Pages restaurant ads can teach you broader lessons about a city, too. Those in the Savannah book, for example, reveal that age and history are highly regarded in the city, with ads for such places as the River's End, "A Restaurant in the Tradition of Savannah's Gracious Past"; the Exchange Tavern, "Elegant Colonial Cuisine on Savannah's Historic Waterfront"; the Johnny Harris Restaurant, "World Famous Since 1924"; even the Canton Restaurant, "Since 1930—Savannah's Oldest Chinese Restaurant."

The listings for Fort Wayne, Indiana, on the other hand, reveal the place immediately as a good place to raise your kids up—a real family-oriented community: At Tourney's Family Restaurant, for instance, "Our Family Is Looking Forward to Serving Yours"; Hilgers Farm Restaurant is "Famous for our Family Style Home Cooking"; the Old Country Buffet offers "Variety and Value for the Whole Family"; the Speedway Café/J.R.'s bills itself as "Fort Wayne's Family Owned Steak House"; Don Pedro Fonda is "One of Fort Wayne's Oldest Family Restaurants"; and on and on.

I've always loved restaurant mottoes in general, whether they ultimately tell you anything about a place or not—and of course the Yellow Pages are full of them. Some are predictably hyperbolic. Grampa's Catfish House in Little Rock, for instance, not only claims to serve the "Best Catfish in Central Arkansas" but adds, "If'n the Kernel [sic] fried chicken like we fry catfish he'd-a-been a general!" The Venice Club in the Milwaukee area grandly promises "The Soul of Italy in the Heart of Brookfield." And then there's the Boar's Head in that aforementioned tradition-minded town in Georgia, which bills itself blithely as "One of the Only True Restaurants in Savannah."

Other restaurant mottoes, in contrast, are charmingly modest. The Dragon Palace in Corpus Christi characterizes itself merely as "One of the First Exclusive Chinese Restaurants in the Uptown Area." The First Edition in Sioux Falls asks only that we remember it for having "The Sioux Empire's Most Raved About Salad Bar." And there are no superlatives at all at the Original Hick'ry Pit in Novato, California—just the promise of "Pork from Pigs That Made Hogs of Themselves."

The Yellow Pages, of course, also record changes in a

community. In today's Des Moines restaurant ads, for instance, not a single establishment uses the word "guinea" or any of its variants, and the "Da-Go Burger" has dagone. The number of pizza places, on the other hand, has swelled to ninety-eight. And, in Des Moines, it's still Anjo's . . .

4. MARKET VALUE

In my ideal world, we would all shop for food every day, and would buy things, insofar as possible, *of* the day. Daily food shopping restores food to the place of conscious importance I think it ought to have in our lives. And buying fresh rather than processed or packaged food keeps the act of food shopping from becoming boring, a travail.

The contents of the supermarket freezer bin and the processed-food shelves remain pretty much the same from day to day, month to month. Shopping for such items is, by definition, repetitious. You make a list, you check it off, you take home the same bright packages you took home last time—ho hum. . . .

Imagine, instead, shopping daily in an old-fashioned market, one composed of stalls and stands, presided over (at least in some cases) by the people who actually grew or made the food they sell. The inventory of items available would change literally daily, according to the weather, the season, the exigencies of the marketplace. You'd never know exactly what you were going to find. You would be challenged—but you wouldn't be bored.

I wrote in my introduction to this book about what I feel is our cultural disconnection from food. Shopping at a market of this kind would reconnect us with what we eat almost automatically. We'd see things in their natural state. We'd encounter species of edibles we've never seen before. We'd be forced to ask, "What do you do with these?" "How long do you cook them?" "Can you eat the green part?"

We'd also have a choice of price, variety, and quality, even for familiar items, that no supermarket can match. Oh, and we wouldn't bring home all that extraneous packaging material that supermarket food is always wrapped in, either; if we shop with our own mesh or canvas sacks, we wouldn't even need grocery bags.

Now, I have nothing against supermarkets. They're wondrous institutions, bright, clean, beautiful, and richly stocked, and we're lucky to have them. They are part of a food-distribution system that is truly elegant in its sophistication and efficiency. But isn't it precisely our insistence on having every kind of food imaginable, whenever we want it, that has led to the development and market primacy of so many frozen, canned, and highly processed foods? Don't we eat such items not only for the sake of convenience, but also because they promise instant gratification—because the recipe calls for peas and you can't get fresh ones all year long and we're not about to wait until they come around again?

It would be churlish (and dishonest) of me to vilify canned and frozen goods unequivocally—and I always think it's a bit silly when I hear ardent lovers of "natural food" reject them out of hand. They serve their purpose, and we all (or most of us) use them sometimes. My own kitchen is seldom without frozen lima beans, frozen black-eyed peas, canned tomatoes, white beans, and, of course, tuna and anchovies.

Anyway, humankind has been "processing" food for thousands of years, and for the same reason people freeze and can food: to preserve it. Drying, curing, pickling, salting, even fermenting are all methods of preservation, and all of them significantly alter both the physical properties and the flavors of food—yet nobody condemns ham or pickles or wine as perversions of nature.

On the other hand, I think we use canned and frozen and other packaged foods far too much. We depend on them. And in so doing, we come to value convenience and predictability more than flavor. The Crown Prince canned-fish company ran a radio commercial a while back, in which the theme was (I paraphrase), "When you go to those fancy fish restaurants, sometimes you have to wait so long for your food that they must be phoning out to some boat to catch your fish to order—so why not buy our canned fish instead and not have to wait?" My God, *imagine* if you could somehow get fish caught to order in a restaurant! It would damned well be *worth* waiting a long time for! Er, but not, of course, very convenient.

Then there's the commercial bakery in Oakland whose motto, writ large on a billboard outside the place, is KIRKPATRICK'S BREAD STAYS FRESH LONGER. What the firm is selling, in other words, isn't the way the bread tastes but the length of time over which it remains edible. There's something very wrong with that notion. Bread's duty isn't to last, it's to get consumed with pleasure.

My wife went to pick up a specially ordered birthday cake one Saturday morning at the La Brea Bakery, arguably L.A.'s best breadmaker. She'd never seen it in action, and she came back wide-eyed. "All those sacks of flour and grains," she said, "those ovens, all the people working, the great smells, the people lined up to buy stuff that just got made—that place was *great*." Of course it was. And nobody cares how long the bread stays fresh, because it's so good that there's never any left the next day anyway.

Old-fashioned markets do exist in some cities, of course, and small farmers' markets are experiencing a genuine revival around the country. Still, few of us have the time or inclination to shop every day. We've got better things to do. Or do we?

5. MR. BLUCHER'S CHILDREN

I was having a late lunch one day at Scaletta in Milan when four young, animated Americans rushed in, apologized to the host for their lateness, then occupied a large table and began chattering. It was easy to discern from their ebullient conversation that the four worked for a particularly successful, high-profile restaurant company in the Midwest, and had spent the morning (and most probably the past few days) visiting other restaurants, taking photographs and notes, seeking inspiration. "So-and-So had an interesting concept," one would say. "The sauces at Such-and-Such were pretty good," another would announce. "I think we can try something like What's-His-Name does," a third would add.

I would bet that the four had already eaten (or at least "eaten") at at least one or two other restaurants apiece that morning, separately, and were now comparing notes. All seemed to be scribbling furiously, in any case. One got up in the midst of lunch to prowl the dining room with his Polaroid, snapping photos. At one point, they proudly showed the restaurant's proprietor pictures of one of their own establishments back home. He muttered something polite.

The next day, I drove out of Milan for lunch at Sole in nearby Maleo. The four were there, too, still snapping photos, taking notes, discussing "concepts," and the like.

Now, I know that these young men were only doing their job, and I'm sure that their research has resulted in new and better Italian food being served in at least one corner of the United States—in fact, I find this company's eateries to be quite good on average, and frequently quite innovative—but nonetheless something about them bothered me.

In the old days, Americans on the Grand Tour used to come home from Europe carting art and artifacts of every kind, sometimes literally stolen or chipped from larger works. The literary exemplar of this particular brand of Ugly Yankee is a Mr. Blucher, who was one of Mark Twain's traveling companions on the journey he records in *The Innocents Abroad*. Blucher was forever collecting fragments of bone and shards of sculpture, hacking them off statues when required, and imputing to them preposterous provenances, with a view toward impressing his aunt back home. Twain notes:

> This person gathers mementos with a perfect recklessness nowadays, mixes them all up together, and then serenely labels them without any regard to truth, propriety, or even plausibility.... I remonstrate against these outrages upon reason and truth, of course, but it does no good. I get the same tranquil, unanswerable reply every time: "It don't signify—the old woman won't know any different."

My four young Americans, I couldn't help thinking, were doing something of the same kind—chipping, stealing, packing up local artifacts to take home and reassemble willy-nilly. However good their intentions might have been, there was something distinctly mercenary about their activities. There was also, I thought, something insultingly perfunctory about they way they were digesting (or nibbling at without digesting) the results of a couple of thousand years of culinary tradition. Like the tourists who run through the Louvre to see the three most famous paintings, they seemed to be saying, "We don't have all day; just show us the best stuff and let us get out of here." They might also have been saying, or at least thinking, too, "It don't signify—the [folks back home] won't know any different." And maybe worst of all, I'm not sure that, in all their haste and desire to assimilate, they even enjoyed their food.

6. NOW, WAIT A MINUTE

"Waitperson" is surely one of the more preposterous and cumbersome of the supposedly "nonsexist" neologisms with which our language has been saddled in recent years. "Waitress" is a gender-specific term, and if female restaurant servers choose not to use it to describe themselves, I think that's fine. But the alternative then ought to be simply "waiter." "Waiter" is not gender-specific. The "er" at the end of the word, that is, is *not* a masculine suffix—at least not any longer; like "or," it simply indicates a person or thing that performs a certain function. I cite as my authority for this statement *The Oxford English Dictionary,* whose entry on "er" reads in part, "The agent-nouns in -*er* normally denote personal agents (originally, only male persons, though this restriction is now *wholly obsolete*)" (italics mine).

There is simply no need for the coinage "waitperson," then. And there is neither need nor excuse for two other coinages I've heard: In a restaurant in Seattle I was once introduced, by the woman who ran the place, to "our maître-person." (Apparently she didn't realize that in the phrase maître d'hôtel it is the former and not the latter word that is gender-specific, and that if she were going to neologize in the first place, perhaps she ought to have turned the phrase into something like "person d'hôtel" or even "person d'." Of course, then we lose the sense that the person so described is in charge of the place. How about "master-person d'," then. No, wait. There's that nasty old "er" suffix again. Okay. Here's the final form, guaranteed to be, as they say, politically correct: "mast-person person d'." Whew. Glad we got that straight.)

And at another restaurant, this one in Los Angeles, I actually heard reference made one evening to the "*maître-dame*"—that is, the "master-lady." (I refrained from asking if this master-lady's name was by any chance

Mistress Sonia, and, if so, if she would mind punishing me for having been such a naughty boy and eaten all my foie gras.) These terms, I am happy to report, do not appear to have become widespread and are too ridiculous even to merit response.

But "waitperson" has become very common in the restaurants of America today, and should indeed, I believe, be responded to, and discouraged, at every opportunity. And you don't have to go all etymological to do it, either. The next time somebody announces himself or herself at your table as a "waitperson," just ask to see his or her driverperson's license, or inquire if he or she is by any chance a jogperson, or perhaps a loveperson of Chinese food.

7. THE MULE DROVER WITH THE KEYS

In old Provençal, a *saumatier* was a horse drover, a man in charge of pack animals. In French, the word turned into *sometier* and then *sommelier*, and came to mean not some sort of early (literal) teamster, but instead a court official in charge of the transportation of supplies. Eventually, since about the most important supply anyone can transport in France is wine, the term took on its present meaning: an individual in charge of hauling wine up from the cellar—a wine steward.

Unfortunately, all too many sommeliers today, in France and America alike, know so little about their supposed métier, or evince such contempt for their customers while practicing it, that they probably ought to be sent back to herding ponies.

I must quickly add that there are also many adept and sensitive practitioners of the trade out there—men (and, increasingly, women) who know their job and discharge their responsibilities with intelligence and grace. (I think immediately of Eric Mancio at Guy Savoy, Didier Bureau at Clos Longchamps, and the appropriately named Eric

Bordelais at Arpège, all in Paris; of Custodio Zamarra at Zalacain in Madrid; and of Mark Slater, who was for some years manager and chef sommelier at Jean-Louis at the Watergate in Washington, D.C.)

But then there are characters like the wine steward in Washington, D.C., who, upon taking my order for what was then a five-year-old bottle of Châteauneuf-du-Pape, added in hushed tones, "If you don't mind, I'd really rather not move your wine across the room in the bottle. I'd like to decant it in the wine room and then present it to you, so I don't disturb it any more than necessary." Now, this was a wine so young and sturdy, mind you, that you could have tossed it across the Potomac without much damaging it—but even the rarest, most sediment-filled old Bordeaux ought to survive a walk of fifty feet or so. Did our sommelier honestly not know this? Or did he hope to impress us with his pretentious mock-concern? Last question: Which would have been worse?

Or like the guy at that two-star restaurant in Paris, who noticed some perfectly harmless tartrate crystals at the bottom of our bottle of St. Joseph Blanc. "Ah," he purred, as if imparting great wisdom, "there's some sugar in your wine." Did he really not know tartrates from sugar? Did he really believe that there is any process by which sugar could possibly drop out of St. Joseph Blanc? Or was he just having sport with us—Americans, who obviously didn't know anything about wine?

Or like the sommelier at that venerable three-star in Burgundy who, after bringing us the wines I had ordered (a white Hermitage and a grand cru Beaujolais), and pouring the first of them for me to taste, ignored our table for the rest of the evening, literally not touching either bottle again. (He was not particularly busy that evening, I hasten to add. I have the impression that he either disdained our wine selection or didn't like Americans in general.)

Or like the wine stewards all over America who, when asked for a particular bottle, reply, "What number is it?" In my opinion, any person who styles himself a sommelier and then asks that question ought to have his or her emblems of authority (which are traditionally a silver *tastevin*, or tasting cup, and crossed cellar keys on the lapel) stripped off on the spot.

The problem here is twofold, I think. First, many so-called sommeliers are simply untrained and unprepared to do their job. They're typically waiters or managers doing double duty instead of the specialists they ought to be. Second, I think both the dining public and wine stewards themselves (and/or the restaurateurs who put them up to it) misconceive the sommelier's role. A wine steward ought to be the diner's friend, or at least the diner's adviser. He should never condescend, never push pricey bottles or gratuitously show off his arcane knowledge. A sommelier's job is to know the food on the menu, know the wines on the list, know his customers, and then know how to put all three together in the way that best serves them all. Any sommelier who can't handle that job ought to pack it in.

Bibliography

FOOD, DRINK, TRAVEL, ETC.

Adams, Charlotte. *The Four Seasons Cookbook.* New York: Ridge Press/Crescent Books, 1971.

Adventures in Good Eating, a Duncan Hines Book. Bowling Green, KY: Adventures in Good Eating, Inc., 1947.

Andrieu, Pierre. *Fine Bouche: A History of the Restaurant in France.* Translated by Arthur L. Hayward. London: Cassell and Company Ltd., 1956.

Androuët, Pierre. *The Complete Encyclopedia of French Cheese.* Translated by John Githens. New York: Harper's Magazine Press, 1973.

Ash, Russell, and Bernard Higton. *Spirit of Place/Provence.* New York: Arcade Publishing, Inc., 1989.

Beebe, Lucius. *Snoot If You Must.* New York: D. Appleton-Century Company, Inc., 1943.

Bertolli, Paul, with Alice Waters. *The Chez Panisse Cookbook.* New York: Random House, 1988.

Bonney, Thérèse and Louise. *A Guide to the Restaurants of Paris.* New York: Robert M. McBride & Company, 1929.

Brady, Roy. *Old Wine, Fine Wine?* Northridge, CA: Santa Susana Press, (California State University, Northridge Libraries), 1990.

Browne, Charles. *The Gun Club Cook Book, or a Culinary Code for Appreciative Epicures*, revised edition. New York: Charles Scribner's Sons, 1939.

Caine, William. *The Glutton's Mirror*. London: T. Fisher Unwin Ltd., 1925.

Capon, Robert Farrar. *The Supper of the Lamb*. Garden City, NY: Doubleday & Company, Inc., 1969.

Case, Frank. *Tales of a Wayward Inn*. New York: Frederick A. Stokes Company, 1938.

Castle, Molly. *Round the World with an Appetite*. London: Hodder & Stoughton Ltd., 1936.

Child, Julia. *From Julia Child's Kitchen*. New York: Knopf, 1975.

Conil, Jean. *Haute Cuisine*. London: Faber & Faber, 1955.

Creasy, Rosalind. *The Complete Book of Edible Landscaping*. San Francisco: Sierra Club Books, circa 1982.

———. *Cooking from the Garden*. San Francisco: Sierra Club Books, 1988.

Deighton, Len. *ABC of French Food*. New York: Bantam Books, 1990.

———. *Où Est le Garlic*. New York: Harper & Row, 1977.

Drury, John. *Dining in Chicago*. New York: The John Day Company, 1931.

Favre, Joseph. *Dictionnaire universel de cuisine practique*. Marseilles: Jeanne Laffitte, 1978. (Reprint of 1905 edition.)

Giraud, Robert. *L'Argot du bistro*. Paris: Marval, 1989.

Guide Gault Millau France. Paris: Médiazur S.A., annual.

Guide Michelin France. Clermont-Ferrand: Michelin et Cie., annual.

Larousse Gastronomique. New American edition, edited by Jenifer Harvey Lang. New York: Crown Publishers, Inc., 1988.

McGee, Harold. *On Food and Cooking: The Science and Lore of the Kitchen*. New York: Charles Scribner's Sons, 1984.

McNeill, F. Marian. *The Scots Kitchen*. Glasgow: Blackie & Son Ltd., 1929.

Meynier, Gil. *Conducted Tour*. Chicago: Thomas S. Rockwell Company, 1931.

Mitchell, Joseph. *Old Mr. Flood*. New York: Duell, Sloan and Pearce, 1948.

Newnham-Davis, Lieut.-Col. *Dinners and Diners: Where and How to Dine in London.* London: Grant Richards Ltd., 1899.

———. *The Gourmet's Guide to Europe,* 3rd ed. London: Grant Richards Ltd., 1911.

———. *The Gourmet's Guide to London.* London: Grant Richards Ltd., 1914.

Rector, George. *The Rector Cook Book.* Chicago: Rector Publishing Co., 1928.

Robert-Robert. *Le Guide du gourmand à Paris,* 9th ed. Paris: Bernard Grasset, 1922.

Robuchon, Joël. *Ma Cuisine pour vous.* Paris: Robert Laffont, 1986.

Root, Waverly. *Food.* New York: Simon & Schuster, 1980.

Saintsbury, George. *Notes on a Cellar-Book.* London & Basingstoke: Macmillan London Ltd., 1978.

Saulnier, L. *Le Répertoire de la Cuisine,* 13th ed. Translated by E. Brunet. London: Leon Jaeggi & Sons Ltd., n.d.

Story, Sommerville. *Paris à la Carte: Where the Frenchman Dines and How.* London: A.M. Philpot Ltd., [circa 1922?].

Street, Julian. *Where Paris Dines.* Garden City, NY: Doubleday, Doran & Company, Inc., 1929.

Tannahill, Reay. *Food in History.* New York: Stein and Day, 1973.

Thorne, John. *Simple Cooking.* New York: Viking, 1987.

Twain, Mark. *The Innocents Abroad.* New York: New American Library, 1966.

Wells, Patricia. *Simply French: Patricia Wells Presents the Cuisine of Joël Robuchon.* New York: William Morrow & Company, Inc., 1991.

Wolfert, Paula. *Paula Wolfert's World of Food.* New York: Harper & Row, 1988.

OTHER WORKS CITED OR QUOTED

Acton, Harold. *Memoirs of an Aesthete, 1939–1969.* New York: Viking, 1971.

Andrews, Robert Hardy. *A Corner of Chicago.* Boston: Little, Brown and Company, 1963.

Bibliography

Benchley, Robert. *My Ten Years in a Quandry, and How They Grew,* 15th ed. New York and London: Harper & Bros., 1936.

Bierce, Ambrose. *The Devil's Dictionary.* Cleveland: World Publishing Co., 1943.

Boswell, James, esq. *The Life of Samuel Johnson, LL.D.,* a new edition with numerous additions and notes by John Wilson Croker, LL.D., F.R.S., Vol. 1. London: John Murray, 1831.

Brodeur, Paul. *The Zapping of America.* New York: Norton Publishing, 1977.

Ford, Ford Madox. *It Was the Nightingale.* London: William Heinemann Ltd., 1934.

———. *Provence: From the Minstrels to the Machine.* Philadelphia: J.B. Lippincott Co., 1935.

Grinstead, David. *The Earth Movers.* Boston: The Atlantic Monthly Press, 1980.

———. *Promises of Freedom.* New York: Crown Publishers, Inc., 1991.

Ibsen, Henrik. *Eleven Plays of Henrik Ibsen.* New York: The Modern Library, 1957.

Kerr, Jean. *Poor Richard.* Garden City, NY: Doubleday & Company, Inc., 1965.

McGinley, Phyllis. *On the Contrary.* Garden City, NY: Doubleday, Doran & Co., 1934.

The Oxford English Dictionary, 2nd ed. Oxford: Clarendon Press; New York: Oxford University Press, 1989.

Potter, Beatrix. *The Complete Tales of Beatrix Potter.* London, New York, etc.: F. Warne & Co., 1989.

Ruskin, John. *Modern Painters.* Boston: Dana Estes & Co., 1873.

Southern, Terry. *Red-Dirt Marijuana and Other Tastes.* New York: New American Library, 1967.

Tennyson, Alfred Lord. *A Collection of Poems by Alfred Tennyson.* Garden City, NY: Doubleday & Company, Inc., 1972.

Thurber, James. *Collecting Himself: James Thurber on Writing and Writers, Humor and Himself.* New York: Harper & Row, 1989.

Vaughan, Henry. *The Complete Poetry of Henry Vaughan.* Edited by French Rowe Fogel. New York: W.W. Norton, 1969.

Recipe Index

Apple Pie, French, 263

Beef
  Boeuf à la Mode Pepita, 178
  Hamburger, The Alice Waters, 187
  Roast, Hash, Orson Welles', 261
  Steak, Deep-Fried, Joe Brodsky's, 114
Brains, Deep-Fried, with Sherry Butter Sauce and Fried Capers, 94
Bread, Steve Hope, 30
Brussels Sprout Soup, Cream of, 15

Calamares Atacados por Piranas Bidimensionales, 246
Caviar, Country-Style, 112
Chicken
  Grilled Breasts with Creamed Corn, 19
  Homecoming, 160
  à la King, 244
Chili, Catalan, 46
Chutney, Orange Marmalade in Peppered Shortbread Cups, Scots Rabbit Curry with, 85
Cole Slaw, Scallop, 75
Crabmeat-and-Mashed-Potato Enchiladas in Sweet Red Pepper Sauce, 65
Croques-Monsieurs, Petits, 228

Enchiladas, Crabmeat-and-Mashed-Potato, in Sweet Red Pepper Sauce, 65

Fettuccine Alfredo, 247
Fritto Misto, Insalata di, 62

Hamburger, The Alice Waters, 187
Homard (lobster) au Whisky, 180

Kidney Bean and Sweet Red Pepper Purée, 84

Lamb
  Baked in Foil, Greek, 31
  Sweetbreads with Chile Caribe and Posole, 96
Lapin à la Minute, 83

Martini, The World's Best, 279
Melon Ice Cream with Blueberries and Candied Walnuts, 67
Mussels, Ligurian-Style Stuffed, 113

Nesselrode Chiffon Pie, 37

Onion Soup, Sweet, 50
Orange and Fennel Salad with Feta Cheese, 64
Oyster and Sausage Bisque, 14
Pepper, Sweet Red, and Kidney Bean Purée, 84
Persimmon Sorbet with Vodka, 116
Pie
  French Apple, 263
  Nesselrode Chiffon, 37
  Raisin, 39
Pork, Roast Loin of, with Lime Cream Sauce, 20
Potatoes. *See also* Sweet Potato.
  Mashed, and-Crabmeat Enchiladas, 65
  Pommes de Terre Bretonne, 32
  Purée de Pommes de Terre, 139

Recipe Index

Rabbit
  Curry, with Orange Marmalade
    Chutney in Peppered Shortbread
    Cups, Scots, 85
  Lapin à la Minute, 83
Raisin Pie, 39
Ranch Dressing, Homemade, 271
Red Wine Sauce, Great, 215
Rigatoni with Morels and Asparagus,
  16
Risotto, Six-Lily, 48

Salad
  Dressing, Homemade Ranch, 271
  Insalata di Fritto Misto, 62
  Orange and Fennel, with Feta
    Cheese, 64
  Scallop Cole Slaw, 75
  Underground, 74
  Vegetable, Cooked and Raw, 76
Salt Cod Stew, Spicy, 98
Sand Dabs, Fried, with Bacon and
  Thyme, 18
Sauce, Great Red Wine, 215

Scallop Cole Slaw, 75
Sorbet, Persimmon, with Vodka, 116
Soup
  Cream of Brussels Sprout, 15
  Oyster and Sausage Bisque, 14
  Sweet Onion, 50
  Sweet Potato Vichyssoise with Three
    Kinds of Salmon, 60
Spaghetti Cacio e Pepe, 167
Squid, Fried, with Tomatillo Salsa, 246
Steak, Deep-Fried, Joe Brodsky's, 114
Sweet Potato Vichyssoise with Three
    Kinds of Salmon, 60
Sweetbreads, Lamb, with Chile Caribe
    and Posole, 96

Thon (tuna) au Cari, 45
Tomatoes in Tomato Sauce, 115

Underground Salad, 74

Vegetable Salad, Cooked and Raw, 76

Wontons, Unusual, 51

General Index

ABC of French Food (Len Deighton), 128
Adventures in Good Eating (Duncan Hines), 197
Aïoli, real, how it is made, 194–95
Alfredo (Rome), 241
Algonquin Hotel (New York), 274–78
Ambassador East Hotel (Chicago), 250–51, 258
Americans
    changing eating habits of, 1–7
    sampling foreign cuisine, 292–93
Andrews, Colman
    Catalan Cuisine, 46
    food preferences, 91–93, 143–44
    gastronomic epiphany, 36–37
    professional food writer, 117–23
    restaurant preferences, 136, 145–60
Anspach, Andrew, 276–77
Apicius (Paris), 174
Appliances, kitchen, 69–73
L'Argot du bistro (Robert Giraud), 283
Arpège, 204
L'Artois (Paris), 171
Arzak (San Sebastián), 136
Auberge de l'Ill (Illhaeusern), 136
Awards, Holiday Restaurant, 117, 119–21

Barker, Alan, 268–69
Beebe, Lucius, 117, 251
Bemelmans, Ludwig, 117
Benzaldehyde (problem), 230–32
The Best of New York, 108
Biba (Boston), 94
Bistro, defined, 281–84
The Blue Bar, Algonquin Hotel, 275–79
Bocuse, Paul, 150
Bodne, Mr. and Mrs. Ben, 274

Brasserie, defined, 281
Brodsky, Joe, 114
Bruderholz Stucki (Basel), 150–51
Bruschetta, 165
La Buca di Ripetta (Rome), 167
Byfield, Ernie and Kitty, 251

Le Cabestan (Casablanca), 154
Cafè de l'Acadèmia (Barcelona), 94
Café Chauveron (New York), 122
California "New American Cuisine," 125–27
Camille (Duplieux), restaurant captain, notebook of celebrities, 252–61
Case, Frank, 274, 276
Caspar-Jordan, Claude, 146–47, 171–77, 180
Caspar-Jordan, Pepita, 174, 176–77, 178
Castle, Molly, 62, 196–97
Catalan Cuisine (Colman Andrews), 46
Catholicism, gastronomic trappings of, 36
Caves Restaurant (Ft. Lauderdale), 108
Cesar Park Hotels International, 274
Champeaux (Paris), 190–91
Chasen's (Hollywood), 261–62
Chateaubriand, the real, 190–91
Château Woltner, 211
Chefs' training, 128–31
Chez Panisse (Berkeley), 92, 186–87
Chinese food nomenclature, 239
Cigars and cigarettes, opposition to, 199–204
Citrus (Hollywood), 83
Claiborne, Craig, 186
Comme Chez Soi (Brussels), 136
The Complete Encyclopedia of French Cheese (Pierre Androuët), 228
Conducted Tour (Gil Meynier), 241

General Index

The Cook and Housewife's Manual (Margaret Dods), 86
Cook Now, Serve Later, 54
Cooking, 56–59, 127–31. *See also* Food.
Cooks Magazine, 185
Corti, Darrell, 167
La Côte d'Or (Saulieu), 136
La Coupole (Paris), 175
Creasy, Rosalind, 11–12
Critics, 103–11. *See also* Restaurant.
Cuisinart, using, 69–71

Dan Tana's (Los Angeles), 110, 119
"Davis Scale," wine evaluation, 227
De Groot, Roy Andries, 157–58
Deligne, Claude, 146, 148
Le Départ (Paris), 228
Dining in Chicago (John Drury), 198
Dishwasher, automatic, 72–73
Domaine de la Romanée-Conti, 211
Dressings, salad, basic flavors, 266–67
Duquesnoy (Paris), 175

"Eaters" (restaurant scouts), 118–20
Eldorado Petit (Barcelona), 156–58
English food nomenclature, 238–39
Enology. *See* Wine.
Er Cucurucù (Rome), 166
L'Espérance (Saint-Père-sous-Vézelay), 136

Farmers' markets vs. supermarkets, 289–91
Fettuccine Alfredo, 237, 241–42
Fisher, M.F.K., 93
Fonds de cuisine, 130
Food
  changes in eating habits, 1–7
  chefs' attitudes toward, 128–31
  cultural disconnection from, 10–13
  fears and misconceptions about, 7–13
  flavored, real and invented, 266
  gastronomic epiphany, 36–37
  nomenclature, creative, 237–43
  popular culture, 54–55
  preferences and prejudices, 90–93
  "processing," 290–91
  processor, about using, 69–71
  spoon, 284–86
Food (Waverly Root), 41
Food & Wine Experience in Aspen, 229
Food & Wine magazine, 229
The Four Seasons Cookbook (Charlotte Adams), 59
Fox, Jimmy, 279
Franzi, Gianni, 113

French food nomenclature, 238
Fritto misto, 62

Gaja, Angelo, 210
Gastronomic societies, 172
Gault Millau, 118, 149, 150–51, 174
Girardet, Fredy, 53, 150–51
Giraud, Robert, 283
Good Food Guide (Richard Binns, editor), 138
"Gourmet" food, 25–29
The Gourmet's Guide to Europe (Lieut.-Col. Newnham-Davis), 190
"Great" vs. ordinary wines, 207–14
Grinstead, David, 279
Guidebook authors, 192–98
Le Guide du gourmande à Paris (Robert-Robert), 193
Guide Michelin, 136, 137, 147, 149
A Guide to the Restaurants of Paris (Thérèse and Louise Bonney), 195
The Gun Club Cook Book (Charles Browne), 191

Hamburgers (cheeseburgers), 183–87; McLeanburger, 7
Harriman, Margaret Case, 277
Harry's Bar (Venice), 152–53, 186
Hazan, Marcella, 91
Henson, Steve and Gayle, 267–69
Hériot, Raymond, 147
Hidden Valley Guest Ranch
  Cle Elum, Washington, 270
  Santa Barbara, California, 267–69
Hidden Valley Ranch Dressing, 267–71
Hochman, Sal, 108
Holiday (travel magazine), 117–19
  Restaurant Awards, 117, 119–21
Hope, Steve, 30

The Innocents Abroad (Mark Twain), 293
International Wine Auctions, London, 220
Ironic (imaginative) food terms, 239–40
Italian food nomenclature, 239

Jamin (Paris), 139

Kitchen appliances, 69–73

Little, Alastair, 286
Livingston, Jock and Micaela, 62
Los Angeles Times, 11–12, 110–11, 268
Lugán, Nestor, 91

Ma Bourgogne (Paris), 135
Ma Bretagne (Casablanca), 154
La Mamounia (Marrakesh), 286

Maxim's (Paris), 180, 193–94
La Mer (Casablanca), 154
Metropolitan Home, 148, 165
Microwave oven, using, 72
Miller, Mark, 94
Mr. Chow (New York), 108
Al Moro (Rome), 166
Musso & Frank's Grill (Hollywood), 104
Mother's food prejudices, 41
  recipes, 33–35

Nation's Restaurant News, 106, 108, 267
Nesselrode, Karl Robert, Count, 37
"New American Cuisine," 125–27
Newnham-Davis, Lieut.-Col., 190–92
Nickolas, Nick, 107

Ogden, Bradley, 94, 186
Old Wine, Fine Wine? (Roy Brady), 219
On Food and Cooking (Harold McGee), 42
Onions, cooking with, 42–44; varieties, 50
Orange marmalade (Janet Keiller), 86
Organ meats, prejudices against, 90–92
Où est le Garlic? (Len Deighton), 43

Paris à la Carte (Sommerville Story), 194
Parker, Robert, wine critic, 212, 232–33
Paula Wolfert's World of Food (Paula Wolfert), 285
Peppers, stuffing, 57–59
Perry, Charles, 94
Au Petit Rocher (Casablanca), 154
Pic (Valence), 136
Picada (Catalan "sauce"), 46
Piccolo Mondo (Rome), 153, 166, 167
Picolit dessert wines, 212
Pinot Noir seminar, 229–30
Piperno (Rome), 166
Port de Pêche, Le Restaurant du (Casablanca), 154–56
Ports (West Hollywood), 62
"Processing" foods, 290–91
"Professional range," using, 71
Puck, Wolfgang, 127, 186
The Pump Room (Chicago), 251
La Pyramide, 136–37

Rabbit, about eating, 79–83
Rainbow Room (New York), 196–97
Ranch dressing, 265–72
Rattlesnake Club (Denver), 240
The Rector Cook Book (George Rector, 1928), 242
Reichl, Ruth, 91, 93, 94, 110

Restaurant(s)
  ads, yellow pages, 286–89
  creativity in, 128
  critics, 103–11
  ordinary, 158–60
  reviewing standards for, 119, 121
  reviews, 105–6
  three-star, 133–39
Richard, Michel, 83, 286
Robuchon, Joël, 139–40, 150
Rome, dining in the 1970s in, 163–67
La Rotonde (Paris), 175
Round the World with an Appetite (Molly Castle), 62, 196

Sabatini (Rome), 166
St. Estèphe (Manhattan Beach, California), 96
Le St-Séverin (Paris), 228
Salad dressings, basic flavors, 266–67
Scaletta (Milan), 292
Schmidt, Jimmy, 246
The Scots Kitchen (F. Marian McNeill), 85
Sedlar, John, 96
Shaw, David, 202
Sheraton, Mimi, 109, 126
Sherman House Hotel (Chicago), 250–51
Shire, Lydia, 94, 186
Silva, Isabelle and Jean-Pierre, 147–48, 149–50
Simon, André L., 219
Simple Cooking (John Thorne), 150
Simply French; Patricia Wells Presents the Cuisine of Joël Robuchon, 139
Skolsky, Sidney, 261
Smoking, pleasures of, 199–204
Sofregit (onion sauce), 44, 46
Sokolin, William, 218, 220–21
Sole (Maleo), 292
Sommeliers, 295–97
"Speed Cooking," 54
Spitzer, Silas, 117–23
Spoon food, 284–86
Sroka, George, 279
Stewart, Martha, 6
Stillman, Alan, 106
Stoddard's Atop Butler Hall (New York), 197–98
Story, Sommerville, 194–95
Street, Julian, 193
Stucki (Basel), 150–51
Supermarkets vs. farmers' markets, 289–91
Sweet potato vichyssoise (with caviar), 59–60
Swiss restaurants, 150–51

General Index

Taillevent (Paris), 135, 136, 145–47
Tales of a Wayward Inn (Frank Case), 276
Taverna Flavia (Rome), 166
Tchelistcheff, André, 200
Thorne, John, 91
The Three Course Newsletter, 138
Three-star restaurants, 133–39
La Tour d'Argent (Paris), 137
Tower, Jeremiah, 186
Troisgros, Pierre, 134–35
    restaurant (Roanne), 133–35, 137, 139, 157–58

Vázquez Montalbán, Manuel, 44
Vergé, Roger, 285
Le Vieux Moulin (Bouilland), 147–50
    specialties, 149–50
Vincenti, Mauro, 167

"Waitperson," 294–95
Wasserman, Rebecca, 148
Waters, Alice, 91, 127, 186–87
Waxman, Jonathan, 94, 186
Welles, Orson, 261–62
Wells, Patricia, 139–40
Where Paris Dines (Julian Street), 193
Who's Who of celebrities, (from notebook of Camille), 252–61

Wilkinson, Bill, 129
Williamson, Mark and Dominique, 112
Wine(s)
    auction, Napa Valley, 213
    auctions, international, London, 220
    bozo, 231–33; jargon of, 232
    collecting for profit, 217–21
    "Davis Scale," for evaluation, 227
    enology and viticulture, school of, 227
    "great" vs. ordinary, 207–14
    jargon, 226
    ritual and vocabulary, 227
    scarcity as price determinant, 211–13
    sommeliers (stewards), 295–97
    tasting, professional, 223–27
    The Wine Advocate (Robert Parker), 212
    The Wine Spectator, 220, 232–33
    Woltner, Francis Dewavrin-, 211
    Woody, Elizabeth, 117

Yellow pages restaurant ads, 286–89

Zalacaín (Madrid), 136
Zapping of America, The (Paul Brodeur), 72